REPORT ON BRUNEI IN 1904

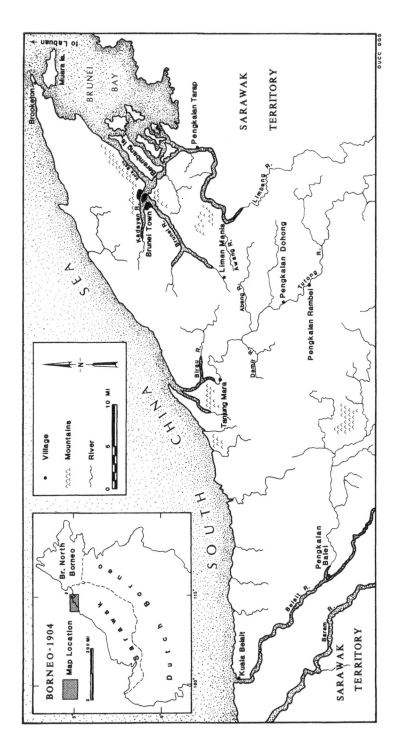

Hinterland of Brunei Town about 1904. Selected place names. (after McArthur's Report)

REPORT ON BRUNEI IN 1904

by

M.S.H. McArthur

Introduced and Annotated by

A.V.M. Horton

Ohio University Center for International Studies
Center for Southeast Asian Studies

Monographs in International Studies
Southeast Asia Series Number 74

Athens, Ohio 1987

Library of Congress Cataloging-in-Publication Data

McArthur, M. S. H. (Malcolm Stewart Hannibal), 1872–
    1934.
    Report on Brunei in 1904.

    (Monographs in international studies. Southeast Asia
series ; no. 74)
    Bibliography: p.
    1. Brunei––History. I. Horton, A. V. M. II. Title.
III. Series.
DS650.6.M37 1987   959.5'503   87–11218
ISBN 0–89680–135–7

CONTENTS

ILLUSTRATIONS

Hinterland of Brunei Town about 1904. Selected place names. (after McArthur's <u>Report</u>)
. . . . frontispiece

Brunei Town about 1904. (Courtesy Public Record Office, Kew, United Kingdom)
. . . . . facing page 100

PREFACE

In April 1904 Malcolm Stewart Hannibal McArthur, a British official in the Malayan Civil Service, was sent to the sultanate of Brunei, a British Protectorate, with instructions to study the situation there and to make recommendations concerning the country's future administration.

Published here for the first time, together with an introduction and commentary by A.V.M. Horton, are the two principal reports which resulted from McArthur's six month stay in Brunei:

(1) Notes on a Visit to the Rivers Belait and Tutong, dated 14 July 1904;
(2) Report on Brunei in 1904, dated 5 December 1904.

These manuscripts were written by an observer comparatively unprejudiced and sympathetic, but not uncritical and offer a unique and exhaustive insight into conditions prevailing in Brunei on the eve of the British Residency there (1906-1959). Although the main findings have been summarized by Professor Nicholas Tarling,[1] it is somewhat surprising that McArthur's reports have yet to be published in full. The texts certainly deserve to be brought to the attention of a wider reading public, particularly in the Sultanate itself, and historians of twentieth century Brunei should find them a useful resource.

II

It might be helpful, at this stage, to present some preliminary details about Brunei, more particularly since McArthur himself was somewhat doubtful about what should be taken as the borders of the country.

Brunei is a small, predominantly Muslim-Malay sultanate situated on the north coast of Borneo. It lies within 4°2' and 5°3' north latitute and 114°4' and 115°22' east longitute. Apart from the loss of 'interdigital' rivers within Sabah (North Borneo) and certain minor adjustments, it has maintained its present borders since 1890. The country is divided by the Limbang basin--annexed by Sarawak in 1890-- into two separate parts, with a total area of 2,226 square miles. The larger, western wing contains the three main "rivers" (districts): from west to east, Belait, Tutong, and Brunei; the Temburong Valley comprises the isolated eastern enclave.

In 1911, at the time of the first census, the sultanate's population totalled only 21,718 people, of whom three-quarters lived in the vicinity of the capital, Brunei Town. Almost ten thousand of these inhabitants lived in the famous Kampung Ayer (River Village) in houses built on stilts over the water. The least populous regions were Belait (1,126 people), and Temburong (1,259 people). Over half the people were Malays and a further quarter were Kedayans; both were Muslim races living mainly in the Brunei district. The remote, outlying portions of the country contained various minority groups, usually pagan, or semi-pagan with a "thin veneer" of Muhammadanism.[2] In addition, there were several hundred Chinese, who dominated such commerce as existed.

III

By 1904 the country had reached the nadir of its fortunes. The Kingdom of Brunei itself may date back to the seventh century A.D., when an exiled Indo-Chinese monarch founded a new realm in Borneo.[3] At any rate, Kota Batu, situated about a mile downstream from Brunei Town, was occupied for a millennium after the seventh century, and archaeological evidence suggests that an extensive trade was maintained with China, especially between 950 and 1450.[4] Chinese records refer to pre-Muslim states on the northwest coast of Borneo, known successively as Vijayapura and P'o-ni. In 1370, the capital of the latter was situated forty-five days' sail from Java and controlled fourteen districts.[5] The origins of the Muslim Sultanate of Brunei remain obscure, but recent research suggests the date of its founding to be 1515.[6] At that time Brunei was fairly powerful, controlling coastal areas of northwest Borneo, parts of Kalimantan, and the Southern Philippines. Although Brunei has given its name, in corrupted form, to the whole of Borneo, it is unlikely that the entire island was ever under its sway. The basis of the country's wealth and power was trade, particularly the export of camphor and gold.[7]

The impact of European colonialism--particularly the occupation of the Philippines by the Spaniards in the late sixteenth century--signalled the beginning of a long period of decline in the sultanate's fortunes which was not arrested until the appointment of a British Resident in 1906. This trend was not finally reversed until after the discovery in 1929 and export from 1932 onwards of oil from the Seria field, which has since transformed Brunei from a poor feudal backwater into one of the richest countries, per capita, in the world.

From the sixteenth to early nineteenth centuries Brunei's outlying possessions fell away, mainly because of encroachments by Spanish and Dutch colonialists. The sultanate was also hampered by domestic strife and warfare against its Muslim rival, Sulu, with whom control of eastern Sabah was disputed. During the second half of the nineteenth century Brunei lost most of its remaining territory in Borneo itself. In 1841 a British adventurer, James Brooke (1803-68), acquired Sarawak proper and began calling himself "Rajah"; the Sultan of Brunei subsequently confirmed him. Thereafter Sarawak expanded "river" by "river" northeastward toward Brunei Town until, by 1906, the sultanate was reduced to two small enclaves, entirely surrounded by Sarawak except along the coastline. Meanwhile, in 1878, a British merchant, A. Dent, and his Austrian colleague, Baron Overbeck, secured the cession of 30,000 square miles of North Borneo (Sabah); later the baron sold his share, and, in 1881, a British Chartered Company was established to govern the newly-acquired territory. The Company itself then began to expand toward Brunei proper, but found its way blocked by Sarawak, which had acquired the Trusan basin in 1884-5, possibly for the purpose of halting the advance of the company. Competition between the second Rajah and the Chartered Company, far from arresting further cessions of territory as some Bruneis apparently had hoped, actually hastened the moribund country's decline. It seemed that the unhappy, bankrupt Sultanate could hardly survive as an independent unit. Indeed, but for the intervention of the British Government in 1905, after receipt of McArthur's Report, it would not have done so.

xi

ACKNOWLEDGEMENTS

The author would like to thank the following: Dr. William H. Frederick of Ohio University, for his interest in this project; Dr. J.B. Post of the Public Records Office (Chancery Lane), for Crown Copyright clearance; Professor D.E. Brown, of the University of California, for suggesting the project in the first place; Messrs. R. Nicholl and W.M. Johnson for permission to quote from their letters; Her Majesty's Government (SSRC/ERSC), for providing the financial support which made possible this research; Ms. Gail HajiSaari of Ohio University for reading the manuscript and suggesting some changes; and Mr. A. Marshall of the University of Hull for reproducing the print of Brunei Town in 1908.

I am grateful to Dr. James L. Cobban, General Editor of the Monograph Series in International Studies and Hope H. Socci for their assistance in the final stages of the preparation of this manuscript. A.V.M. Horton is solely responsible, of course, for the material which appears here under his own name.

PART ONE

BRUNEI 1904-1908

M.S.H. MCARTHUR AND THE FOUNDATION OF THE

BRITISH RESIDENTIAL SYSTEM

by

A.V.M. Horton

INTRODUCTION

When M.S.H. McArthur's Report on Brunei in 1904 arrived in London early in 1905 Whitehall greeted it with unanimous approbation: "far the best that has ever been written" on the subject, "excellent," and "exhaustive and very useful" were three of the reactions.[1] Sir Frank Swettenham congratulated himself on having recommended McArthur for the mission and the government of Singapore for having appointed him.[2] Yet, apart from a handful of civil servants and perhaps even fewer historians, no one has seen this important document, along with the complementary Notes on a Visit to the Rivers Belait and Tutong.

This introduction aims to place the Report in its historical context. After indicating the task given to McArthur and outlining his stay in Brunei, I shall give details about the envoy himself and examine the dire straits into which the Sultanate of Brunei had fallen at the time of his arrival. Next, I shall identify some important themes in the Notes and the Report. The introduction concludes with an account of McArthur's tenure of office (1906-8) as the first British Resident in Brunei. Where appropriate I indicate the paragraphs in McArthur's Report and his Notes on a Visit to the Rivers Belait and Tutong to which my comments refer.

THE PURPOSE OF MCARTHUR'S MISSION AND THE REACTION OF THE RAJAH OF SARAWAK

In his commission as acting consul, dated 22 April 1904, McArthur was informed that the British government had, for some time, been receiving reports of the "unsatisfactory character" of the Brunei administration.[3] The Foreign Office recommended that he spend three months in the sultanate to study conditions in order to make recommendations for the country's future administration. He also was directed to investigate the various complaints against the sultan and his officers and should he

3

find conditions as bad as had been represented, he was authorized to warn the sultan of "the consequences likely to ensue from a continuance of bad administration."[4]   In addition--at the request of the high commissioner--the exact nature of his mission was to be concealed from the Brunei Malays.[5]

The aged Rajah of Sarawak, Sir Charles Brooke, GCMG (b. 1829; r. 1868-1917) believed that Brunei lay within his sphere of influence and that the British government would not oppose its final absorption within his raj.   Indeed much of the correspondence contains a view that the "consequence likely to ensue from a continuance of bad administration" would involve, simply, a hint to the sultan that, if necessary, the United Kingdom might no longer stand in the way of the rajah, for it was only thanks to British protection that the Sultanate survived at all.[6]

Sir Charles would not have contradicted the statement, made by one of his officers, that Brunei was "a blot on civilization and a canker in the heart of Sarawak."[7]   The rulers of the sultanate, in his opinion, were idle, oppressive, grasping and unjust; they reduced their subjects to misery and could not show "one foot of contentment" throughout their remaining dominions.[8]   Regular British colonialism was equally unsuitable.   Officers would be sent from Malaya who were inexperienced and lacking in knowledge of conditions in Borneo; they would introduce a "complicated system" and fail to govern in the people's interests.   The upshot would be bloodshed.[9]   He felt that British colonialism would result in the imposition of alien legal and education systems, and, worse still, would be accompanied by large-scale capitalist enterprise which was sure to swindle the indigenous population out of their land and other possessions.   The rajah felt his own philosophy of "respect for local custom, and a gradual, selective approach to change" or, in his own words, "letting system and legislation wait upon occasion" was far better adapted to the needs of Borneo.[10]   The "honester part" of the Brunei people continued to look to Sarawak for protection, and Sir Charles felt duty-bound to come to their support.[11] In any case for sixty years, he and his predecessor had been the "sole workers towards civilization" on the northwest coast of Borneo, and it seemed to him only just and proper that the British government should enable him to round off his life's work by permitting him to absorb the rump of Brunei and devote his final years to establishing peace, order and justice there.[12]

As he grew older Sir Charles became increasingly intolerant of the slightest opposition to his wishes.[13] Hearing of McArthur's appointment and fearing a possible change of British policy, he protested to the Foreign Office: the new acting consul, he said, would not be able to prepare a "reliable report" in less than one or two years.

> I don't wish to imply that Mr. McArthur is inexperienced, nor to call into question his abilities, but the Brunei natives and the surrounding of the Sultan are such an accomplished set of flatterers and liars, that it is as well to be guarded when framing a report. . . . Only a knowledge of their character over some years' experience can enable anyone to know how to deal with them.[14]

Sir Charles could not understand "why Mr. McArthur has been sent to report on the Brunei Government, being without experience and a stranger to those parts," and he remarked that it appeared the reports of the three previous consuls who had been favorably disposed towards Sarawak were "to be put aside as untrustworthy."[15] This was indeed the case. F.H. Villiers a foreign office mandarin explained to the Secretary of State as follows:

> For a long time past we [the Foreign Office] have had difficulty in obtaining correct information about the state of affairs [in Brunei], or, rather, in checking the contradictory reports to which conflicting interests have given rise. We have had a consul for Brunei but the salary has not been sufficient to prove an attraction, and the climate has been declared so bad as to necessitate residence in Labuan. For these reasons and some others of a personal character, the duties of the post have not been satisfactorily performed.[16]

McArthur would not have disputed the rajah's assessment of the truthfulness of Brunei nobles (Report 37). But Sir Charles himself was not entirely innocent, perhaps, of that mendacity which he imputed to others and the three previous consuls

5

had been strangers to Brunei, no less than McArthur. The rajah did not mind strangers so long as they uncritically echoed his own opinions. In truth, he now feared that his lifetime's ambition to swallow up Brunei was in jeopardy.

In this instance the rajah's representations were disregarded, and McArthur's mission went ahead as scheduled.

C.N. Crisswell remarks in his biography of the second rajah that Sir Charles "remained convinced that Mr. McArthur was biased against Sarawak and the Acting Consul, for his part, never visited Sarawak nor sought the rajah's opinion."[17] But this, surely, is the whole point: the rajah had left no one in any possible doubt about where he stood in the matter. McArthur's task, on the other hand, was to ascertain, as far as possible, the real attitudes of the Brunei people. In my opinion he reported honestly on the situation as he found it, even when the facts were distasteful to him (Report 112-3, 117). It might be argued that he coveted the possible future post of British resident but there is no evidence for this and, in any case, his career was already progressing steadily, for he had the reputation of being "one of the coming men of the Straits' service."[18] At the time, Brunei was hardly an attractive posting and even Peninsular Malays regarded the country as a "savage land" beyond civilization.[19] Moreover, McArthur was not the only candidate for the office of British resident.[20] Allegations of anti-Sarawak prejudice need not be entertained seriously. Indeed, it is the greater impartiality of the acting consul which makes him a more reliable reporter than previous British consuls.

MCARTHUR IN BRUNEI:
3 MAY TO 10 NOVEMBER 1904

The newly-appointed acting consul, along with three Malay assistants, left Singapore on 27 April 1904, reaching Brunei on 3 May. During the following afternoon, Sultan Hashim (reigned May 1885-May 1906) granted him an audience. McArthur quickly realized that the allotted three months would be insufficient for the task in hand: not only had he been struck by illness soon after arrival, but the difficulties of communication in a country with no roads precluded visits to all the outlying stations. An extension was granted, but progress was further delayed by the tragic smallpox epidemic of June to August 1904, which may have decimated the population of the capital. In any event, McArthur did not depart from Brunei until 10 November 1904, after a residence of slightly more than six months.

During his first month, the acting consul was very busy. He spent the second half of May studying the archives and meeting the pengirans (nobles). The latter, he reported, were "most friendly," but they conversed at such length that he found his work interrupted.[21] On 27 May he paid his first visit to Limbang, Brunei's erstwhile "rice store and richest asset."[22] The annexation of Limbang by Sarawak had caused great bitterness in the sultanate; its loss had been "the final step" towards the ruin of Brunei. Although impressed by the neatness, cleanliness and prosperity of Pengkalan Tarap (Limbang Village), particularly in comparison with the "filth and squalor" of Kampung Ayer, he was surprised to find "so few signs of cultivation" along the banks of the river below Pengkalan Tarap. During this first month, the acting consul also made three trips to Berembang Island (opposite Kota Batu), where the rajah owned a coal and oil works and had begun to usurp certain government functions.

In the second half of June and early July, McArthur toured Belait and Tutong districts to collect what information he could; his impressions, written on 14 July, are recorded in the first text published here.

On his return to the capital, he found the smallpox epidemic raging at its height: in the second week of July there were said to have been sixty deaths a day.[23] One eye witness later described the "heroic efforts," during this emergency, of the acting consul, who "went round Brunei daily in a large canoe" making "heartening speeches" which encouraged the people not to despair.[24] Towards the end of July medical assistance was summoned from Singapore and three doctors remained in Brunei throughout August. They had, however, arrived "too late to do much good."[25]

For the remainder of his stay in the country, September to November, McArthur continued to collect general information about the sultanate. It was probably during these months that he visited the Temburong and Lawas districts. Meanwhile he had also to conduct the ordinary consular business. In early June, for example, he was instructed to prevent the sultan from granting any "improper" oil concessions. There were also several tiresome debt

7

cases involving British subjects which had eluded settlement for months. Fugitives from justice also presented a problem since Brunei had no gaol. Various other matters, including petitions for loans from Sultan Hashim and the Pengiran Bendahara (chief minister), had to be investigated. The acquisition by Sir Charles Brooke of certain lands at Kota Batu provoked a lengthy correspondence.

McArthur departed from Brunei on 10 November. Once back in Singapore, he prepared his final Report, which was completed on 5 December 1904.

M.S.H. McARTHUR (1872-1934)

Regrettably, little is known about McArthur, and, to the best of my knowledge, there are no "M.S.H. McArthur Papers" in existence. He was, however, an extremely prolific and conscientious official reporter, as the files in the Public Record Office testify.

Writing in the early 1920s, F.N. Butterworth,[26] formerly (1901-13) engineer and then manager of the cutch factory in Brunei Town, remembered that the affable acting consul was "a dapper little fellow with dark, round eyes and a small chin." During the day, Butterworth added,

> he wore white duck (suits) like most of us Europeans. But in the evenings he adopted native garb and, being of a sallow complexion, looked very like a Malay. His knowledge of the Malays, so far as could be gathered from his conversation, was profound. He loved their company, and on going to his quarters of an evening one would usually find some native or other squatting on the verandah, smoking a palm leaf cigarette and talking about Brunei.[27]

McArthur's superiors in the Colonial Service certainly entertained a favourable opinion of his abilities: "modest and capable . . . entirely unprejudiced . . . one of the few men left in Malaya who have taken the trouble to get a better knowledge of Malay than that required to pass an examination" was Sir Frank Swettenham's verdict.[28] Another High Commissioner judged that McArthur was "a very careful and sound fellow."[29]

The acting consul also won the respect of

Sultan Hashim. For many years before 1904, relations between Sultan and consul[*] had been strained, principally because of the tendency of the latter to forward the interests of Sarawak at the expense of those of Brunei. Furthermore, in consequence of the alleged unhealthiness of Brunei Town, consuls tended to reside in Labuan, and hence lost touch with opinion in the Sultanate (Report 60). McArthur discovered that the raison d'être of the consul in Brunei was generally believed to be "something to do with Sarawak" (Notes 12).

On 4 May 1904, McArthur had his first interview with Sultan Hashim, who appeared "very infirm" as a result of a recent accident when the floor of his Istana gave way, precipitating him onto some nibong stumps under the building. The acting consul reported that His Highness

> expressed himself pleased to hear that I proposed to make Brunei my headquarters for a few months. I informed His Highness that I had decided on this step as I considered that only by living on the spot for some little time could I hope to make myself acquainted with the place and people.[30]

Toward the end of the month, the acting consul received a message that Sultan Hashim wished to visit him. The elaborate preparations made by McArthur ensured that the occasion was a great success.[31] His highness "kept up a very friendly conversation," he reported; but business was not discussed. On the following day the Sultan granted McArthur an audience in order to thank him. The impact of the new acting consul's consideration for his highness was doubtless highlighted by the contrast with former consuls, who were variously brusque, disrespectful, or drunk, and all of whom furthered the cause of Sarawak. (Indeed, one acting consul was a retired Sarawak officer.) Several petitions exist in the files from Sultan Hashim requesting the removal of this or that consul.[32] On 20 September 1904, by contrast, the sultan appealed to the high commissioner to confirm McArthur in the substantive post of British consul.[33] After McArthur's recall to Singapore, his highness requested McArthur's return to Brunei because he had

---

[*] See below, p. 13, for the role of the consul.

9

"exceeding great liking for him on account of his discretion, courtesy, and gentle disposition."[34] This indicates that McArthur had the personality to deal successfully with Brunei Malays, whom the British found--and continue to find--very "difficult."[35] It seems that Sultan Hashim had found in McArthur the "sympathetic official like Sir Spenser St. John [consul in the 1850s]" whom he had continually petitioned the British government to appoint. McArthur supported the sultan's stance on some issues, such as Limbang, the Muaras, and Kota Batu. But despite his greater sympathy and understanding, the strictures he passed concerning the chaotic condition of Brunei, the nature of the ruling class, the incompetent financial administration, the oppression of the subjects, and the absence of usual governmental institutions, differed from his predecessors' reports only in tone and emphasis. Unlike his predecessors, however, the acting consul managed to remain on cordial terms with his highness.

McArthur also appears to have been popular with the people of Brunei generally, and when he revisited the country in 1918, after an absence of ten years, he received a friendly reception.[36] Yet the only group of people within Brunei for whom he had a good word were the Bisayas of Belait and Tutong, an "industrious and peaceable race," of proverbial honesty, pleasant to meet and

> free from that assumption of superiority
> which generally seems to accompany a
> mixture of Muhammadanism and ignorance,
> and which makes it difficult to more
> than tolerate a Brunei Malay or a
> Kedayan (Report 30).

Malcolm Stewart Hannibal McArthur was born in 1872, the son of a general.* After leaving Oxford University, McArthur joined the Malayan Civil Service in 1895, holding a succession of increasingly important posts, mainly in Penang and Singapore until he was sent to the Sultanate of Brunei in 1904. After an interval in Singapore, he returned

---

* I was unable to trace any "General McArthur" in "Who Was Who" (1897-1916; 1916-1928); presumably he died before 1897. Nor have I discovered any details about other family members and possible descendants.

10

to the sultanate in November 1905 with D.G. Campbell
(1867-1918), Resident of Negri Sembilan, to obtain
Sultan Hashim's consent to a new treaty, making
provision for the appointment of a British "Resident" to conduct Brunei's administration. This was
achieved quickly and with little difficulty. From
January 1906 until April 1908, McArthur himself was
the first British Resident in the country. Among
the posts he occupied after returning to Malaya were
Under Secretary, Federated Malay States (1916-1919),
and Acting British Adviser, Kedah (1919-1922). He
retired on 4 October 1922.[37] Although his career
was by no means unsuccessful, neither was it outstanding.

For some years after 1908 McArthur remained an
authority on Brunei affairs to whom at least one
High Commissioner turned for advice.[38] As mentioned, he had the opportunity to return to Brunei
in 1918 on the occasion of the Coronation of Sultan
Muhammad Jemalul Alam.[39] McArthur died on 20
February 1934.[40] His name is perpetuated by the
name of a Brunei street. In the late 1960s, he
still was remembered by aged Malays as "the man who
had pacified Brunei."[41] In a wider sense, the
continued existence of Brunei as a separate country
is his real memorial.

BACKGROUND TO THE 1904 MISSION

Nicholas Tarling has written the definitive
account of the virtual partition of Brunei by
Sarawak and North Borneo during the second half of
the nineteenth century.[42] The impoverished sultan
and pengirans ceded one district after another for
annual payments of "cession money," most of which
was spent immediately on the upkeep of retainers,
the basis of a Malay chief's power.[43] Since cession
money was "an easily negotiable form of property,"
the pengirans did not hesitate to dispose of it for
many years in advance, and often sold it outright
for a lump sum down, which was "immediately squandered." As a result they had become "practically
face to face with beggary."[44]

In 1904 Brunei retained only four major river
systems, the sultan and nobles were virtually
destitute, and there remained serious popular unrest
in Belait and Tutong which began in 1899. In short,
a crisis existed and it was feared that the bankrupt
kingdom was doomed to extinction.

It was alleged that extortionate taxation and

the plundering and enslavement of inhabitants by the
sultan and his pengirans which increased in intensity in Brunei's remaining dominions in proportion
to the amount of territory which was lost, provoked
continual unrest. Such unrest disturbed not only
Brunei itself, but its neighbors as well. Successive consuls complained that Sultan Hashim continually ignored their legitimate representations and
described his record as follows:

> one of broken promises, lawless acts and
> outrages against British subjects,
> denial of justice or redress, and the
> protection of wrong doers . . . The
> representations of H.M. Government have
> been invariably ignored, the warnings of
> successive High Commissioners have
> passed unheeded, and the efforts of the
> consuls to obtain justice and satisfac-
> tion for British subjects have been
> wearisome and futile, and I know of no
> single instance where any result has
> been achieved except by the presence of
> one of H.M.'s Ships in Brunei.[45]

The tasks of government remained unfulfilled.
There was, for example, no public treasury and no
money was spent on the public welfare; there were no
police, nor even a gaol, and serious crime was
allowed to pass unpunished. It was said that Brunei
Town was perceptibly disappearing because government
oppression was driving the people abroad, while
pengirans connived at cross-border cattle-
rustling.[46] Worst of all, the rival royal faction,
led by two wazirs (senior ministers) the Pengiran
Bendahara and Pengiran di Gadong, never accepted
Sultan Hashim. These ministers ignored the sultan's
authority, compelling him "to merely sit [sic] upon
his throne with a nominal authority that he is
unable to exert, regarded as an interloper by his
Ministers of State, who afford him no loyal support
or faithful service."[47]
Conversely, it was argued that all could be
placed in order if only London permitted the rajah
to incorporate within his realm all the territory
between Baram and Trusan. There was no one, besides
Sir Charles Brooke, "for whom the natives of Brunei
have greater respect and confidence, or whose
knowledge and experience in dealing with the natives
of Borneo can compare with his; and His Highness
could effect the change in Brunei in a manner no one

else could."[48]

I have referred to these claims and allegations at some length to enable the reader to appreciate the impact of McArthur's conclusions. To give just one example: he discovered that the rajah far from being "respected" was "generally disliked" in Brunei (Report 112).

The internal condition of Brunei was of concern to the United Kingdom because of the sultanate's strategic position on the flank of the sea lane between India and China and the associated fear that, if a rival colonial power established a foothold in Brunei, it would be enabled thereby to threaten this increasingly important trade route.[49] The coal deposits at the mouth of the Brunei River, moreover, were considered an important asset.[50]

Official Anglo-Brunei ties commenced in 1846-47. The Friendship Treaty of 27 May 1847 confirmed the earlier cession to the United Kingdom of Labuan, an uninhabited island in Brunei Bay. Provision was also made for the appointment of a British consul to Brunei.[51] A further step was taken in 1888 when Brunei became a British Protectorate, control of its foreign policy being taken over by the United Kingdom, whose interests were supervised by the governor of the Straits Settlements, now appointed, ex-officio, "High Commissioner" for Brunei. (The details were left to the consul on the spot.) The sultan sought in this agreement a means to prevent further territorial encroachment, especially by Sarawak. The United Kingdom's principal purpose, on the other hand, was the exclusion of any possible foreign interference in Brunei. The ultimate fate of the sultanate, therefore, was a matter of indifference to London, so long as its territory remained within the British sphere of influence. Indeed, Whitehall's preferred solution to the 'Brunei problem' was the country's partition between Sarawak and North Borneo, which had also become British protectorates in 1888.[52] The proposed boundary was to be the watershed dividing Trusan from Lawas: in other words all the territory now (1983) belonging to Brunei fell within the portion earmarked for Sarawak. Hence, when Sir Charles Brooke annexed Limbang in 1890, the British government acquiesced in this accomplished fact. Lawas, although taken over by North Borneo in 1901, was transferred to Sarawak four years later.

Although Sultan Hashim's continual protests about the seizure of Limbang won him some sympathy in official circles in Singapore and London, the

13

consensus remained in favor of the "Sarawak settlement." The imperial government was reluctant to assume the burden of administering Brunei because its information was that the country was unlikely to be financially self-supporting. One of the most telling aspects of McArthur's Report, therefore, was to indicate that Brunei was "more valuable than we [HM Government] have ever thought it to be" and that its future might, after all, "ultimately be one of prosperity were present abuses abolished" (Report 146).[53] Previous consuls, and the rajah, who had understated Brunei's actual and potential worth, stand indicted at best of ignorance, if not of deliberate distortion of the facts.

NOTES ON A VISIT TO THE RIVERS
BELAIT AND TUTONG

These Notes were prepared by McArthur in early July 1904, after an eighteen day tour of the two districts concerned. The main concerns of his paper were trade, the condition of the people, and the political situation.

With regard to trade and customs, McArthur concluded as follows:

> In considering the relation of the amount paid [by the Chinese revenue farmers] for the lease of customs duties to the volume of trade in these rivers, it must always be remembered that the former depends in no way on the latter, the determining factors being always the shrewdness of the lessee and the financial difficulties of the authorities at the time the lease is made (Notes 11).

This confirms the point made at the end of the last section, namely that the revenue being received by the sultan and pengirans was only a fraction of the potential receipts if the districts were placed under more efficient management.

To understand the political situation in Belait and Tutong it is necessary to return to the years preceding McArthur's visit. In 1899 there had been an uprising in each district in reaction to heavy taxation imposed by the Brunei authorities in order to finance the celebrations connected with the wedding between Sultan Hashim's grandson and the Bendahara's daughter. These festivities continued

14

for the next three years. There was an underlying political motive, namely, the attempted reconciliation of the two rival royal factions (Report 64). The disaffection led indirectly to McArthur's 1904 Mission, as shall be demonstrated presently (below pp. 21-3).

In 1899 the Orang Bukit (Bisayas) murdered several of the Bendahara's poll-tax collectors in Belait. Some of the Orang Bukit crossed over into Baram (Sarawak) to ask that Belait be brought under the rajah's rule. This request was refused.

The murdered tax collectors were "Burong Pingais." Burong Pingai, one of the wards of Brunei Town, was inhabited by the chief Malay traders of the country, who had established 'colonies' elsewhere along the coast. When 150 relatives of the murdered men failed to persuade Sultan Hashim to bring the murderers to justice, they crossed over into Belait, also seeking Sarawak rule. The Sarawak flag was hoisted in Burong Pingai itself.[54] The rajah's officers then had a great difficulty preventing a clash on their own soil between the Orang Bukit and the Burong Pingais. At the same time a forced trade tax (dagang serah) in Tutong caused the resident headman, Dato di Gadong, to appeal for Sarawak control. It was reported that both districts were "practically independent" and that attempts by Brunei pengirans to reassert their authority would have been met with force. Sir Charles Brooke took advantage of the situation to appeal to the United Kingdom for permission to incorporate the disturbed areas within his raj; but he was disappointed.[55]

During 1900, an uneasy calm appears to have been preserved, but violence flared up again in Tutong district early in 1901. The leader of the rebellion was again Dato di Gadong. The facts of the disturbances are difficult to establish with certainty since the British consul of the day, G. Hewett, was notoriously pro-Brooke and, perhaps, not entirely scrupulous in his methods.[56] His own reports, moreover, contain apparent contradictions.

At first Hewett reported that the disturbances were "entirely due to the cruel outrages and extortions of the Brunei Government," the renewal of violence having followed further attempts

> to exact contributions, in the shape of
> girls, buffaloes and anything that is of
> value, towards the monstrous extrava-
> gance which has gone on unchecked for

15

some two years now in connection with the marriage.[57]

The "final strain" was the imposition of a tax of two dollars per head on buffalos and the refusal of the people to pay. This led Dato Kalam--described elsewhere by a Brooke officer as "that notorious buffalo thief"[58] of Limau Manis--to join and conspire" with Dato di Gadong in revolt.[59] Meanwhile, all 146 of Dato Kalam's followers who had remained at Limau Manis situated at the head of the Brunei River, about ten miles from the capital were robbed of everything. Their homes were destroyed, and, they themselves were driven, destitute, out of the country. Hewett reported that the Tutong headmen had appealed for Sarawak rule and, subsequently, a "large gathering" of Tutong people declared that under no circumstances would they again submit to the Sultan's authority.[60]

In apparent contradiction to the foregoing, Hewett also declared that there was "collusion" between the Brunei authorities and the "two so-called 'rebel' datos."[61]

Sultan Hashim had sent an expedition, commanded by his son-in-law, Pengiran Tajudin, to deal with the Dato di Gadong. But, Hewett explained, no attempt had been made to attack the "offending datos," the force confining its activities to "indiscriminate looting and burning of houses and committing wanton murder and outrage."* At the mouth of the Tutong all persons were prevented from entering or leaving. Hewett was outraged that Chinese traders (British subjects by registration) had "all their goods seized" or were obliged to supply Pengiran Tajudin's followers on credit. People lost their crops, moreover, because they were afraid to emerge and reap them.

Meanwhile "a fable of hostilities" was being enacted with the rebels. According to the consul, Pengiran Tajudin and the rebel datos had arranged that the latter would abandon their fort and retire to another they had prepared in the ulu (up-river). After this had been done, Pengiran Tajudin "boldly attacked" and captured the empty fort. Thereafter the object was "to plunder the inhabitants" for both

---

* Hewett was implicated in two of the atrocities which have blackened the British record in Borneo: the Kinabatangan massacre of 1890 (130 dead) and the devastation of the Inanam Valley in 1897.

16

sides, Pengiran Tajudin from below and the datos from the ulu.

Hewett's J'accuse continued with the claim that the whole charade had been planned in advance by the Pengiran Bendahara (Pengiran Anak Besar, c. 1829-1927) in the hope that the rajah would pay him the Limbang cession money out of gratitude[*] and that Sultan Hashim had been neither ignorant of the fact nor unwilling to profit from the circumstance.[62] The Bendahara, Hewett explained, had sent the headmen word to resist the buffalo tax, plus ammunition for the purpose. This resistance was the excuse for the subsequent attack upon the people by the Brunei authorities after the sultan's chop (signature) imposing the buffalo tax had been withdrawn. After trouble had been "successfully started" in this way, the Bendahara continually urged the Tutong people to resist, while Sultan Hashim continued to attack them with the force led by Pengiran Tajudin. Four men were "murdered in cold blood" in Birau, a tributary of Tutong, and one hundred families from there fled to Limbang. The consul added that, with the chief wazir (vizier) "instigating rebellion" and conspiring against the sultan, and the latter taking advantage of the fact to plunder his own peaceable subjects it was

> impossible to avoid the conclusion that they recognize clearly that Brunei cannot survive much longer as an independent State, and are anxious to seize everything of value while there is yet time.[63]

By July the disturbances had spread to Belait. The Pengiran Pemancha (Pengiran Muhammad Salleh, d. 1912), the junior wazir, had gone into the district "ostensibly for trading purposes," but really to stir up the Belait people to attack Tutong and so give the Brunei authorities a pretext to plunder their houses while they were away.[64] The consul received reports that the Pemancha had succeeded in inducing a party of five hundred Belait people[**] to

---

[*] See below, pp. 30-1.

[**] Is this not remarkable, in view of the previous reports that both Belait and Tutong were "practically independent" and that any attempt by

17

attack the Tutongs; but Hewett thought the number was probably an exaggeration.[65] At the end of September he was able to confirm that Belait had been treated "in the same way" as Tutong and that the state of both 'rivers' was "identical,"[66] meaning that both districts were the scene of strife, trade was at a standstill, the inhabitants had been "robbed of their possessions," and the authorities had borrowed against annual cession payments for many years into the future.[67]

In September 1901, according to Brooke sources, Dato Bakong, "the Belait chief who for three years has refused to submit to the authority of Brunei," surrendered to the Pemancha to whom the Bendahara had transferred his rights. Other chiefs were said to have had a meeting with the pengiran.[68] By November the last reports from Tutong were that no further attack would be made by Pengiran Tajudin if the people surrendered and paid a fine. Most of the chiefs gave up, "not having arms or ammunition to continue the struggle," while others moved into Limbang in order to avoid paying the indemnity. Datos Kalam and di Gadong were not included in the amnesty and were to be put to death if either were caught in Brunei territory. Both received shelter from the Limbang authorities, Dato di Gadong declaring that the people would continue the struggle as long as they could.[69] It was stated that about two hundred families had moved into Limbang from Tutong at one time or another during 1901, though some returned after the disturbances had died down.[70]

During 1902 the Dato di Gadong, who had himself been responsible for a number of atrocities including multiple murder,[71] crossed back into Tutong, where he was killed "by order of the Sultan of Brunei" in about July.[72] Dato Kalam proved as

_____

pengirans to reassert their authority would have been met by force? An expedition of five hundred people from Belait would have represented practically the entire adult population of the district. (The 1911 census enumerated 1,126 persons, but it was thought that this number was underestimated.) The best explanation is probably that, in 1899, the consul was referring to the small portion of Belait district owned by the Pengiran Bendahara, which was subsequently transferred to the Pengiran Pemancha. The latter, who retained the remnants of an assured income, was less extortionate than the senior wazir.

much of a nuisance to the Sarawak authorities as he had been to those in Brunei. Eventually, in 1904, he was captured and "ended his adventurous career [as a buffalo thief] with three years' imprisonment" in Kuching.[73]

In 1904 McArthur, having read the reports of his predecessors, expected to find everywhere in Belait and Tutong "great misery and want and grave discontent"; but these expectations were not realized.[*] There were no signs of great poverty; on the contrary, every house seemed well-furnished, the people had ample food, and could even afford small luxuries. With regard to taxation, their discontent was that they sometimes had to pay up to twenty dollars annually, whereas by custom as practiced in Sarawak they should have paid only two dollars. The acting consul might have added that taxation was exceptionally low across the border. Furthermore, in the provinces of North Borneo which he visited, McArthur found that there was

> far greater poverty and distress than in Brunei, [and] that the people complain bitterly of the oppressive taxation introduced by the Chartered Company and are full of regrets for the "happy-go-lucky" times of Brunei rule, when . . . though they might in some years have heavy calls made upon them, in others they were hardly molested at all (Report 105).

McArthur was informed that perhaps half the population of Belait and Tutong had emigrated during the previous decade and that more would have done so but for sentimental attachment to their place of birth. Furthermore, not all emigration from Brunei was due to oppression. The Kedayans, for example

---

[*] This is puzzling. After going to great lengths to establish that the Orang Bukit had no "definite grounds for complaint," McArthur added that they still looked to Sarawak for relief: but if they had no complaints, why should they have turned to the Brooke State for the amelioration of their condition? (Notes 12). In concluding his Notes (paragraph 16), McArthur declared that "discontent is general." being unable to do so myself, I leave it to the greater ingenuity of readers to resolve these apparent direct contradictions.

19

were a nomadic group to whom the rajah offered
financial inducements to settle in Sarawak, and
escaping the obligations of serfdom was, in itself,
a great gain. Despite these factors, some Kedayans
after a short experience of life in Sarawak, preferred to return to Brunei.

The Belait chiefs whom McArthur met had no
complaints against the Pemancha, except that he took
more than his due in poll tax. Exactions in Tutong
were greater. During the vacancy in the office of
Pengiran di Gadong, ownership of the district and
its serfs had reverted to the Crown. Sultan Hashim,
being at his wits end for money, made continual
demands on the people of the province; however,
McArthur found that he was only just beginning to
collect the indemnity imposed after the failure of
the 1901 Revolt. Although the people complained
bitterly of poverty and distress, and acting consul
felt that the actual conditions under which they
lived did not seem to support their statements.
They were certainly the victims of scandalous
extortion, but the scale of the exactions had been
"the subject of some exaggeration" in the past
(Report 29).

McArthur suggested, also, that the 1901
disturbances in Tutong "were not entirely spontaneous, but were stirred up and fostered by
intrigues, the headmen hoping to gain something by a
change of allegiance" (Notes 14). One headman
volunteered the information that they had been
promised active assistance by Sarawak and had
revolted relying on these (largely hollow) promises.
With regard to the Birau "murders," Pengiran
Tajudin claimed that the four men had been taken in
open rebellion and had been summarily executed after
attempting to escape. If this were true, the acting
consul added, the rebels "could hardly expect
clemency from the authorities of a State such as
Brunei" (Notes 15). Nor did McArthur find that
Pengiran Tajudin was the monster portrayed by
Hewett. In 1904 the nobleman was instrumental in
vaccinating the people of Tutong against smallpox[74]
and during the Anglo-Brunei negotiations of the
following year he played an important part as an
intermediary.[75]

In conclusion, McArthur agreed that the people
of Belait and Tutong were "taxed most unreasonably"
by a government which did nothing for them in
return. Elsewhere he added that the Bisayas were
kept peaceable only "by the idea which prevails
among them that the country is soon to be merged in

Sarawak" (Report 30).

Meanwhile, in the spring of 1901, news of fresh violence in Tutong had moved the Foreign Office to suggest that it had become more than ever desirable that the British government should be prepared with "a scheme for the future government of Brunei to take effect at the Sultan's death. . ."[76] At length it was agreed that the High Commissioner, Sir Frank Swettenham, should travel there in April 1902, in order to prepare a report on the problem for consideration by the Foreign Secretary.

This plan was overtaken by events. In July 1901, Consul Hewett urged that the only remedy to the worsening situation in Tutong and Belait was the conclusion of some arrangement whereby the two districts should come under the protection of the Sarawak Government. The rajah, he suggested, might be invited to make a liberal offer to the sultan for their transfer.[77] The Brunei monarch was likely to accept because of his straitened financial circumstances. The British government, for reasons of humanity, superseded its previous decision, and agreed instead to try Hewett's plan.[78] Sir Charles --who blamed the continuance of strife in Brunei on the British government's refusal to allow him to intervene to restore peace there[79]--offered annual cession money of $3,000 for the rivers, or $4,000 if Brooketon (Muara) were included. Lest anyone doubted the liberality of these terms, he pointed out that nothing could be found in the districts that might be called assets or public works of government and that everything would have to be "laid out at great expense on starting."[80]

In November 1901 Hewett was instructed to open negotiations with Sultan Hashim on behalf of the rajah. These negotiations proceeded slowly and ended without agreement being reached. In June 1902 the scope of discussion was enlarged to include the surrender of the whole sultanate to Sarawak. The rajah proposed that he should take over the administration of Brunei and that the Sarawak flag should be hoisted there. The sultan and wazirs would be permitted to retain the personal honors and titles due them, and would be paid annual pensions: $12,000 to the Sultan, and $6,000 each to the two remaining wazirs. After their deaths, half these amounts would be paid to their descendants. Hewett reported that the Sultan and wazirs were in favor of accepting "this most generous offer" from the rajah;[81] but, in fact, the terms were rejected in a decidedly uncompromising tone and this rejection was

21

repeated with equal force to McArthur himself in 1904.[82] The reason for Sultan Hashim's refusal, according to Brooke's sources, was the opposition of the junior ministers, some of whom were money-lenders who had the monarch in their financial power.[83] This would not have been an insuperable obstacle if the sultan had intended seriously to accept the rajah's terms. In 1903, under pressure of unauthorized attempted gunboat diplomacy by Consul Hewett, Sultan Hashim appeared to waver; but this was short-lived. There can be no doubt that one of the major aims of Sultan Hashim's policy was the preservation of his country and dynasty.[84] It should be remembered that he was under constant pressure to sell out his country from Consul Hewett, who played on his fear of starvation. Knowing his junior ministers would never allow him to accept the rajah's offer, he simply played along with the consul. In addition, he may have wished to expose the unpatriotic Bendahara: hence the sultan's insistence that Consul Hewett should induce the senior wazir to lay the rajah's terms before the State Council.

In mid-1903 when Hewett's strategy collapsed, Sir Frank Swettenham gathered the opinions of his senior colleagues and suggested that the best course to adopt with regard to the future of Brunei would be as follows:

> to instruct the consul to live at Brunei and to endeavor to secure the sympathies of the Sultan and his people and give them good advice, being strictly impartial in all his dealings whether those where British subjects are concerned or not.[85]

The British government elected to delay taking a decision until Sir Frank should have arrived home on leave at the end of the year.[86] In fact, he took the opportunity to retire, but he continued to advise the British government on Brunei matters.

The Foreign Office, which still favored the "Sarawak settlement," suggested to the rajah that he might consider improving the terms which he had offered to Brunei: for example, by making the proposed annuities progressive as the revenues allowed, or by paying the Limbang "cession money." But Sir Charles declared that Sarawak's finances could bear no further burden.[87] It was decided, therefore, to recall Hewett whose service was

22

considered unsatisfactory by the British government, and who was persona non grata to the sultan and in his place to send McArthur, who was to undertake to prepare the report which Sir Frank Swettenham had postponed in 1901-2.

The next two sections suggest some of the main themes of McArthur's final Report and outline his recommendations for the future and the extent to which they were implemented. Finally, this monograph reviews McArthur's term as British Resident in Brunei (1906-1908) in order to evaluate the accuracy of some of the statements made in his Report.

REPORT ON BRUNEI IN 1904, PART ONE

McArthur's Report follows a logical progression designed to convince the British government that their only honorable alternative was to appoint a British Resident on the Malayan model to undertake the daunting task of reforming the Brunei Sultanate.

The paper may be divided into two main sections. In the first (paragraphs 1-102) the author attempts to establish that the state of affairs in the country was sufficiently dire to warrant some form of outside intervention; in the second (paragraphs 103-146), he argues that the only solution likely to accommodate most interests would be, as mentioned, the establishment of a Residential system. In making this recommendation McArthur was not being a 'yes-man' whose conclusions had been fixed for him in advance. His immediate superiors, the Foreign Office and the new High Commissioner, Sir John Anderson, were in favor of the 'Sarawak settlement'.[88] Admittedly, opinion in the Colonial Office had been shifting in favor of a Residency. Sir Frank Swettenham commented after receipt of the Report as follows:

> I agree with all he says, and although he does not know it, I have myself, at different times, written to the Foreign Office in the sense of the opinions he expresses in regard to the Sultan, the Rajah of Sarawak, and the British North Borneo Company. (emphasis added.)[89]

The Report describes a semi-feudal society in disintegration, in the final stage of its long decline. The country had been unable to cope with the new circumstances created in the second half of

23

the nineteenth century by aggressive, albeit unofficial, British imperialism (Report 101).

In his intelligence-gathering the acting consul was hampered by the necessity to maintain the secrecy of his mission and by the fact that a consul was not supposed to take any interest in the internal affairs of the country. McArthur had the assistance, however, of three peninsular Malays, who had accompanied him on a similar mission to Kelantan the previous year, in the hope that they would be more likely than a European to gain the trust and confidence of the Brunei people, who were often described as "suspicious" of foreigners. Further, McArthur spent only a few days in Belait and Tutong and admitted "a lack of acquaintance of the conditions under which the lower classes live." He acquired sufficient knowledge, nevertheless, to be able to comment that "nearly all my preconceived ideas of Brunei have been upset during my residence in the State." His historical passages (as opposed to the majority of his writing, which was based directly on his own experience) are weak, perhaps being derived largely from hearsay; but, as McArthur commented, the sentiments expressed, even if historically inaccurate (which may not necessarily be so) help to explain the attitudes of the Brunei people.

The acting consul found little to admire in the sultanate. The few individuals who escape censure are unsuccessful types, underdogs too scrupulous to thrive in the conditions prevailing in Brunei: for example, Teoh Ah Gau, the worthy Chinese businessman, "devoid of cash profits, but rich in book debts run up by traders who took advantage of his lack of business instincts to postpone payments of their dues" (Report 57); or Pengiran Muda Muhammad Tajudin, whose unrealistic pretensions to the succession made him the butt of local wit, but whose relations with his serfs "were not marred by any excesses on the one hand or disaffection on the other" (Report 17, 71).

McArthur, of course, represented a power close to its imperial apogee: 1904 was a mere six years after the humiliation of the French at Fashoda and seven after Queen Victoria's Diamond Jubilee. It might be argued that McArthur shared the prejudices of his time and class, for example, a disdain for non-British methods of administration revealed in statements such as "however exceptional is the depravity of the Brunei aristocracy" or "they [the Brunei ruling class] cannot be expected to realize

how repugnant all their methods are to civilized
minds. . . ." Such lapses are rather too frequent
for comfort. McArthur personally felt that it was a
pity that Brunei "was not finally disposed of years
ago" but he attempted to write "without exaggeration" and more temperately than previous consuls
about the evils existing in the sultanate. In a
letter to Sir Frank Swettenham the acting consul
commented as follows:

> I am afraid it is a most inadequate
> (report), but the whole thing seems to
> me to be in such a muddle that it is
> difficult for anyone (and, more particu-
> larly, so junior a man as myself) to say
> definitely what ought to be done. . . .
> I do not think I have anything to add to
> what I put in my Report. I have been as
> plain-spoken as I can.[90]

Among the major concerns of McArthur's Report
are the weakness of central authority, poverty and
taxation methods, the Chinese, Sultan Hashim, and
the loss of Limbang.

The weakness of central authority. McArthur
discovered that there was "no Government in the
usual sense of the term--only ownership" (Report
54). Brunei had no salaried officials (unless the
aged and illiterate Pengirans Bendahara and Pemancha
could be thus dignified), no public institutions, no
police, no coinage, no roads, no public works (apart
from a wooden mosque) and only the "semblance" of a
judicature.[*] Instead, the country was "an aggregation of small and semi-independent fiefs acknowledging one head" (Report 8). All the land and the
people living thereon was held by the sultan and
pengirans according to three forms of tenure:
kerajaan (crown lands), kuripan (lands held by the
wazirs ex-officio); and tulin (private hereditary
domains). The capital was kerajaan, but the Malays

---

[*] However Sultan Hashim had attempted (in 1887-
1888) to introduce his own coinage--to take just one
example. The British authorities pressurized him to
withdraw it. He found, also that Chinese traders
were not keen to accept the new tokens. (Source:
CO 144/64 (26094); CO 144/66 (items 1684, 3169, and
7447); and FO 12/78 pp. 23, 153, 174, 214, 226, 231,
and 261).

living there enjoyed a greater degree of personal freedom than the serfs living in the rest of the country.

Sultan Hashim possessed only "the shadow of power" because he was not allowed "by constitution and custom of Brunei" to interfere in the internal administration of kuripan and tulin domains.* The sole prerogative retained by the Crown was the right to prevent alienation of a domain to a foreign power, but his consent was rarely withheld because His Highness was usually too poor to forego the fee charged for attaching his seal to such transactions. Sultan Hashim, having "no real power except over his own districts and people," had been blamed unfairly in the past for oppression, much of which was the responsibility of pengirans. McArthur cited one instance when Sultan Hashim was forced by a British consul to pay a debt to a Chinese trader because he (the Sultan) had failed to compel the Pemancha who was liable to do so. The acting consul thought this was most unjust:

> The curious constitution of the country makes the Sultan only supreme in name, and his position is so much a matter of accommodation with ministers as strong as himself, that it seems unfair to expect him to risk an open breach with

---

* Upon succeeding to the throne in 1885, Sultan Hashim left vacant his former office that of Pengiran Temenggong. Similarly after the death of Pengiran Muhammad Hassan (reported in January 1900), the office of Pengiran di Gadong remained unfilled. The kuripan revenues, therefore, reverted to the Crown. Sultan Hashim held Temburong, Muara Damit and Brunei districts as kerajaan. The Pengiran Bendahara held Bukit Sawat as kuripan, which he leased to the Pengiran Pemancha from circa 1900-1910 for $8,000 in cash. The Belait was tulin of the Pengiran Pemancha; Muara Besar the tulin of Pengiran Omar Ali; the Labu the tulin of Pengiran Muda Muhammad Tajudin (Pengiran Muda Muhammad Tajudin); and finally Limau Manis the tulin of the heirs of Pengiran di Gadong. There were, of course, numerous smaller tulin districts within these larger areas enumerated above. In 1910-11 W.H. Lee-Warner, the Assistant-Resident, found no less than 105 tulin claims--albeit some of them fraudulent--to be settled.

them (Report 42).*

Poverty and taxation methods. By 1904 Brunei
had lost most of its richest economic areas. Brunei
Town itself produced little apart from cutch, fish,
and some craftsware. In the surrounding district,
the rajah ran coal-mines at Muara (Brooketon) and
Buang Tawar but this brought little revenue to the
sultan. The Kedayans practised shifting cultivation
of padi. Collection of jungle produce including
bark for the cutch factory provided a livelihood for
many Kampung Ayer folk. The sparsely-populated
outlying districts were self-sufficient in food-
stuffs, the labors of the serfs there representing
"the sole source of income" for the impoverished
Brunei rulers.
     There was no State treasury as such, the
revenues of a particular district belonging to the
kerajaan, kuripan or tulin owner as the case might
be. It was difficult to distinguish between
"personal perquisites," the results of ownership,
and the revenues which would, "in a properly
governed country," accrue to the government.
McArthur complained that there were none of the
items "which generally go to make up a revenue to
government," such as land rents, port and harbor
dues, customs and licenses, and fines and fees of
office. The pengirans, he claimed, were "incorrigibly idle and constitutionally dishonest" and had
been living "with increasing difficulty on the
proceeds of [the] gradual disintegration of the
State, being too lazy or too incompetent to do an
honest stroke of work" (Report 37). In the past
bankruptcy and starvation had been deferred by the
alienation of further territory to Brunei's
acquisitive neighbors, but by 1904 there was little
more to be sold. The only way starvation could now
be avoided would have been by increased taxation of
the people, who were already ripe for revolt, at
least in the outlying districts. As more Brunei
territory had been ceded, taxation in the remaining
parts of the sultanate necessarily had become more
concentrated. This contributed to an uprising which
occurred in Limbang in 1884-1890 and to the unrest
in Belait and Tutong after 1899. The rebels, moreover, no longer had to fear the Kayans of Baram
(transferred to Sarawak in 1882), who had been used
formerly by Sultans of Brunei to keep other tribes

_____

* See below, p. 230, note 58.

27

in obedience.[91]

Treatment of the subject serfs outside the capital varied according to the character of their owners. The sufferings of the people increased if the owner took a personal interest in his property; fortunately, many pengirans were indolent and inefficient and left all they could to local headmen who, being of the same race as the serfs, were not invariably cruel. The acting consul, however, was horrified by the scale of contributions generally exacted by the pengirans. The traditional sum of two dollars annually from each household in poll-tax was "merely the irreducible minimum and a convenient basis for every other kind of exaction which the ingenuity of their owners can conceive" (Report 93).

On the other hand, the Muruts--found mainly in the most remote ulus--lived too far off in the jungle to be the victims of regular oppression. Those Kedayans whom McArthur managed to engage in conversation made no complaints of marked oppression, their yearly payments being the equivalent of only $1.50. (But, apparently, "any Brunei Malay considers himself at liberty to steal from them, or abuse any power over them which circumstances may give them.") The Malays of the capital--about half the total population of Brunei--did not pay poll tax or the other exactions. They were undoubtedly poor, however, as a result of large families, the effects of the loss of Limbang (see below), their preference for independence in earning a livelihood, and--principally--the system of monopolies, which forced up the prices of imports.[92]

The Chinese. The plight of Brunei's rulers was made worse by their own financial incompetence and their dependence upon foreign traders. The principal traders of the country were Chinese, registered as British subjects in Labuan, who had obtained, very cheaply, mortgages on the revenues of Brunei for many years ahead. Sultan Hashim, for example, in exchange for small advances of cash, would alienate to money-lenders the right to collect a certain item of revenue, such as import duty on this or that product. The monopoly was then let and sublet by successive middlemen so that prices of goods to the consumer were forced upwards. This caused great distress to the ordinary inhabitants of the capital, since almost everything had to be imported.

In the past, British consuls had been outraged by the treatment accorded to Chinese shopkeepers and money-lenders and, on a number of occasions, British gunboats had been sent to Brunei, at the request of a consul, to extract from Sultan Hashim, payment of the debts he was alleged to owe them.[93] In fact, the alleged mistreatment of Chinese traders was one of the principal charges of misrule brought against Sultan Hashim. McArthur was less sympathetic towards the Chinese, whom he described as aliens rather than the real inhabitants of the country. Previous consuls, he argued, had attached too much importance to the occasional losses of these British subjects, who, generally, were making substantial profits. British Chinese cupidity, in his opinion, was responsible for much of the poverty in the country since they had bought up, at very little cost, all the revenues of the sultanate, for many years to come. In other instances, moreover, Sultan Hashim had been forced to pay up by the British, even when he had not been responsible for the original debt.

The high cost of living caused by monopolies was driving Brunei Malays further afield in search of employment although the establishment of the cutch factory in 1900-1 had curbed the exodus to some extent.

Sultan Hashim. McArthur took a much less unfavorable view of Sultan Hashim than previous consuls. The latter along with some Sarawak officers often failed to take account of His Highness' difficulties, caused by his virtual powerlessness vis-a-vis his ministers. Most of the rapine attributed to His Highness was actually the responsibility of pengirans over whom he had no control. Indeed, his chief fault was his leniency towards offenders against his own laws. When he attempted to arrest criminals, they would simply seek the protection of a powerful chief, which meant that the sultan could take no further action. Sultan Hashim's unsympathetic treatment by British consuls, who resided outside the sultanate in Labuan and often acted in the interests of the rajah of Sarawak, had caused him to look upon representatives of the British government in Labuan as an enemy. But his Succession in 1885 had been the result of popular choice and to the people he was simply behaving in the natural manner of a Brunei ruler. Sultan Hashim himself lived in great poverty, most of his receipts being squandered by hangers-on.

29

Limbang. McArthur stressed the disastrous
impact on Brunei Town caused by the loss of Limbang,
the "Life of Brunei," which Sir Charles Brooke had
annexed in 1890. There had been a revolt simmering
in the district since 1884, and this provided an
excuse for the rajah who claimed the following: the
district had been de facto independent ever since
1884; the people were oppressed by unjust taxation
and had refused to pay anything further to Brunei;
the headmen had raised the Sarawak flag of their own
accord; and Sultan Hashim was preparing to exact his
revenge which would have caused fearful bloodshed if
Sarawak had not intervened. The facts, however,
contradict these claims: (1) the disturbances had
been confined to a relatively small part of the
Limbang while most of the district had remained at
peace; (2) the people of Limbang had never repudiated the authority of the sultan and were quite
willing to pay the scale of taxes as arranged in
1884 by the mediator, W.H. Treacher, but the sultan
would not accept them until the rebels had been
punished; (3) even the headmen appeared to be
wavering in their support of Sarawak; and (4) the
Brunei ministers signed at least three petitions
requesting the return of the district, while Sultan
Hashim's letters to the British government on the
subject were innumerable.
    The Limbang was the true river of Brunei Town.
The Brunei River, so-called, was actually an arm of
the sea, salt throughout its length, with no ulu.
In these circumstances Kampung Ayer folk depended on
the large, fertile Limbang for food, clothing, and
materials for housing and fishing. Since 1890,
however, the Sarawak authorities had imposed export
duties on these materials, so that Brunei people
could no longer afford to obtain them from Limbang.
Furthermore, petty traders, such as collectors of
jungle produce, found their livelihood undermined.
All four sago factories in Brunei Town had been
obliged to close down, because they were no longer
able to meet competition from their Sarawak rivals,
who obtained the raw materials free of export duty.
McArthur estimated that the annexation of Limbang
had cost Brunei $200,000 annually in trade (the
trade in the remainder of the country he put at only
$500,000, not including coal export of $112,000 from
Brooketon). The acting consul agreed that Sarawak
control had eliminated the worst excesses of Brunei
rule in Limbang, but the rajah's intervention had
punished innocent as well as guilty, and the
annexation of Limbang by Sarawak was "a real loss to

all Brunei, and not only to its unworthy owners."

The Brunei pengirans complained bitterly about the rajah's usurpation. McArthur, however, believed that their grievance was not so much the loss of the district, but rather that they had not received financial compensation for their former rights. The rajah had offered $6,000 in annual cession money, but Sultan Hashim, who owned little or no property in the "river" himself and had refused to recognize its annexation and would not permit the pengirans to touch the money. In 1895, the British government ruled that Sir Charles Brooke had no further obligations to meet in the matter.[94]

These comments are not exhaustive; further aspects of the first section of McArthur's Report will be mentioned later. Meanwhile, an important point is McArthur's stress on the variety obtaining in Brunei, despite its reduced circumstances: the different districts, peoples, classes, economic conditions and so on, all of which required separate description.

The acting consul warned that the sultanate was decaying through internal causes and feared that if nothing were done by the United Kingdom to rescue the country this would only postpone for a short time the final loss of Brunei's independence and increase the suffering of the inhabitants of the State, while encouraging the squandering of all its resources (Report 103). McArthur felt that the British government had a clear obligation to act decisively, one way or another:

> When it is remembered that these evils
> flourish under nominal British protec-
> tion, and that it is that protection
> alone which keeps Brunei in existence as
> a separate State, it seems obligatory on
> His Majesty's government to take some
> steps to ameliorate them, either by
> insisting on internal reform or by
> withdrawing all semblance of suzerainty,
> when Brunei would rapidly be absorbed,
> piecemeal, by its neighbors (Report
> 100).

REPORT ON BRUNEI IN 1904, PART TWO

In the second part of his Report (paragraphs 103-146), McArthur discusses possible future alter-natives for the ancient Kingdom of Brunei. One

alternative was to trust to the personal influence
of the consul on the spot to check abuses, but this
was rejected as impracticable, since the consul
would have no means of enforcing his advice, while
the sultan would be subjected to internal pressure
to disregard outside interference.   To hand the
country over to North Borneo (Sabah) was equally
unacceptable, because the Chartered Company was
administratively inefficient, commercially
motivated, and over-exacting in taxation.

The British government, for several years, had
intended to incorporate Brunei within Sarawak; but
McArthur found that this was "the only solution of
the problem of which it may be said with certainty
. . . would not meet with the approval of the rulers
of Brunei."   This was confirmed the following year
by H.C. Belfield, a Malayan Civil Service colleague:

> They [the Sultan and Chiefs] observe
> with concern and mortification that in
> addition to the seizure of Limbang
> district, the Rajah has established a
> footing for himself at Brooketon, at
> Buang Tawar and at Kota Batu, in each of
> which places he has superadded to his
> private rights of ownership the exercise
> of official jurisdiction without the
> sanction of the authorities of the
> State.
>
> They have unreservedly stated to me
> their opinion that the Rajah will not be
> satisfied until he has absorbed the
> whole of Brunei, and they would be
> willing to make substantial concession
> to any suggestion of control by the
> British Government rather than that
> opportunity should be left to the Rajah
> to further extend [sic] his sphere of
> influence at their expense.[95]

The ordinary people also disliked and feared
the rajah.   A contributory factor was the influence
of their chiefs, but the principal reason was their
understanding that the rajah's regime depended on
the support of Iban warriors, of whom they had a
great terror.   More positively, most Brunei Malays
did not wish to see their ancient sultanate and
dynasty blotted out from among nations.   Hence,
although the 'Sarawak settlement' was the most
convenient and cheapest solution from the British
government's point of view, it was morally impos-

sible to enforce.

McArthur felt that a British Residency would be less obnoxious to the rulers of Brunei than loss of identity as a mere part of either Sarawak or North Borneo. This would also meet the needs of the oppressed. Although the Bisayas of Belait and Tutong looked to Sarawak rule, the acting consul attributed this to their ignorance of other governments, and he argued that their interests could be equally protected by the British government. McArthur suggested that Labuan Island, which had been poorly administered by the Chartered Company, ought to be resumed by the Colonial Office and its administration combined with that of Brunei. The resumption of the island was essential, because it was the focus of Brunei's trade and provided the easiest means of communication with the sultanate's outer districts. McArthur agreed that the initial expense of setting the new administration on its feet would be heavy but he felt that its future could be one of prosperity.

The High Commissioner, Sir John Anderson, accepted the conclusions in the Report and recommended to the British government that they should proceed accordingly.[96]

G.V. Fiddes, in the Colonial Office, was inclined to let matters take their course without any British interference:

> Imperial interests seem perfectly safe in any event. . . . On the merits of the case, the squalid politics of Brunei do not excite enthusiasm and I should have no hesitation in voting . . . [to] do nothing.[97]

His colleagues, however, were persuaded by the arguments in favor of a Residency.

Sir John had suggested that the United Kingdom should find the L20,000 ($200,000) which he estimated would be necessary to start the new administration of Brunei. This was to be of a very simple character and self-supporting thereafter. Sir John thought that the sum mentioned was not an excessive amount for His Majesty's Government to pay

> to retrieve the condition of a country which has certainly not derived any benefit in the past from its position under British protection, and has, indeed, suffered, because its position

33

and its regard for British protection
and justice has rendered it easy for its
neighbors to encroach on its territories
with serious results to its resources
and revenues.[98]

Whitehall, for its part, could see no reason for
asking the British taxpayer to find the money. The
Secretary of State for the Colonies, A. Lyttelton
ruled that a loan bearing interest for Brunei should
be sought from the Federated Malay States (FMS) and
that "an attempt should also be made to recover the
Limbang," without which, it was feared, Brunei would
never pay well.[99]

At the end of 1906 C.P. Lucas listed the main
reasons why the British government had supported
McArthur's recommendation that a Resident should be
installed in Brunei: (a) as far as could be judged,
the people of the country opposed the rajah and (b)
no reason was seen why the spectacular success of
British administration in the FMS should not have
been repeated in Brunei. Lucas himself wanted the
British government to have a footing in Borneo, in
the expectation of the collapse of the British North
Borneo Company (BNBC) and possibly Sarawak also, to
facilitate the incorporation of all British Borneo
(Kalimantan Utara) into one larger colony "for the
benefit of the human beings concerned."[100]

The second point is important. For many years
Sarawak had seemed a model for the administration of
a Malay State, but later it was overshadowed, in
Colonial Office eyes at least, by British administration in Malaya. Rajah Charles, in comparison,
began to appear "disappointed and unprogressive";
and he had "quite enough" territory already.[101]

During 1905, arrangements were made for the
recovery of Labuan from the BNBC and for the
appointment of a joint Brunei-Labuan Resident. It
should be noted, however, that although the two
posts were held by one man until 1921 (apart from
1915-17), Brunei and Labuan remained separate
entities: the former was a Malay sultanate under
British protection; the latter a Crown Colony
transferred to the Straits Settlements.

Who was to be the first Resident? In January
1905 Sir Frank Swettenham had suggested McArthur.
Sir John Anderson agreed that the former acting
consul was "a very careful and sound fellow," but
some of his senior advisers had suggested that "if
we are to have a Resident, Mr. Chevalier is the best
man." Sir Frank, whose opinion had been requested

by the new High Commissioner, declared that Chavalier was "about the best of the district officers now left in the Federated Malay States" but was "too good and too senior to send to Labuan." Hence McArthur was preferred. Chevalier replaced him while he was on leave in 1907 and was Acting Resident again from 1909 to 1913.[102]

Back in 1905, it remained to re-negotiate the 1888 Treaty with Sultan Hashim. McArthur, reappointed acting consul in October 1905, asked that a senior officer accompany him to Brunei to undertake this task because such an individual would be more likely to be able to complete negotiations than he would by himself. Donald George Campbell,* Resident of Negri Sembilan, became available for this purpose at the end of October 1905.

Sir John's instructions to the two envoys were set out in a letter dated 9 November, which provided a blueprint for the early years of the Residency system.[103] In view of the lawlessness in Brunei Sultan Hashim was to be warned that if he refused to accept the terms offered, the British government would leave him to his fate. In that case Brunei would probably have been annexed by Sarawak and its royal dynasty blotted out. Assuming that Sultan Hashim desired His Majesty's assistance in averting such an end, it was to be made clear to His Highness that the whole of the administration and the whole powers of legislation and of taxation were to be considered on the advice of the Resident. Instead of the irregular revenues which they had hitherto received, the sultan and wazirs were to accept fixed annual payments, and they were to understand that the amounts of such payments might be revised (reduced) in the case of their successors in the light of the actual costs of the administration. Tulin rights and monopolies were to be investigated carefully and bought out, in order to provide a revenue for the new regime. Similarly, mortgages of cession monies were to be redeemed, and Sarawak and North Borneo were to be notified to pay the amounts to the Resident in future. Finally, Sir John wanted the Treaty signed before his projected arrival in Labuan on 1 January 1906.

---

* Donald George Campbell (1867-1918) C.M.G. 1912. 1883: Jointed PWD, Selangor. 1890 District Officer. 1904: Resident, Negri Sembilan. 1910-18: General Adviser, Johore. 1918: died 25 June. (CO List, 1918, p. 543).

The negotiations proceeded smoothly and on 5 December 1905 Sir John was able to telegraph to the Colonial Office that His Highness had signed the Supplementary Agreement to the 1888 Treaty, accepting a British Resident. Sir John added a tribute of his own:

> Considering the special difficulties of dealing with so suspicious a people as the Malays of Brunei, I think that the speedy success of negotiations is a great tribute to the tact and ability of these gentlemen.[104]

The two envoys had arrived in Brunei Town at noon on 16 November. On the 18th Campbell presented to the Sultan a letter from the High Commissioner outlining the situation. Two days later His Highness replied that he was always willing to follow the advice of the British Government; but there were many matters to be considered and it would be impossible for him to give an answer during the month of Ramadhan. Sultan Hashim raised the question of Limbang and the usual reply was given-- that the matter could not be reopened. Hence Lyttelton's instruction on this point was ignored. The remainder of the month was spent discussing various points on which His Highness required definite assurances. Eventually, on 3 December 1905, Sultan Hashim and the wazirs attached their seals to the Treaty.[105]

The document they signed was exactly the one which had been drawn up in the Foreign Office the previous July, apart from one change of wording: instead of the Sultan having to accept the Resident's "advice" on all matters except those relating to "the Muhammadan religion and Malay Custom," the last three words ("and Malay custom") were not included in the signed version.[106] This was a significant omission, since "Malay custom" included, among other things, the Brunei methods of land tenure and taxation which the British wished to abolish.

In order to facilitate the signing of the Treaty, Sultan Hashim was loaned $3,000 repayable in installments as his allowance fell due. At the same time he was given assurances on various matters. It was agreed that His Highness and the wazirs would continue to receive any private cession money payments from Sarawak and North Borneo, but that all other revenues would go to the government. Yearly allowances of $12,000 to the Sultan and $6,000 each to the two wazirs were granted with a promise that, should the revenue allow, these allowances "might properly be raised in the future" thus reversing Sir John Anderson's instruction on this point.[107]

At a final interview, however, the wazirs complained that they were not receiving adequate compensation for the rights they had surrendered. As a result a supplementary document was drawn up, which they apparently found to be more satisfactory.

Sir John himself arrived in Brunei Town on 2 January 1906 to sign the new treaty on behalf of HM Government. Sultan Hashim, he reported, gave the impression that he was very glad to be relieved of the burden of attempting to govern Brunei and, at the end of the inaugural ceremony, he shook the High Commissioner warmly by the hand.

Sultan Hashim had invited the assembled nobles to say whether they had any objections to raise. On this occasion the only matter brought up concerned the position of the Muhammadan religion, and they were apparently satisfied with the assurances given.[108]

In August 1906, however, Sultan Muhammad Jemalul Alam, who had succeeded his father the previous May, along with the Regents, presented to the High Commissioner a petition listing five demands, the adoption of which was essential for the "increased happiness and peace" of Brunei.[109] In a commentary written for the guidance of the High Commissioner, McArthur noted that the document, which was "written in a somewhat peremptory style," dealt with questions "which were certain to arise as soon as an attempt was made to introduce a (from the European standpoint) more enlightened form of administration."

With regard to the first demand that Islamic religious courts should be constituted for the hakim (judges), McArthur declared that it was well known that the British authorities had promised not to interfere in any matter concerning breaches of Muhammadan religious law. The real object, he thought, was to ensure the presence on the bench of a hakim, on the grounds that what the Brunei authorities were pleased to call Muhammadan religious law provided penalties for all kinds of offences, from murder to failure to attend Divine Service. McArthur, who had had now become Resident, suggested that in reply it might be stated that provision was being made for the trial of offences against Islamic law by kathis to be appointed by the sultan, but the government did not propose to invoke the assistance of the former Brunei judges in the trial of other offenders, except possibly as assessors.

The adoption of the second proposal, that warrants should not be issued against persons of standing, was out of the question because it would have made a farce of the attempt to administer justice.

The third demand, concerning the recovery by the government of absconded slaves, opened up a very difficult subject, for every person of substance in the sultanate had some domestic slaves. Men lived a fairly independent life, but women were constantly being bought and sold as concubines. This situation was indefensible, but slaves constituted valuable property and McArthur feared that it would be impossible to free them all. He believed, however, that as the "reformed administration" grew in efficiency, the situation would settle itself: more slaves would run away from owners, who would find it impossible to recover them. Hence, while the government would do nothing to free slaves, it could not countenance slavery in any form and would do nothing to assist the recovery of those who had absconded.

The fourth demand, requesting that the Brunei flag should fly over all government buildings, was the only one of the five considered reasonable enough to be accepted.

The final demand, that the High Commissioner uphold his assurances that the customs and laws of Brunei would be kept inviolate and unaltered forever the Resident claimed was a case of "willful misrepresentation." He had had frequent arguments with the Pengiran Bendahara on the subject, and had pointed out that if no changes were to be made, the Pengiran's allowance would automatically cease, because the previous constitution had not provided for its payment. McArthur suggested that the reply to the proposal might be as follows:

> every country has from time to time to alter and revise its laws, that any new laws introduced in Brunei will be laws approved by the Sultan, and that the ridiculous statement attributed to [the High Commissioner] was never made, the whole object of intervention being the amendment of existing customs and so-called 'laws' which were ruining the

country.*

Sir John replied to the petition along the lines indicated above. He did not quite understand why the sultan had been led to put it forward

> unless someone who desires to cause trouble between my friend and me has been saying things to my friend which are not true. I advise my friend not to listen to such people but to seek advice and information, in accordance with the Treaty made with his father, from the Resident only.[110]

Sir John regretted the style of the petition, but doubtless this was to be excused by his friend's youth.

There were further intrigues in Brunei fostered by Rajah Charles Brooke in 1906-1907 which shall be considered in a moment. After McArthur's term of office, a serious clash took place between the British and the young sultan concerning the Land Code of 1909. Sultan Jemal's allowance was cut and at one point he evem was threatened with deposition. Later, however, when he had liberated himself from the influence of the old generation of wazirs who were acting as Regents, his relations with the Residents became more cordial. In 1920 he was knighted and his early death, aged about 35, in 1924 was much regretted.

MCARTHUR AS BRITISH RESIDENT IN BRUNEI
(1906-1908)

Relations with Sarawak. In a dispatch dated 25 January 1906, Sir John Anderson proposed that McArthur, who was also Deputy Governor of Labuan, should "be British Resident (in Brunei) and visit Brunei regularly but an officer permanently on the spot [would also] be necessary.[111] The first Assistant Resident, as this officer was styled, was F.A.S. McClelland (1873-1947), who arrived in Brunei in May 1906. Dato Roberts was appointed to supervise public works in Brunei and Labuan and there was a Chief Police Officer for both territories. No

---

* CO 144/80 (36822) McArthur to Anderson, 10 August 1906, paragraph 7.

other British officers were employed during McArthur's term, unless the Labuan doctor be included.

Before the new Resident could devote his full attention to the reorganization of the administration, he had to deal with the pretensions of the Rajah of Sarawak. Sir Charles was staying at his Cirencester mansion when word arrived that a new UK-Brunei Treaty had been signed. He complained to the Foreign Office that this development was unjust to him adding that the Resident "could not really advance the place and people, except perhaps in the mere fact of keeping the sultan from committing any untoward or oppressive acts."[112]

R.E. Stubbs, a Colonial Office clerk, declared that the decision of His Majesty's government did not require the approval of Sir Charles Brooke. It was essential that the rajah should not be given any grounds for supposing that the new order was likely to be reversed as he might stir up trouble in Brunei in order to show that the new government was unpopular.[113] Indeed, this is exactly what Sir Charles did attempt to do.

In his Report McArthur had stated that the Brunei rulers and people were opposed to the disappearance of their ancient country and dynasty; partisans of the rajah, on the other hand, declared that the Brunei people favored Sarawak control and opposed the Residency.[114] The 1906-1907 intrigues, therefore, provide an opportunity for us to decide which of these interpretations was correct.

For the time being the rajah was informed that in appointing a Resident, the British government had had the most complete regard to all the circumstances of the case, including his own claims and had acted upon advice given with full knowledge of the place and of the people. It was their duty to respect the well-known wishes of Sultan Hashim, who desired to maintain the independence of his country. The Secretary of State, moreover, had no reason to suppose that British rule in Brunei would be any less successful than it had been in Malaya; nor could it be admitted, as Sir Charles had claimed, that the Resident would be ignorant of Borneo or would inaugurate a complicated administration. Finally, the British government looked with confidence to the cooperation of the Sarawak government in making the new system successful for Brunei and for the adjoining British protectorates.[115]

This was expecting too much. The rajah's disappointment at the turn of events was too deeply rooted for him easily to acquiesce in the new situation. He blamed McArthur personally for his failure to incorporate Brunei within Sarawak, and, being a "vindictive old man," he desired to see the new Resident come to grief in Brunei. As the High Commissioner commented:

> He [Sir Charles] never has been a scrupulous person, and, surrounded as Brunei is by Sarawak territory, there can be no doubt if he gives the wink we [HM Government] shall have trouble.[116]

One matter particularly incensed Sir Charles: they were paying the sultan and his officers the exact amount that he had offered.[117]

This was only superficially true. McArthur devoted a long section of his Report to the Sarawak offer and concluded that: (a) even in his current reduced circumstances, the sultan was already receiving (admittedly by mortgaging future revenues and by cession of territory) approximately the same amount offered by the rajah; (b) that no allowance had been made in the Sarawak offer for tulin claims; and (c) that present needs rather than true value had been the criterion upon which Sir Charles had based his terms. Finally, the annuities promised by Sir Charles, instead of increasing as the future revenues of Brunei might allow, were to be cut in half at the death of the present recipients. In accepting the British offer, on the other hand, Sultan Hashim did not personally have to meet tulin claims from his own allowance. He and his descendants had the prospect of an increased rather than reduced annuity in the future, and, the sultanate and dynasty were preserved (which would not have been the case had the Sarawak offer been accepted).

The early death of Sultan Hashim (10 May 1906) gave Sir Charles his opportunity. The old sultan, who had been in bad health for some years, began to fail visibly in March 1906. Early in April he took to his bed complaining of severe internal pains and never appeared in public again. McArthur addressed a letter to His Highness requesting him to nominate his successor. The Resident took this step, partly to prevent intrigues concerning the succession, which did not follow the rule of primogeniture, and partly to allay the worries of the Kedayans, who feared that no royal ruler was to be appointed at all. In early April McArthur was summoned to a private audience by Sultan Hashim, who had rallied a

41

little. His Highness questioned him closely as to
whether His Majesty's government really intended to
uphold his dynasty after his death and seemed very
relieved by the Resident's assurances. It is
notable that no request was made for Brunei to be
placed under the protection of Sarawak.

McArthur then was handed a letter, Sultan
Hashim's will, to be read before the State Council.
Its contents had been kept secret, and McArthur
found on arrival that the Council was full of conjecture about the nature of the decision. Sultan
Hashim's final wishes were that he should be succeeded by his oldest legitimate son Pengiran Muda
Muhammad Jemalul Alam, that the succession should
descend in the future in his line, and that the two
remaining wazirs were to be Regents during his
minority. These were endorsed unanimously by the
council. The Pengiran Bendahara, who had claims of
his own to the throne, failed to conceal his disappointment that he was not even to be sole Regent
and McArthur feared that this may have had the
effect of "making him more willing to intrigue with
others."[118]

McArthur, who devoted a section of his Report
to the succession (paragraphs 69-71), does not even
mention therein Pengiran Muhammad Jemal. The
Resident had seen very little of the designated
heir, for in 1906 he was a youth aged about 17, and
held no official position.[119] McArthur felt that it
would have been impolitic not to retain the sultan's
allowance, although he knew that the High Commissioner wanted it reduced, because His Highness
(Sultan Hashim) had left seven illegitimate sons
unprovided for.

Sultan Hashim's illness continued until 10 May
1906, when he died. Sir Charles, who was in Brunei
at about this time, took advantage of the situation
to attempt to demonstrate the unpopularity of the
Residency system and the preference of the Brunei
people for his own rule.

The first intrigue concerned the obsequies of
the late sultan. The Resident had made provision
for a public funeral at $1,000. Dato Roberts was
instructed to pay the Regents $500 immediately on
the sultan's decease and a further $500 when he was
satisfied that the first sum had been properly
expended. A few days later McArthur, who was ill in
Labuan, received a letter from Deshon, one of the
rajah's officers, to the effect that Brunei chiefs
had been to Sir Charles, apparently in great distress because they could raise no money properly to

carry out the funeral ceremonies. The rajah, out of
pity for them, made a free gift of $500 but Deshon
would not divulge to whom the money had been paid.
When the newly-arrived Assistant Resident inquired
in Council as to the rajah's gift, "everyone indig-
nantly denied having received a cent of it."[120]
(The recipient, in fact, was the Pengiran
Bendahara.)

Meanwhile, the rajah had been gathering
signatures for a petition and forwarding to the
British government the Bendahara's complaints.

A little later the British government received
a letter from Sir E. Sassoon, M.P., enclosing a note
from the Bendahara and commentaries thereon by C.A.
Bampfylde (another Sarawak officer) and a petition
from "all the people of Brunei." Sir E. Sassoon had
been asked to bring to the attention of the Foreign
Office the State of opinion prevailing among the
people and chiefs of Brunei:

> Enveloped as this decayed Sultanate is
> by the growing territory of Sarawak,
> where, in contrast to a position of
> unhappiness, their own kindred live in
> prosperity and content, it is not
> surprising that the chiefs and people
> of Brunei ask to be allowed to live
> under a rule which the experience of
> their friends and relatives has taught
> them to regard as sympathetic and bene-
> ficient.[121]

The Pengiran Bendahara's grievances do not
appear to have been particularly substantial. He
complained, for example, that McArthur had ordered
the Assistant Resident to Brunei in a man-of-war to
inquire who had received the payment from the rajah.

> We were much surprised, wrote [the
> Pengiran Bendahara], for from the first
> we had kept this matter from the Sultan.
> We were shamed to have to acknowledge
> the receipt of this money. (Emphasis
> added.)[122]

It is interesting to note that the wazir considered
his own deception to be of less importance than its
exposure by the Assistant Resident, i.e. disrespect
by a social inferior to an aristocrat. His other
four complaints in this letter were demonstrated to
have been factually inaccurate. Elsewhere he

complained that the Resident no longer consulted him on matters of policy. McArthur conceded that this was to a certain extent true because he "found it necessary on every occasion on which official matters [had] been discussed to disagree with [his] extraordinarily selfish views."[123]

Bampfylde, in his commentary on the Pengiran Bendahara's letter claimed that the rajah had done nothing wrong in offering his gift, and the whole affair had involved an unprecedented piece of bullying (by McArthur) and a studied and wholly gratuitous insult to the rajah, emphasized by the uncalled-for dispatch of a man-of-war. McArthur, he added, had seized on the incident

> to impress upon the Bruneis his superior authority and to endeavor to weaken the rajah's influence. It was a tactless act and can only have been prompted by jealousy, but it is an act that will bring Mr. McArthur into a contempt amongst not only the Bruneis but the people of Labuan.[124]

After refuting the Bendahara's claims, McArthur explained that after Sultan Hashim's death he had telegraphed to the High Commissioner that someone should take his place during his incapacity in Brunei during such a critical time. McClelland was sent in HMS Thistle because there was no other ship to take him from Singapore. The Resident considered that this afforded

> an excellent opportunity to counter-balance the impression caused in Brunei by the visit of the Zahora (the Rajah's 'yacht') and therefore asked the commander of the Thistle to take Mr. McClelland across to Brunei.[125]

The Zahora was armed, a gun being prominently mounted in her bow, and was run on regular man-of-war lines. McArthur felt that it was advisable that "the people of Brunei [should] see that other Governments also possess such ships," (presumably, so that they need not feel intimidated by Sir Charles Brooke).[126]

Sir E. Sassoon also presented to the Foreign Office a petition dated 11 May 1906 (the day after Sultan Hashim's death) from the servants of the Rajah, all the people of Brunei, together with the chiefs of the villages who did not at all approve of being governed by the Resident, under whose rule nothing but trouble was experienced. Under the Sarawak government, on the other hand, the people were prosperous and contented, commodities were cheap and trouble was not brought down upon the rakyat (people). In view of this the people of Brunei trusted a thousandfold to be placed under the Brooke State, so that they might have been relieved of their troubles. McArthur replied that, apart from the signatures of, at most, four of the eleven headmen of Kampung Ayer, he could trace none of the other twenty-six signatories and that they were certainly not leaders of society in Brunei. The majority of people, McArthur claimed, were satisfied with the change of administration. He was also able to demonstrate that the intrigue was not spontaneous, but was made on the initiative of the rajah himself.[127] Finally, commodity prices had actually begun to fall since the installation of the Resident at the beginning of the year.

It is difficult to believe that the people of Brunei genuinely sought Sarawak rule, as claimed by Bampfylde both in these documents in the Public Record Office and in his History of Sarawak.[128]

First, as Sir Frederick Weld had pointed out in 1887, acceptance of Sarawak control would have meant

> nothing less than the extinction of the ancient kingdom of Brunei, and the probable ruin of his (the Sultan's) town and dispersion of his people. It is hardly in human nature to 'willingly' accept this, and nothing could be more evident than that he would never accept it.[129]

F.N. Butterworth, a contemporary observer and a sympathizer with Sarawak, noted that the Brunei people were "intensely patriotic and very proud of their city."[130] H. Chevalier (Resident 1909-13) reported that the Brunei Malay had "a greater pride of race and country than any Malay [he had] come across so far."[131] If these observations are true, the people can hardly have wished to see their country disappear within another. Confirmation of this is provided from Brooke sources: on 1 July 1913, for example, the Sarawak Gazette lamented that, during the rajah's recent visit to Brooketon,

very few visits or messages were received from the Brunei capital, where
all at one time before the occupation by
the British Government used to be so
friendly whenever a Sarawak flag or man
appeared in their river.[132]

In the 1940s and 1950s, moreover, British officers
serving in Brunei met strong resistance to attempts
to coordinate more closely the administrations of
Brunei and Sarawak (the latter having become a
colony in 1946).[133] It seems, therefore, that we
may safely agree with McArthur when he commented in
1904 that a British Residency was less obnoxious to
Brunei Malays than incorporation within Sarawak.

In 1906 the Sarawak pressure group continued
to work for a reversal of the British government's
decision to appoint a Resident in Brunei. Sir
Charles Dilke and Sir Charles Jessel addressed
letters to the Foreign Office in support of the
Rajah.[134] Sarawak's most persistent advocate,
however, was Sir E. Sassoon, who bombarded government and newspapers with letters, and in 1906-8,
tabled several sets of questions concerning Brunei
in the House of Commons, sometimes at the least
excuse. In April 1906, for instance, a report had
appeared in The Times under the headline "Incident
in Brunei." The baronet demanded further details.
It transpired that the episode had been of absolutely no importance of political significance. The
Resident suggested that certain persons outside
Brunei, disappointed at the recent course of events
there were "only to anxious to misrepresent" all
that occurred in the sultanate.[135] A policeman had
gone to call a Malay to the Residency on charges of
having evaded payment of customs duties. The headman of this ward, whose mortgages on State revenue,
had been compulsorily redeemed by the new administration, instigated other inhabitants of the hamlet
to attempt to intimidate the Government, leading
them to suppose that this was an arrest and not a
summons to trial. The crowd drove the policeman
from the hamlet and pursued him to the Residency
wharf. McArthur directed them to disperse but they
paid no attention to this order. Upon threatening
to ask the policeman to open fire, however, the
crowd melted away. The Resident then inquired into
the customs fraud, and ordered the defendant to pay
the amount due to the customs farmer. The latter
did so at once. Subsequently, the matter was taken
up independently with the State Council, who summon-

46

ed the headman and fined him $500. The incident, moreover, proved the goodwill of the pengirans, a number of whom had come to assist the Resident. Finally, Sultan Hashim himself caused it to be notified publicly that he was ashamed that some of his subjects should have shown disrespect to McArthur.[136]

The credibility of Sir E. Sassoon was undermined further by his letter published in The Standard of 10 December 1906, in which he referred to Brunei as a state in the Malayan Peninsula.[137]

Sir Charles Brooke, however, did not give up all hope of achieving his objective, and when McArthur went on leave in 1907, the rajah took the opportunity to renew his petition for the incorporation of Brunei within Sarawak. Prompted solely by an earnest desire to have matters in and around Brunei put on a surer and better footing so that some improvement in the state of affairs there might be effected, he suggested that Lord Elgin, Secretary of State for the Colonies, might invite the Acting Resident (Chevalier) to prepare a full report on the condition and prospects of the sultanate. The rajah added that Brunei was worth nothing to him (Report 109), but it would benefit the people of the north-west coast if they were all under one administration. Hence, although Brunei would be a liability, Sir Charles was willing to undertake all responsibility and losses in this respect. His only conditions were that a thorough transfer should be made, in consideration of monthly allowances to the sultan and his chiefs and that the latter "should have no power or authority over the people and in the affairs of the State other than [he] should deem fit and proper to invest them with."[138] The British government declined the rajah's offer and reiterated their reasons for appointing a Resident. Lord Elgin regretted that he could not "reconsider the matter or hold out hope that the policy [would] be revised and the State of Brunei incorporated with Sarawak."[139] As late as 1910, however, the rajah, reportedly, was entertaining such hopes.

Meanwhile there were many other outstanding questions between Brunei and Sarawak which needed to be settled before an effective administration could be introduced in the sultanate. In a dispatch dated 13 February 1906 McArthur raised the Limbang issue.[140] After reviewing the importance of the district to Brunei, the circumstances of its seizure in 1890 and the consequent rapid decline of Brunei thereafter, McArthur expressed the opinion that the district was an integral part of Brunei and that some arrangement would be necessary if anything were to be made of the State in the future. He realized that the full recovery of the district was out of the question, that reversal of roles with the Rajah of Sarawak, instead of the powerless Sultan of Brunei, as victim, would no doubt rouse too great an outcry.

McArthur suggested instead that the Limbang River itself should be made the boundary between (West) Brunei and Sarawak administration from its mouth up to the Madalam confluence. This arrangement would (a) settle once and for all the disputed ownership of land between Brunei and the Limbang and the island of Berembang and (b) short of leaving the rajah in undisturbed possession, cause the minimum of inconvenience to the Sarawak Government. Control of the upper Limbang would give Brunei two main advantages: (1) a means of communication to Belait and Tutong; and (2) a more effectual control over the export of jungle produce from Brunei territory, which was being sent from ulu Tutong without any duty being paid to a Brunei government dependent on customs revenue for much of its income. The Sarawak authorities had refused to help in this matter. The establishment of a system of internal customs in Brunei being difficult, McArthur concluded that the sultanate's interests would be best served by obtaining control of one bank of the Limbang River down which the goods were carried. The Limbang boundary had already proved a fruitful source of disagreement and the district had never been voluntarily ceded; hence the Brunei government was justified in asking for a definite and favorable settlement.

Stubbs agreed that Sarawak's seizure of Limbang had been an outrage, in which Her Majesty's Government would never have acquiesced if their representatives had kept them properly informed. The fact remained, however, that H.M. Government had acquiesced and to take the territory back now without compensation would be an injustice to Sarawak. As an alternative Stubbs suggested a territorial exchange and, if this were not agreed upon, he said a joint Sarawak-Brunei Commission would have to be insisted upon to determine the borders.[141] It was decided to await the death of Rajah Charles before re-opening the issue.[142] In August 1906 the High Commissioner suggested that the rajah should be called upon to pay the $6,000 annual cession money, but this proposal was not accepted, for the reason given above: that the British government had already acquiesced in the situation and released the rajah from any further obligation.[143] (See above, p. 31.)

When Sir Charles died in 1917, well after McArthur had left Brunei, the issue was revived, but it was felt that the new Rajah, Vyner Brooke (1874-1963; r. 1917-1946), would suffer a severe blow to his prestige if he were to surrender Limbang so early in his reign. It was shown, moreover, that Sarawak had sustained a loss of $120,000 in its administration of the district since 1890. And so nothing was done.[144]

McArthur was slightly more successful in his attempts to recover full administrative rights for the Brunei government over Muara Damit at the mouth of the Brunei River. In February 1906 McArthur drew the attention of the High Commissioner to the powers being exercised by the rajah there, some of them illegally.

Sir Charles was obliged to withdraw his "Administrator of Brooketon" (Muara), where he owned a coal mine as well as land rights and revenue farms. The rajah regretted, however, that

> after so many years of unquestioned administration in Borneo, he should now, for the first time, be met with an accusation of irregularity and that doubt should be thrown upon the justness of his actions.[145]

Undoubtedly, some people (presumably the Resident and High Commissioner) wished to damage his reputation. Stubbs argued that it was ludicrous that Sir Charles should presume to appoint an administrator of territory which even he admitted belonged to another country.[146] The rajah, therefore, was made to understand that he could not be allowed to do so, nor could the claim be conceded that some people wished to damage his reputation.[147]

McArthur sounded the Sarawak Resident of Limbang about discussions concerning further outstanding questions to do with Muara Damit, such as the stationing of Sarawak police there and the maintenance of a Sarawak magistrate.[148] Sir Charles immediately took up the matter with the Colonial Office: he wished to know whether McArthur was authorized to negotiate for the taking over of this concession, to inaugurate a system of jurisdiction, and to put police in place of the small force which he had hitherto maintained there. The position of Brooketon, the rajah added, could be of no use to the British government, the colliery settlement was compact and peaceful, and any change could not be beneficial to anyone concerned. Why, he demanded, should the present state of the place be disturbed?[149]

In a second letter, this time to Sir John Anderson, the rajah declared that the British government should either leave him to work the coal as before or purchase from him the coal rights and deed of land concession, but not one without the other: "In [that] event [he] would at once hand over and clear out."[150] This offer was made, however, in the full knowledge that Brunei was bankrupt.

Sir John Anderson noted that the position created by the British government's implied recognition of the rajah's revenue rights in Muara Damit was extremely anomalous and difficult. He pointed out that while Sir Charles held all the sources of revenue enumerated in his concession, he was under no obligation to contribute one cent towards the administration by Brunei of this territory, and that he had, in fact, established without any legal warrant an administration of his own, which had been exercising both civil and criminal jurisdiction there. Now that a reformed administration had been instituted in Brunei, Sir Charles might no longer plead the justification of necessity, and he had been informed by the British government that the usurpation must cease. But

> unless some method can be found of obtaining a contribution from the Rajah towards the expenses of the new administration, it must, so far as the Muaras are concerned, be inefficient and intermittent.[151]

The rajah's occupation of the district had deleterious consequences for the administration of the sultanate as a whole. McArthur pointed out that, not only were the actual revenues of Muara district lost to Brunei, but attempts to collect revenue in the Brunei watershed were rendered hopeless by the existence of a foreign power at the mouth of the river:

> Brunei has depended in the past, and will have to depend for some time to

come, on the revenues derived from import and export duties. At present goods are landed at Brooketon, from which depot they are distributed over the countryside without paying any dues to the government.

For example, buffaloes were being exported from Brunei to Sarawak via Brooketon, without payment of the duty of one dollar per head. McArthur urged, therefore, that Sir Charles Brooke's monopoly of revenue rights in Muara be cancelled, the question of any compensation to be settled afterwards, by arbitration if necessary:

> The question is, for the Brunei Government, not merely one of monetary profit and loss, but of effective administration of the State.[152]

Acting upon McArthur's information, Sir John Anderson contended that the January 1887 Agreement by which the rajah held his rights in Muara district did not preclude the Brunei government from imposing export duties there. The only other sources of income which had not been hypothecated to Sarawak were poll tax and shipping dues. Hence, from 1 January 1907 an export duty of 25 cents per ton was to be imposed on coal, and from the same date the rajah would be required to withdraw his police from the district and his post office. Another reason for asserting the Brunei government's rights in Muara was that the High Commissioner's efforts to abolish slavery in the sultanate would be undermined if the prohibition could not be enforced throughout the State, and the rajah, apparently, continued to permit domestic slavery.[153]

Stubbs agreed that it would be a good thing to buy out the rajah, but there was no money.[154] Sir Charles agreed to withdraw his police but described the proposal to levy a coal export duty to be quite contrary to the spirit of the concession, and, in view of the heavy losses he was sustaining already at Brooketon, he threatened to close down the mines. Once more the rajah lamented these and other complications, as they appeared to be to him, that were then taking place in and around Brunei.[155]

The Colonial Office was anxious that the rajah should keep open his mines and they feared that he had them in a "cleft stick" in this matter for, as Stubbs explained, if the mines were closed

51

Sir C. Brooke will make capital out of
the incident by using it in support of
the intrigues in which he is now engaged
with a view to swallowing up Brunei and
we shall gain nothing--since, if the
mines are shut, there will be no duties
collected.[156]

Stubbs took up the suggestion that the wild,
unknown Temburong district might be given to Sir
Charles in exchange. If the Temburong were considered too valuable to be given for the farm rights
alone, the rajah should either make a money payment,
or return such part of the Limbang as would make a
more convenient frontier.[157]

McArthur, however, vehemently opposed any
exchange involving Temburong district. The region
contained no tulin property apart from the Labu, and
was the only tract of territory which had come under
the control of the new administration unencumbered
by such rights (see below, p. 55). The watershed
had never been fully explored, but the district was
said to be rich in damar, timber, jungle produce,
gold and mineral oil. Indeed, a timber-cutting
company was interested in working the district and
royalties of $7,000 a year were in prospect (a
considerable sum, when it is realized that Brunei's
entire revenue in 1907 was only $51,777). The
Temburong, moreover, was the most accessible of the
outdistricts, being only three hours by launch from
the capital. Finally, any transfer was opposed by
the Sultan and chiefs, and would destroy that confidence in the British which he had been attempting
so laboriously to build up since January 1906.[158]

Sir John Anderson, in May 1907, conceded
reluctantly that the present state of things would
have to continue for the present. The main
difficulty with such a 'do-nothing' course lay in
the character of the rajah who had not yet abandoned
hope of obtaining control of Brunei and was still
intriguing there and using his agents to gather
signatures to petitions.[159] (An export duty on coal
was eventually imposed on 1 January 1921, the
Brooketon mines having achieved profitability for
the first time in 1917. Rajah Vyner (r. 1917-46),
however, closed the colliery in 1924 and his coal
mining concession lapsed the following year.)

Another dispute with Rajah Charles in 1907
concerned the gambling farm which he had established
in Muara Damit. McArthur had no doubt that the
Brunei government was entitled to claim the revenue

52

from any such farm and "seeing how few rights [the Brunei government had] left there, [he did] not think that any should be allowed to lapse."[160] On this occasion, however, the rajah's stance was upheld by Sir Frank Swettenham, as it was again in 1914.[161] The really strong argument in the rajah's favor was that if Sultan Hashim had believed himself to have retained the right to this farm, undoubtedly he would have sold it, just as he sold every other source of revenue.[162]

Gambling, however, did have deleterious consequences in Muara district. Chevalier reported in 1910 that the indigenous magistrate at Brooketon

> has to spend most of his time in Court, there being more litigation in the Court of Requests at Brooketon than there is at Brunei [Town]. This is probably due to indebtedness among Malays owing to the existence of a farm in which Malays are allowed to gamble.[163]

This is confirmed in the following table.

Table 1. Brunei: Court Cases 1912-1913

Year	Type of Case	Muara District (1)	All Brunei Sultanate (2)	(1) as % of (2)
1912	Civil	237	428	55.37
	Criminal	41	254	16.14
1913	Civil	166	304	54.61
	Criminal	49	310	15.81

Source: CO 824/1, Compiled by author from Brunei Annual Reports.

These figures are all the more remarkable when one considers that Muara district in 1911 contained only 6.6 percent of the Brunei population (1,447 out of 21,718 people). Normally in British-protected States gambling was restricted to adult male Chinese, when it was permitted at all.[164] In this instance, however, the government was powerless to intervene. Stubbs believed as follows:

If only Rajah Brooke will leave the
place [Brunei] alone, it ought to turn
the corner soon . . . I believe . . .
that the whole of the Muara concessions
are causing [him] a very heavy loss:
and it is only his pride and his hope
that he may yet be allowed to absorb
Brunei that prevents him abandoning
them. I have great hopes that his son
will be more reasonable, and Sir C.
Brooke is over eighty.[165]

Hence the Muara question was not settled
during McArthur's term. It was not until 1924,
after three years of negotiation, that agreement was
reached whereby Sarawak would surrender the revenue
farms, including gambling and <u>chandu</u> (opium) in
exchange for a reduction of certain cession money
payments to the Brunei government. Finally, in
1931-2, agreement was reached whereby Rajah Vyner
also gave up his land rights in Muara Damit, except
for his bungalow and its grounds.

Finance. One of the most pressing tasks of
the new government in Brunei was to abolish the
former land tenure system in order that one
authority might be exercised throughout the country
and revenue raised for a newly-created, albeit
simple, central administration.
As mentioned already, the surrender of
kerajaan and kuripan rights had been secured during
the 1905 negotiations. Tulin claims, on the other
hand, presented a more formidable difficulty as did
the resumption of trade monopolies. McArthur also
sought to introduce institutions such as a public
treasury, a public works department, a police force,
a gaol, and so on, all of which had been lacking in
pre-Residential Brunei.
Such internal reform was delayed, however, by
the difficulties with Sarawak (just described) and
by the death of Sultan Hashim. The latter event was
most inopportune as far as the new administration
was concerned: he had reigned for over twenty years
and his knowledge of what had been done in the past
and the weight of his authority (when bolstered by
that of the Resident) had been "of great assistance
in the peaceable introduction of reforms and
changes."[166] The confusion consequent upon his
illness and death, it was reported, retarded the
work of reorganizing the administration.[167] During
Sultan Hashim's final illness all public business

remained at a standstill. McArthur continued to
redeem such monopolies as to the genuineness and
value of which he was satisfied but he had to give
up all attempt to deal with the ownership of land
because Sultan Hashim's seal was abstracted during
His Highness' sleep and affixed illegally to documents which the Sultan never saw. For fear of such
forgeries, the Resident was obliged to leave
unsettled a great many matters, including the
resolution of tulin claims, which might otherwise
have been tackled, and he voiced the fear that
little progress had been made during the first six
months.[168]

(a) Tulin property. Tulin rights were powers
of administration and taxation, held as hereditary
property by local families, but usually mortgaged to
Chinese traders.[169] The only district of Brunei
relatively free of such property was the Temburong.
Redemption of tulin rights did not begin in
earnest until 1907.[170] The sorting out of claims
was an intricate process because many had been
forged, particularly during the final illness of
Sultan Hashim. The rights were gradually taken over
by the Government by arrangement with the owners,
who received instead fixed annual allowances
(political pensions) in place of their previous
receipts. In some cases, tulin owners preferred to
sell out to the government for a capitulated sum.
Two claims were bought outright in this way during
1907, payment in one case being $2,500 and in the
other $2,000.[171] Assessment continued in 1908 and
1909, computations in some instances being referred
to the High Commissioner for final pronouncement.
In 1910 Lee-Warner, the newly-appointed Assistant
Resident, found 105 "claims-in-chief" and another
500 sub-claims which remained outstanding. The
tulin issue appears finally to have been settled
during his first term (1910-11).[172] During the
years 1906-1909 at least $7,045 was spent on the
redemption of tulin rights,[173] but for the main
period of settlement, 1910-11, figures are not
available. It was estimated in 1907 that "at least
$6,000 annually" ultimately would have to be paid as
political pensions.[174] In 1915, $5,141 was listed
under this heading; in 1920, $7,709; but in 1925
only $4,064.

More important than tulin rights in terms of
revenue for the new administration was the redemption of monopolies.

(b) Monopolies. At the beginning of 1906 most
of Brunei's revenues were in the hands of monopo-

55

lists, chiefly Chinese, who had obtained the right to collect them by payments of cash to the sultan.[175] In some cases the monopoly of trading in certain articles had been granted, in others the right of charging duty on imports or exports had been sold outright, no limit being fixed for the rates to be charged by the monopolist. The only commodity not thus exploited was rice, the staple food. Even in the case of rice, in 1904, a British trader, James Hatton Hall unsuccessfully attempted to persuade Sultan Hashim to sell him a rice monopoly. I have mentioned already (p. 28 above) that the letting and sub-letting of such monopolies forced retail prices up. For, as McArthur reported, it was to the interest of the original monopolist to sublet the monopoly and so receive a fixed income from other traders, rather than go to the trouble and expense of maintaining a private preventive staff. The result was that many goods sold in the sultanate were of an inferior quality and "cost more than double what better kinds would fetch in Singapore."[176]

The more valuable monopolies were leased to just two Chinese traders, Chua Cheng Hee and Cheok Yu, who enjoyed the additional advantage of being able to import their own goods free of tax. Let us consider imports of sundry goods. At the end of 1904 McArthur reported that Chua Cheng Hee had acquired the right to levy five percent duty on such imports from 1901 to 1929 (for which right he had paid $15,000), plus the right to collect additional two percent duties during the years 1904 to 1910 (for $8,800). In addition Cheok Yu had purchased, for $7,500 in cash, the right to levy five percent duties on the same articles from 1905 until 1910. McArthur, writing in 1904, noted that one of these leases was chopped and dated 1905. This is the most extreme example, but it does give an indication both of the financial plight of Brunei's rulers at the time and of the nature of the task facing the first British Resident in Brunei.

Since no administration was possible as long as these monopolies remained in existence, a loan of $200,000 was obtained from the Federated Malay States to enable the government to buy them out. Many were redeemed in 1906, but others (affecting outlying districts were not touched until the following year, as Table 2 indicates.

56

Table 2. Brunei: Monopolies (1906-1908)

	Monopolies Redeemed by the Government		Revenue Accruing to the Government
Year	Number	Cost ($ Straits)	($ Straits)
1906	27	61,105	19,850
1907	4	9,360	30,155
1908	n.a.	1,544	28,897
Totals	31+	72,009	78,902

Source: CO 824/1. Compiled by author from Brunei
        Annual Reports.

These statistics appear to suggest that by
1908 a profit of $6,893 had already been achieved if
interest due on the loan is excluded.
Of the 27 monopolies redeemed in 1906, the
most valuable were indicated in Table 3.

Table 3. Brunei: Compensation paid to monopolists
          in 1906

Compensation paid ($ Straits)	Description of Monopoly
11,699.54	Sundry goods (10% import duty)
9,952.50	Opium
9,000.00	General import and export (Tutong)
9,000.00	Spices and Java tobacco
3,750.00	"3% import duties"
2,848.47	"Belait import/export and opium etc"

Source: CO 824/1. Brunei Annual Report for 1906,
        p. 7.

Lesser amounts were paid in 1906 for the
redemption of monopolies of market boat tax (leased
until 1920), kerosene (leased until 1922), import
and export duties (Temburong), cattle export, sugar
(leased several times over up to 1909), and so
on.[177]
The procedure adopted was to offer monopolists

their original purchase money less an amount proportionate to the number of years they had held
their monopoly already. An exception to this rule
was Sir Charles Brooke, who was allowed to retain
his revenue monopolies in Muara district.

After monopolies affecting the import trade of
the capital had been cleared off in April 1906,
customs regulations were introduced substituting a
fixed and moderate scale of import duties for the
restrictions which had been in force. These regulations were extended to Tutong district as soon as
monopolies there had been similarly dealt with. In
1906 time did not allow clearing off the import
monopolies in the other two districts, and no export
monopolies at all were redeemed before November of
that year.[178] It is recorded that the initial
customs regulations, which were "tentative and
temporary," were repealed, and at the end of 1906 a
new Customs Enactment was passed and made applicable
to the entire State.[179] Some trade monopolies
affecting the outlying districts were redeemed early
the following year.[180] The combined results of
these measures was to reduce retail prices in the
capital and permit a greater degree of free trade.

Toward the end of 1908, the original Malayan
loan was already virtually exhausted. By 1914 no
less than $439,750 had been borrowed, of which
$72,009 had been used for the redemption of
monopolies.

(c) Cession monies. Another possible source
of income for the new administration was the annual
cession money paid by Sarawak and North Borneo for
districts which had been ceded to them. After 1906,
therefore, the Brunei government set about buying up
these rights which, like monopolies, had often been
mortgaged for many years in advance. By 1914,
$174,377 of loan expenditure had been devoted to
this purpose and, before 1928, a further $80,870 of
ordinary revenue had been used likewise. Government
receipts from redeemed cession monies amounted to
$21,646 in 1915 and remained above $18,000 annually
in the years 1916-1918.

(d) Ordinary Revenue: 1906-1908. Ordinary
government income amounted to only $28,173 (not
including 'personal account' of $43,941.80) in 1906,
rising to $51,777 in 1907, but falling back to
$43,529 in the following year. The allowances
payable to the sultan and wazirs alone absorbed
$24,000 annually.

In 1906 the main source of government income
came from revenue farms (licences). Three such

58

farms--opium and spirits ($4,950), import duty on tobacco ($6,050), and kerosene and matches ($1,200) --accounted for no less than $12,210 of the 1906 income. Other customs duties, collected directly, brought in a further $7,270. Additional receipts came from mines, posts and poll tax.[181]

In 1907 the opium, gambling and tobacco import farms were leased for three years at an annual rental of $16,800. But, as Butcher has shown, the revenue farming system was falling into disrepute in Malaya at this time.[182] Hence in Brunei we find that the duty on spirits, let to a farmer during 1906 in conjunction with opium, was collected by the government from the following year. Similarly, the farm for kerosene and matches was also discontinued.

In 1908 it was found that the revenue farmer was unable to meet his liabilities. The agreement, therefore, was terminated on 31 July 1908. Securities were realized, but of $2,300 due, only $1,430 was collected.[183] After 1 August 1908 a new chandu farm was instituted, and this appears to have been the only important one in existence after that date. The farm was leased to Cheok Boon Seok, producing $12,000 in 1912.[184] (The former leading Chinese traders, Cheok Yu and Chua Cheng Hee, appear to have faded into obscurity after 1906.) As a result of the first International Opium Conference, held at The Hague in 1912, it was decided that the manufacture and sale of opium should become a government monopoly. Hence, from 1 January 1913, the Brunei government received all chandu imported into the country from the government of the Straits Settlements' factory in Singapore, and a Government Monopolies Department, headed by E.G. Goldfinch, was created.[185] During 1913 the sale of chandu increased (by about 10 percent) and produced a net profit to the government of $25,070.50 in 1913, rising to $58,975 in the year 1924, when it represented over twenty percent of total government income.[186] It was demonstrated that an increase in the price of chandu had done little to reduce consumption (as hoped in 1912), but it had swelled the receipts of the Brunei administration marvelously.

To return to McArthur's term of office, poll tax produced a mere $1,112 in 1906. In his 1904 Report he had reckoned on $15,000 annually from this source, but great difficulty was always experienced in collecting this tax, and nothing even remotely approaching that figure was ever received. Compilation of registers was not even completed during the first Resident's term, and the figures for 1909 ($4,265) were described as very disappointing.[187] Indeed, the amount was so small and the cost and trouble of collecting it so great, that it was hoped the tax might be abolished altogether.[188] The Kedayans were the most troublesome people with regard to this tax. Being very mean and parsimonious by nature, they made constant appeals for exemption on one ground or another.[189] It was subsequently discovered that Kedayan headmen had not been collecting the tax as fully as they ought to have been.[190] Another reason for the low yield, was that exemption was used as a carrot to attract people to take up land for cultivation.

One major source of income in McArthur's day came from the sale of postage stamps, many of which were bought up by European collectors. In 1907, out of Brunei's total revenue of $51,777, no less than $14,587 (28.17 percent) was derived from this source. Indeed, more might have been done to exploit this avenue: in 1908 and 1909, the income was only $3,766 and $1,870 respectively, but at the time of a new issue in 1912 the amount jumped to $15,957.

During McArthur's term, land revenue was derived chiefly from Sir Charles Brooke for his coal rights and from the Island Trading Syndicate for the area occupied by their cutch factory. In the absence of the necessary staff, it was not yet possible to carry out a survey of occupied lands, and no rents were as yet assessed although rough demarcation was in progress in the vicinity of the capital. As mentioned, the government attempted to encourage agriculture and land settlement (and thereby to swell government receipts from land rents) by remitting poll taxes for new landowners.

(e) Conclusion. McArthur, during his term of office, laid the foundations for the creditable expansion of Brunei's revenue which occurred after his departure from the sultanate. By 1910 a small surplus of ordinary income over expenditure had been achieved for the first time, and an income of six figures was achieved for the first time in the following year. In 1913 income amounted to $165,082, almost a fourfold increase since 1908. Progress was delayed by the First World War, but apart from 1914 and 1920-1 Brunei has always achieved a surplus balance. Loan repayment, however, did not commence until 1920.

Economic Development, 1906-08. At the beginning of the Residential Era the main industries of
the Brunei people included fishing and the collection of mangrove bark in the case of the inhabitants
of the capital and the export of jungle produce from
the outlying districts. Over 300 Malays were
employed in Sir Charles Brooke's coal mines at
Brooketon and Buang Tawar. Another local industry
was boat and tongkang building, but while considerable skill was shown in the manufacture of these
vessels, they were built only to meet domestic
demand. A factory for the manufacture of cutch had
existed in Brunei Town since 1901. This industry
employed large numbers of Malays (400 in 1904), but
the amount of work fluctuated according to vagaries
of the world market: in 1907, for example, the
factory was practically closed for most of the time
because the industry had been adversely affected by
tariff imposed by the United States of America.[191]

In 1906 six oil prospecting licences were
granted. Various extensions were made the following
year and a considerable amount of work was done.
But operations were delayed by wet weather and the
consequent difficulty of transporting machinery in
the interior, so that one of McArthur's successors
commented on the desultory nature of operations.
Indeed, it was not until the formation of the
British Malayan Petroleum Company in 1922 that
matters really got under way. Mineral oil was
exported in small quantities from Buang Tawar, a
spring of oil having been struck accidentally during
the course of coal-mining operations there. The
usual flow was only about four barrels a month.[192]

Early Residents looked to the timber industry
to provide a substantial source of income for the
Brunei government, but here again hopes were dashed.
A number of Chinese woodcutters established themselves in Temburong district. The river contained
large areas of good timber, but it appeared difficult to find any but a purely local market for it
during McArthur's term in office. In 1908 a large
number of railway sleepers were prepared by the
North Borneo Trading Company, but because of
differences with the local Chinese contractors, work
ceased and the sleepers were not exported. A few
Chinese sawyers continued to cut timber and plants
for local use.[193]

Rather more successful was the encouragement
given to Brunei's craft industries, which seem to
have enjoyed a revival under the Residential System.
At the Agricultural Show at Kuala Lumpur in August

61

1908 a few months after McArthur had returned to Malaya Brunei silversmiths, brassworkers and weavers carried off most of the prizes, and the Brunei government itself also won an award.[194]

Brassware and silverware were restricted to certain families and guilds, the members of which kept the secret of the trade very much to themselves. Craftsmanship was traditional, having been handed down from generation to generation. The individual workman was "closely bound by the rules of his trade, very little scope being left for originality of design or method."[195] The work they produced, however, was very beautiful and sometimes elaborately patterned. The craftsmen were concentrated, in particular, in the Sungei Kedayan ward of the capital.[196]

Brassware was the more extensive craft of the two, its practitioners numbering more than two hundred. Silversmiths were less numerous because their trade required greater skill and was more difficult to learn. After 1906 the demand for weapons declined, but the smiths proved adaptable and concentrated more on the production of cigarette cases, ashtrays and finger bowls.

There were also a number of Brunei potters, whose wares were strictly for home consumption. Butterworth recalled that he never heard any Brunei Malay, apart from the potters themselves, boast about the indigenous pottery.[197]

In 1908 some government assistance was given to stimulate the sarong-weaving industry, by which a considerable number of Malay women earned their livelihood. The import duty on the raw materials required for this work was removed and it was hoped later to further reduce the cost of these materials by enabling weavers to purchase them from the government at cost price, which represented a saving of perhaps twenty percent.[198]

The craft industries appear to have remained buoyant under the British Residency, and a fairly substantial export trade was even built up.[199] In the 1930s, however, weaving began to decline because Brunei producers were unable to adapt to meet Japanese competition.[200] The export of brassware and silverware slumped during the Great Depression, and since the Pacific War these crafts have been dying out, because young people are not inclined to undertake a long apprenticeship when higher wages for less labor are available elsewhere. Nowadays only a few old men keep alive these ancient crafts.[201]

One of McArthur's great objects in 1906 was to persuade the river villagers to abandon their crowded and unhealthy surroundings in Kampung Ayer-- where the population may have been decimated during the 1904 smallpox epidemic[202]--and to settle instead on terra firma, where they might take up cultivation, both to their own benefit and to that of their country. In fact, however, the first Resident made virtually no progress in this direction. Very little cultivation was undertaken, although a number of fruit plantations were cleared and reoccupied during the early years of the Residency. The soil was declared generally to be fertile,[203] especially in Tutong district, and it was hoped that as soon as road communication had been established, people who were earning a casual livelihood by the collection of jungle produce would realize the natural advantages of the sultanate and would recommence permanent cultivation of the soil.[204] Lee-Warner, Assistant Resident 1910-1914, took up McArthur's proposals with zeal, and even contemplated forcible measures to induce river villagers to settle on dry land. Fortunately, these ideas were not pursued.[205]

In 1906 four applications were received from Europeans for large areas of land for rubber planting, but three of them were speculative and not pursued. The passing of the Land Code produced a number of claims to agricultural land, the prevalent idea among the aristocracy of Brunei apparently being that land would have a great value in future. No real development of the country was possible, however, until the resolution of tulin claims, which, as we have seen, was not completed until 1911.

In 1908 para rubber planting commenced in Labu district (Temburong). Labor for agricultural purposes was plentiful in Brunei Town itself, but in the outstations population was so scanty that the alternatives were either to induce Malays to migrate from the capital or to import labor. Efforts were made to induce farmers to adopt improved methods of rice planting, especially in the direction of irrigation. Those who did so were well satisfied with the resultant heavier crops and it was expected that others would follow the lead given.[206] By 1910, river villagers had taken up cultivation for the first time and it was already proved that it would be popular and permanent.[207]

The Island Trading Syndicate which owned the cutch factory declined during McArthur's term, but production picked up in 1909 and 1910 and plans were made to open another works in the Rejang district of Sarawak. Similarly, coal output in 1906-8 was restricted because of lack of demand. The collieries continued to run at a loss, which, was all the more to be deplored as the bulk of the coolies were Brunei Malays who earned a steady livelihood under sympathetic masters.[208] (Indeed, it was not until 1917 that the Brooketon colliery produced even a small surplus on a year's working.) Coal and cutch remained Brunei's principal exports until the early 1920s, when they were overshadowed by rubber. Since the 1930s, however, all else has been rendered insignificant by receipts from oil.

Administration 1906-1908. The traditional system in Brunei was characterized by the weakness of the central government and the virtual autonomy enjoyed by nobles in their own districts. The pengirans' territorial power was effectively broken, however, when all land was taken into State ownership and they were relieved of their former powers of administration and taxation. In due course this made possible the creation of an efficient central authority, whose writ ran throughout the country, although McArthur's effective control was not always exercised in the outlying districts.

Indigenous chiefs were placed in charge of the outlying areas as soon as the redemption of monopolies provided employment for government servants. In 1907 there were six such officers stationed in different places. The Resident complained that their ignorance and inexperience made it impossible to hope that they would be of much assistance in the general development of the district of which they were in charge.[209] Their duties consisted of little beyond the adjudication of petty civil cases and the collection of customs duties and poll tax. No government official at all was stationed in Belait until September 1907, because of the delay in coming to terms with the previous tulin owners. In the case of Temburong, a Malay magistrate was appointed early in 1907, but had to be prosecuted and dismissed for extortion after a few months leaving the district without a government representative for the remainder of the year because of the difficulty of finding a suitable replacement. Similarly, the customs clerk at Limau Manis had been dismissed. In 1908 the station there was abolished and the administration of the district combined with that of Brunei. All revenue from Tutong, other than

64

customs, was collected in the State capital. Even so, the Native Officer, a Sarawak Malay of advanced age, had to be retired in 1908 because of numerous and well-founded complaints regarding his administrative methods.[210] No doubt these dismissals represented the unfamiliarity on the part of the Malays concerned with the new ways expected of them: what seemed like extortion to European eyes, was only the time-honoured methods of the Malay. Other Malay officers, particularly Pengiran Anak Hashim in Belait,[211] were considered very worthy, and G.E. Cator (Resident 1916-21) often praised the fairness and justice of the Malay magistrates during his term.[212]

The cardinal feature of British policy in Brunei, as in other Malay States, was the maintenance of the position, authority and prestige of the sultan.[213] Sultan Muhammad Jemalul Alam, who succeeded his father in May 1906, was a minor and the two wazirs acted as regents. Great care was taken to ensure that the ancient constitution was preserved as far as possible.

All legislation was passed by the Sultan-in-Council. According to the Pengiran Bendahara, nine Malays had a constitutional right to sit on the State Council: the sultan who presided; the Pengirans Bendahara, Pemancha, Shahbandar, and Kerma Indra; the Jawatan Abu Bakar; the Dato Perdana Menteri; the Tuan Imam, and finally the Orang Kaya Laksamana.[214] (Doubtless, the other two wazirs--the Pengirans Temenggong and Di Gadong--also had a right to a seat on the State Council, but in 1907 their offices were vacant.) The dominant voice, however, was that of the Resident, whose advice, by the 1905-06 Treaty, had to be accepted on all questions in Brunei, except those affecting the Muhammadan religion.

Three meetings were held in 1908 but only one in the following year, when relations between the young sultan and the Resident were at a low ebb. One irascible Resident declared that meetings of the State Council were rarely necessary or advisable in the present State of Brunei. Their old age precluded the presence of the Pengirans Bendahara and Pemancha and the attitude of the other leading nobles showed that they were incapable of forming any opinion for themselves, discussion of which might tend to the benefit of the country.[215] Elsewhere it was added that the consideration of proposed laws by the Sultan-in-Council was an innovation in a State where formerly sultan and chiefs were laws unto themselves.[216]

An Enactment was passed in 1906 providing for the establishment of civil and criminal courts and for the administration of justice throughout the State as far as possible on the lines in force in the Federated Malay States.

For the first four months of 1906 Brunei was policed by one Pathan and one Sikh. Arrangements were then made to establish a combined force for Labuan and Brunei, nine Sikhs being stationed in the sultanate as soon as accommodation became available. Later, three Malays were engaged, "but the difficulty of recruiting and the lack of suitable candidates made it impossible to bring the [numbers] up to reasonable limits."[217] At this time the services of the police were not required for anything beyond "routine guard duties."[218] By 1908, small contingents of Malay constables had been established in each of the outstations.

Fortunately, there was little crime in the sultanate. Only twenty-one cases came to court in 1906 (ten criminal, eleven civil), resulting in the imprisonment of six persons. Most of the crime reports in the first years of the Residential Era concerned theft, but there was an occasional murder or amok. The Chief Police Officer until 1917 was a certain H.G. Crummey, who had the misfortune to contact leprosy while serving in Brunei.

One of McArthur's further reforms was the establishment of a Public Works Department under the control of Dato Roberts. The number of projected works was drastically curtailed, however, by the need to observe stringent financial economy and the difficulty of obtaining material and skilled labor.

The site of the former British consulate was cleared of jungle and a temporary building put up to accommodate European officers (Report 25). Work commenced on a permanent Residency in December 1906 and was completed the following July. (This building, the bubongan dua-belas, or the house of 'twelve roofs,' has just recently been vacated by HM Government.) A wharf was also built at the Residency.[219]

Among other things, the first Resident was also the founder of the New Capital on terra firma. He declared that he wanted a clean, dry village with 'suburbs' of kampung houses and that he wanted to discourage houses in the river.[220] Hence the plain at the back of the sultan's palace was opened up and a town site there was laid out consisting of two short streets with lamps. In addition a canal was

66

excavated beside the main street for the use of small boats. Finally, a supply of potable water was obtained from a concrete tank constructed about one mile beyond the township and relayed to the New Capital through three-inch cast iron pipes. In fact, only a beginning was made with the land town during McArthur's term of office, and, although approximately 10,000 people lived there at the close of the Residential Era, the population of Kampung Ayer remained even greater.

During 1908 five miles of road trace was cut towards Tutong from the terminus of an oil prospecting trace, thus connecting Tajau, on the Brunei estuary, with Birau, a tributary of Tutong, making a distance of ten miles in all. A further short length of road was made at Tutong, connecting the government station with the village. But it was not until 1927 that the Tutong-Brunei Town road was finally opened.[221] There were no motor vehicles in Brunei before 1924. Unskilled labor was paid 35 cents a day.

In his Report McArthur said nothing specific about medical and educational matters and when he became Resident, his plans in this direction were nullified by the necessity of exercising absolute economy.

In 1906 no medical institutions and no sanitary measures were in existence and it was claimed that neither would have been understood or appreciated by the population. Such medical aid as was required by government officials was obtained from the Colonial Surgeon (Dr. Adamson, d. 1912) in Labuan.[222] A stock of simple medicines was kept by the Assistant Resident, who treated many Brunei Malays for minor ailments. Butterworth, manager of the cutch works, claimed to have provided a similar service.[223] Eventually, in 1911, a government dresser, Leong Ah Ng (also the postmaster, ?1911-1929), was appointed and his attention was in constant demand.[224] It was not until 1929, however, that a hospital and a resident doctor were established in the sultanate. Fear of a renewed outbreak of smallpox was ever-present, but it was not until the First World War (1914-18) and beyond that vaccination became publicly acceptable. In the interval, fortunately there had been no repetition of the 1904 disaster.

No developments took place in the field of education before 1911, when it was reported that preparations were being made to start a first school in the sultanate. There was no further mention of a school until 1914. It was most difficult to find anyone literate among Brunei Malays, so this led to the employment of foreign Malays. By 1914 there was a small Malay vernacular school at Brunei Town with about thirty boys attending. Hitherto classes had been held in the mosque, but in October 1914 it was removed to a building used formerly as the Monopolies Office. The schoolmaster, Awang Yahya, died in 1915, which set back the cause of education once again. In the same year a start was made with vernacular education at Muara, and an allowance was made to a local Malay who opened a school for about a dozen boys in his own home. It was declared that education in Brunei needed all the encouragement the government could give it. Of the four Malay magistrates in office in 1916, three were from Sarawak, and the same was true of most of the Malay clerks. The Resident considered that it was desirable that when they retired, there should be Brunei people to take their place and assume their proper share of the responsibility for the administration and development of their country.[225] It was noted that some of the more influential Malays had begun to send their children regularly to school from an early age.

By 1917, when Brunei Town school had more than fifty pupils, and two boys from the highest standard were taken into government service as apprentices. The experiment proved a success and was repeated in following years. A further step was taken in 1919 when Brunei began to contribute to the cost of the English school recently opened in Labuan, which reserved a certain number of places for students from Brunei. Successful completion of the course enabled individuals to qualify for even higher posts in the administration.

By 1918 further Malay vernacular schools had been opened at Tutong and Belait. These institutions did not aim at providing a high standard of education, but they did provide children with elementary training and also taught them discipline, punctuality, and cleanliness, qualities in which their parents were markedly lacking.[226] The school at Tutong proved unexpectedly popular and efficient and one Resident remarked that children there appeared generally to be more intelligent than Brunei Malays. The principal difficulty throughout the Residential Era was the shortage of trained teachers. Finally, the first Chinese vernacular school in Brunei did not appear until 1916.

68

CONCLUSION AND EPILOGUE

M.S.H. McArthur is perhaps the key figure in the history of twentieth century Brunei. His balanced Report refuted the prevailing orthodoxy and convinced the Straits' and British governments that it would have been unjust to hand over Brunei to Sarawak. The United Kingdom had the awesome responsibility of possessing the power of life or death over the moribund sultanate and in electing to regenerate the dying State, HM government surely chose correctly. As a result, an ancient culture was preserved which has since enjoyed an opportunity to blossom anew. For Brunei to have been allowed to disappear would have been a loss, not only to Bruneians, but to mankind as a whole. In any case, Brunei was a British Protectorate in 1905 and was thus entitled to expect protection. The United Kingdom shouldered its responsibilities only in the nick of time and for that present-day inhabitants of the sultanate might spare a thought for the individual who made it possible: if not for McArthur, the Seria and offshore oilfields would have been in Sarawak.

From 1906 the task of reformation was hindered by opposition from Rajah Charles Brooke's faction and by the final illness and death of the aged Sultan Hashim. McArthur's efforts to obtain the restoration of Limbang and the recovery of the revenue and land rights in Muara Damit from the Rajah proved unavailing because of lack of support from His Majesty's government. But the first Resident did establish the foundations for a reformed administration. He managed to set the country's finances on the road to recovery by buying up monopolies, tulin rights, and mortgaged cession monies to provide a revenue for the State. The former territorial power of the nobles was broken by taking all land into State ownership. An effective central administration was established, with all government and legislation in the name of the sultan. Indigenous chiefs found some difficulty in adapting to the new methods expected of them, although as far as possible the traditional social structure was retained intact.

Civil and criminal courts were established on the lines of those in existence in the Federated Malay States. A rudimentary police force was introduced, and a number of public works--mainly temporary, apart from the British Residency--were completed.[227] A beginning was made with the

69

construction of a new site for the capital on dry land, but little progress had been made in this direction by 1908. The coinage of the Straits Settlements was adopted as the only legal tender. In short, it was demonstrated that Brunei could become a viable State, even within its reduced limits; this was confirmed after the discovery of the Seria oilfield in 1929.

Economic growth, more particularly land settlement, was delayed pending the resolution of tulin claims, which was not achieved until 1911, and by the disinclination of the river villagers to settle on dry land. The revenue farm system was more or less eliminated by August 1908, with the exception of the chandu farm, which persisted until the end of 1912, and the rajah's rights in Muara district, which were not surrendered until 1924. Meanwhile, the elimination of monopolies had reduced the cost of living for the people in the capital.

There were some economic set-backs: revenue from the poll tax was disappointing, and postage revenue was not exploited as much as it might have been. Nor was the timber industry as successful as had been hoped; applications for rubber land were few; and the coal and cutch industries, which provided Brunei with its most valuable exports at this time, experienced a depression during McArthur's tenure of office. On the other hand, Brunei's traditional craft industries appear to have enjoyed a revival.

The introduction of European control in a Malay State could be a hazardous business, as indicated by the case of Perak in 1874-5. No doubt the fates of Birch (the murdered first Resident) and Sultan Abdullah were a lesson to both sides in Brunei. Older Brunei pengirans may well have remembered, also, the 1840s when British warships bombarded Brunei Town, and on one occasion, obliged the sultan to flee into the jungle. It was a significant achievement on the part of McArthur that he was able to introduce the Residential System in Brunei peacefully and comparatively smoothly, notwithstanding all the difficulties placed in his path by the Brooke faction. It is noticeable that after McArthur's departure there was a deterioration in the relations between Sultan and Resident. By and large--and particularly in view of the harsh words they received from McArthur--the pengirans also merit their share of praise, as a subsequent Resident later acknowledged:

In retrospect I marvel at the patience
and courtesy with which the proud
aristocracy of Brunei accepted the
shocks which we young officers must have
administered to their sense of fitness.
There was much to do and so little
material to work with that we could not
always tread with a nice regard for
corns.

But accept it they did, not with the
resignation of despair, but with unfail-
ing goodwill and appreciation that our
activities, crude though they might
seem, were inspired by a genuine wish to
serve their State.[228]

In 1918 McArthur returned briefly to Brunei as
the High Commissioner's representative at the pupsa
(Coronation) of Sultan Muhammad Jemalul Alam. Sir
Arthur Young reported that the former acting consul
was "not only well acquainted with the country and
its customs, but [was] also a personal friend of the
sultan and popular with the people."[229] McArthur
was greeted, certainly, by endless guards of honor
from many different groups in the community.

The Coronation has been described several
times already.[230] McArthur noted particularly the
tumult at the moment of the Pengiran Bendahara's
proclamation of His Highness as Yang di Pertuan had
been "so spontaneous an exhibition of loyalty and
homage that no spectator could have failed to be
thrilled by it." Sir G.E. Cator agreed:

It was impossible for even the most
stolid Englishman not be moved by the
passion of loyalty evoked, and among the
Brunei people it was evident that
tension was strung to its highest
pitch.[231]

These two statements make it even more difficult to
believe the rajah's and Bampfylde's claims that the
people of Brunei wished to be placed under the
protection of Sarawak.

The former Pengirans Bendahara and Pemancha
had died in 1917 and 1912 respectively, but on the
day after the Coronation, McArthur's time was
entirely occupied in receiving formal calls from
their successors in office and from many other
pengirans apparently anxious to renew acquaintance
with him.[232]

71

Sultan Muhammad Jemal, learning that McArthur must leave the following day, arranged an audience for him despite the fact that custom forbade a newly-crowned sultan to leave his private apartment until three days after the pupsa ceremony. The former Resident was most favourably impressed with His Highness's bearing and manner. In 1908 the sultan had been a shy and rather clumsy youth whom it seemed impossible to interest in any matter brought before him. Since that time, he had developed into a young man of intelligence, and the courtesy of his demeanor created a most favorable impression. Evidently both his highness and the current Resident (G.E. Cator) were working in close cooperation. The dinner party in the Council Chamber on the Sunday evening

> which was well carried out on European lines was another surprise to me, and helped me to realize how great has been the development of Brunei during the last ten years and how much the outlook of its people had broadened in that period.[233]

McArthur concluded his account of the Coronation by placing on record his appreciation of the progress which Brunei has made during the past ten years, and his admiration of the work which must have been done by the Resident to produce such good results.[234]

PART TWO

NOTES ON A VISIT TO THE RIVERS BELAIT AND TUTONG

JUNE-JULY 1904

by M.S.H. McArthur

Sources and Usage
    The sources for the texts presented here are
as follows:
    1.   Notes on a Visit to the Rivers Belait and
Tutong by McArthur is taken from FO 12/126, pp. 146-
152.
    2.   The dispatches covering McArthur's Report
are taken from CO 144/79 (10323).
    3.   McArthur's Report on Brunei in 1904 is
taken from FO 572/39 pp. 4f-48.

                              *

    Original spellings have been retained exactly,
despite the fact that there are some divergences
from general modern usage: Laboh, Kadayans and
Tamburong, for example, usually appear nowadays as
Labu, Kedayans and Temburong respectively.   To
facilitate reading McArthur's practice of putting
Malay words inside quotation marks has not been
followed; rather, the modern practice of italicizing
these words has been substituted.

GOVERNOR SIR JOHN ANDERSON[1] TO THE MARQUESS OF LANSDOWNE,[2] NO. 16 (CONFIDENTIAL), 10 AUGUST 1904:

My Lord,

I have the honour to transmit, for your Lordship's information, a copy of a despatch from His Majesty's Acting Consul at Brunei covering a Report on his visit to the Rivers Belait and Tutong.

The Report discloses a serious state of affairs on the Tutong, which, especially in view of the attitude of the people towards Sarawak, may result in serious disturbances at any time if any encouragement, authorized or otherwise, was held out to them on behalf of the Rajah of that State.

Pending receipt of Mr. McArthur's final Report I defer making any recommendations on the subject.

I have &c
[Signed] JOHN ANDERSON

Inclosure No. 1

ACTING CONSUL MCARTHUR TO GOVERNOR SIR JOHN ANDERSON, NO. 24 (CONFIDENTIAL), 14 JULY 1904:

Your Excellency,

I have the honour to forward the accompanying notes on a recent trip to the Rivers Belait and Tutong. I left Brunei on the 15th ultimo for Labuan and left Labuan on the 17th in the steamship Taganac, which I had to charter at a charge of 75 dollars, to take me and my boat and crew to the Belait. I engaged two extra paddlers for the trip, paying them 40 cents each a day. I spent nine days on the Belait, and then sailed along the coast to Tutong, spending six days there and returning to Brunei overland, leaving my boat to be brought round by sea as soon as the weather was calm enough. Finding no great distress or discontent near the mouths of these rivers, I thought it better to travel as far up them as I could, and this consider-

ably delayed my return, causing me to be absent from
Brunei when the Rajah of Sarawak visited Brooketon
and Buang Tawar at the end of the month.

2. I inclose a sketch map giving more
information than that shown in the map lent me by
Mr. Marks, a duplicate of which is in his office.[3]
That map gives an incorrect idea of the size and
importance of these rivers, and I hope that the
rough sketch I inclose, which is copied in the main
on an enlarged scale from a Sarawak map of the Baram
district, may prove useful.

3. The Belait was pantang or tabu on account
of smallpox. All traffic was suspended at the time
of my visit, and I was thus somewhat handicapped in
my inquiries. In spite of the pantang I was
received with great hospitality by the Orang Bukit
and have carried away a pleasant recollection of
their unaffected welcome and their readiness to
assist me. I found the people of Tutong and the
Kedayans inland far less civil and obliging.

4. So conscious am I of the negative results
of my inquiries and the discrepancies between my
account and those of my predecessors that I have
kept back my report, written immediately after my
return, to see whether further reflection would lead
me to modify it. I have found no reason to do so,
and must therefore leave it to those better quali-
fied than myself to reconcile or account for the
differences.

5. I regret to say that my request to the
Labuan authorities for information as to trade has
proved unsuccessful, the reason given being that no
correct records are kept.[4] This is surprising, as
they would, one would imagine, be required for the
calculation of import and export duties.

I have &c
[Signed] S. McArthur

Inclosure No. 2

M.S.H. MCARTHUR: "NOTES ON A VISIT TO THE RIVERS
BELAIT AND TUTONG (JUNE-JULY 1904)"

GENERAL

1. The River Belait flows into the sea about
100 miles to the West of the Brunei River.[5]   The
Tutong lies nearly midway between the two.   The

76

mouth of each river is closed for about three months in the year (January, February, and March) by the sand rolled up by the sea. At other times both are open in fair weather to tongkangs and shallow-draft steamers, though the surf gets up very suddenly on the first approach of a squall. I am informed that both bars are more practicable than that of the Baram, over which the Sarawak steamer, the Kakak, plies periodically, running up to Claudeton.[6] Small boats can always get in and out by watching for a favourable opportunity. Once the bar is passed each river provides a good waterway, the Belait having a depth of some fathoms right up to Pengkalan Balei, where it is about sixty yards broad, and even beyond as far as Siong, where, however, it narrows considerably. Above this point it is impeded by rapids and snags, and only very small boats can travel beyond Pengkalan Dato' Bakong. The mouth of the Tutong is practically an estuary, being formed by the junction of three tidal rivers, the Tutong, the Talamba, and the Birau. The Tutong is also deep and navigable by tongkangs or small steamers as far as Tanjong Maia. Above this point it narrows and shoals rapidly, and I found it full of snags and much impeded by fallen trees, through which a way for my boat, drawing only about 18 inches, had often to be cut. I found it impossible to get the boat above Pengkalan Dohong, having to borrow a small canoe to continue my journey to Pengkalan Rambei. If the obstructions on both rivers in the shape of fallen trees and submerged roots were cleared it would be possible to take an ordinary tongkang, drawing, say, six feet, up to Pengkalan Siong on the Belait or to the mouth of Sungei Damit on the Tutong.[7] The tributaries of both rivers, except the Mangaris, are too small for anything but the native dug-out canoes, and even these have frequently to be dragged over obstacles.

2. Both rivers, up to Pengkalan Balei on the Belait, and Tanjong Maia, on the Tutong, present the ordinary features of Malay tidal rivers in nipah, mangrove, mud and mosquitoes. There are besides patches of sago palm. The upper reaches are clear and rapid, with sandy banks, on which, where not cleared for cultivation, grows low scrub.
The headwaters flow through heavy jungle, which keeps them shaded and gloomy.

3. The land watered by both rivers appears to be most fertile, sago, cocoanuts, padi and fruit trees growing freely. Little planting is, however,

done in the immediate neighbourhood of the rivers, owing to the heavy floods which come down after rain in the interior, overflowing the banks and uprooting everything.

4. There are various paths leading from each pengkalan or hamlet. Some of these lead to settlements further inland, and some, ultimately, to Sarawak territory. Judging by those which I had occasion to use, their origin is due more to the chance excursions of buffaloes than to any desire for roads on the part of the inhabitants. The rivers and streams are, in fact, practically the sole means of communication, and it is to this fact and to the consequent length of time occupied in reaching them that I attribute the comparative freedom from extortion enjoyed by the inhabitants of the Belait. All trade is carried on by water, Labuan being its natural terminus, and there is thus little necessary connection between Brunei and these outlying portions of the Sultan's territories.

5. The principal villages and hamlets on the Belait are Kuala Belait, Pengkalan Balei,[8] Pengkalan Siong and Pengkalan Dato Bakong. Pengkalan Balei is the local centre and the residence of Pengiran Lumbor, the agent and tax collector of Pengiran Pemancha, the owner of the river. It is a village of abut sixty houses and about 400 inhabitants, most picturesquely situated at the junction of the Mangaris with the main stream. It is cleaner than Brunei (Town), and shows every sign of prosperity, sago being worked, fruits and vegetables grown, and boats and tongkangs built all along the banks. It possesses a row of five well-built plank shophouses, with large sheds for the storage of sago, rotan and getah. The shops compare favourably with those of Brunei, though at the time of my visit trade was at a standstill owing to the river being closed to traffic on account of smallpox. The other villages call for no special comment, except, perhaps, Pengkalan Dato Bakong. I visited this place just at the commencement of the 'harvest festival' and possibly the fact that the place was en fete may have given it a fictitious appearance of prosperity. It is a village of some ten houses, some holding five or six families, built on a sandy bluff overlooking the river. I noticed a profusion of gongs and brassware, and expensive silk and gold thread sarongs. Everyone was feasting, and I regret to say than when I left, nearly everyone was

overcome by _borak_, an extremely nauseous drink, made locally from _padi_ of which I also was forced to partake. The ceremony of _mengalei padi_ which I watched for some time, was both strange and picturesque. _Padi_ was strewn about and scattered everywhere in heaps, and on my remarking on the waste, I was told that the crops had been exceptionally good and that there was no fear of scarcity. My Malays were, or professed to be, much scandalized at all the proceedings.

6. The chief villages on the Tutong are Peniatung, at the mouth of the Talamba, Tutong,[9] a little below the mouth of the Birau, Tanjong Maia, Pengkalan Sungei Damit, Pengkalan Sungei Abang, Pengkalan Kuala Layong, Pengkalan Dohong and Pengkalan Rambei. Tutong, the principal place, struck me as being most squalid. It is build on mud, and consists of a row of crazy shops and sago sheds. The smell is disgusting. The shops are apparently poor: they are certainly dirty. The Chinese seemed rougher than those at Pengkalan Balei and less prosperous. Peniatung and Tanjong Maia are apparently prosperous Malay settlements. The other hamlets are small. There is a marked difference between the distribution of population on the Belait and on the Tutong. On the former one can travel all day and pass no houses. On the latter houses and little gardens and herds of buffaloes are to be seen every hour or so.

POPULATION

7. It is not easy to estimate the population of either river.[10] The Belait was almost deserted except at the _pengkalans_ at the time of my visit, whereas the Tutong, which has, so far, escaped smallpox, was, in comparison, crowded with people taking _padi_ about, collecting jungle produce or fishing. The people of Belait are said to be numerous away from the river, and the _pengiran Pemancha_ is generally credited with a revenue of about 4,000 dollars from the river in the shape of poll-tax. Allowing for the inevitable exactions, this could give a population of from 1,000 to 1,500. The population of the Tutong is less scattered, but the river is smaller, and I think the numbers would be about the same. Many of the former inhabitants of both rivers have sought happier homes in Sarawak territory, and I was told by Chinese who had been

trading for years with both rivers that the population is less by half than it was ten years ago. A
number of deserted and overgrown plantations goes
far to support this statement. Those of the
inhabitants whom I questioned on the Tutong said
that if it were not for their attachment to the
place of their birth they also would emigrate.
Every inducement is offered to immigrants into
Sarawak, free passages being given when asked for.
Once arrived in Sarawak territory, the immigrant is
free of all taxes except an annual head tax of two
dollars, and it is not surprising to find that a
steady flow of immigration is kept up in consequence.

CHARACTER

    8. The character of the <u>Orang Bukit</u>, Dusuns,
or Bisayas, as I have heard them variously called,
is simple and almost childlike. They would be, I
should think, a most tractable race to govern, being
peaceful and industrious, and they certainly possess
traits, such as sincerity and frankness, in which,
though despised as Kaffirs, they compare most
favourably with Malays, more particularly with those
of Brunei, who seem to be the least civil and pre-
possessing of their kind. The lower reaches of the
Belait and Tutong are inhabited by Brunei Malays and
Chinese from Labuan, nearly all engaged in trading
with and cheating the inhabitants of the <u>ulu</u>.
    Inland, on the hills, there are a certain
number of Kadayans, in whose favour there is little
to be said, if those whom I met in the populous
settlement of Lugus are fair examples. They are
Mahommedans, apparently very suspicious of strangers
and certainly very grasping. They appear to be
fairly well off, years of extortion and the experience which they have brought having driven them to
make their homes so far from the rivers that access
to them is difficult and extortion on a large scale
almost impossible.

CONDITION

    9. As far as I could judge, there is, on the
whole, less real poverty among the Dusuns than among
the Malays of Brunei. Every house seems well fur-
nished with gongs and brass cannon; the plantations
are flourishing; the rivers supply fish for food,

and the banks are dotted for miles, on the Tutong especially, with neat <u>padi</u> granaries. They seem also to possess a good supply of buffaloes. Some of the better houses even had plank walls of sawn timber, which must have been purchased from downstream. For these reasons, however scandalous and unjust may be the extortion practised by the Brunei authorities, I cannot say that I think it has as yet caused general misery or actual want. As an instance of prosperity I may mention the general possession of Brunei-made brass <u>sireh</u> boxes. Every householder possesses one, which is produced as soon as a stranger enters. They cost about 6 dollars or 7 dollars in Brunei (town), and are sold in Belait and Tutong for 15 dollars each. They cannot be called necessaries, and their purchase, where any cheaper receptacle would serve the purpose, argues, I think, a certain amount of wealth. The chief grievance in regard to the taxation to which they are subjected seems to be that it is uncertain in its incidence and dates, and that they never know when they may be called upon to pay something further for a royal wedding or funeral or for the expenses of a Chief's visit to replenish his purse. They compare with the certainty and fairness of taxation under the Government of Sarawak, and are proportionately dissatisfied.

TRADE

10. In attempting to form some estimates of the value of the trade and resources of these two districts I have had necessarily to depend to a large extent on the information given me by interested traders, who seem unable or unwilling to tell the truth regarding their profits. Most of them, of course, informed me that they were carrying on business at a loss. The produce of both districts consists of sago, <u>getah</u>, <u>rotan</u> and hides, and the Labuan traders, in whose hands most of the trade is, import in return, cloth, brassware, salt, tobacco and sundries.[11] On both rivers there are extensive tracts of padi land, the land being on the whole flat or gently undulating, and evidently fertile. I am informed that fifteen years or so ago padi formed an export, and I see no reason why, if the country were settled and populous, the same condition should not prevail in the future.[12] There is said to be antimony up the Sungei Mangaris, and oil at Kelakas, near the mouth of the Tutong.[13] The main products

81

are, however, jungle produce, chiefly sago (which practically grows wild), getah and rotans. The Chinese traders state that neither of the latter articles now fetch any price in Singapore, and that it is hardly worthwhile to export them. The getah is principally getah durian, which is, I am told, the same as getah taban. This is bought from the Dusuns for about 40 dollars a picul, and is said to fetch 60 dollars or 70 dollars in Singapore. I was under the impression that getah taban was worth about 400 dollars a picul in Singapore, but possibly that exported from these rivers, which are said to have great reserves of it still untouched in the interior, is not free from impurities. The import and export duties from Belait are leased to a Labuan trader names Goh Ah Lai[14] for 900 dollars per annum. He states that he makes a profit of about 400 dollars per annum out of them. He values the imports and exports at about 10,000 dollars each. On enquiry at the shops at Pengkalan Balei, however, I was told that sago alone was exported to the value of about 20,000 dollars per annum, that the exports of getah reaches 8,000 dollars, and those of rotan about 3,000 dollars per annum. This would give a total export of about 30,000 dollars per annum as against the 10,000 dollars estimated by Goh Ah Lai. I am inclined to consider the figures given me in Pengkalan Balei by various agents of the Labuan firms as more reliable than those given by their principals, whom I met in Labuan. The imports are said to be approximately the same value as the exports. This is to be expected, as trade with the Orang Bukit is more or less a matter of exchange. Since, however, the exchange is always in favour of the Chinaman, the import figures would always be less than those for exports. Goh Ah Lai's shop alone at Pengkalan Balei is said to import from 10,000 dollars to 15,000 dollars' worth of goods per annum.

11.   The import duties of the Tutong are leased by one Chi Ki Yi for ten years for 2,000 dollars. He puts his receipts at 220 dollars per annum. Rival traders estimate them at 2,000 dollars per annum. The duties charged are 5 per cent. ad valorum. His own imports, untaxed, amount of 7,000 dollars annually. He is also the lessee of the export duties, for which he pays 900 dollars annually. These are charged at the rate of ten per cent ad valorem and bring him in a profit, at his own showing, of 500 dollars annually. He himself

82

exports sago to the value of 15,000 dollars, untaxed, and estimates other exports of rotan and hides at about 1,000 dollars per annum. His figures, if correct, would give an annual import value of about 11,000 dollars and an export of 20,000 dollars. In considering the relation of the amount paid for the lease of customs duties to the volume of trade on these rivers, it must always be remembered that the former depends in no way on the latter, the determining factors being always the shrewdness of the lessee and the financial difficulties of the authorities at the time the lease is made. I am told that the British North Borneo Company keep a record of goods imported into Labuan, showing their origin, and I have applied to the Company for information to enable me to check the figures given by interested persons. As, however, it is doubtful when or whether I shall obtain this information, the Company being notoriously averse to publishing reliable statistics, I will not detain this report for them.[15]

POLITICAL SITUATION

12. Of the political situation on these two rivers I find it difficult to write with any assurance, and it will, I hope, be remembered that in such a brief visit I could not expect to obtain more than a general, and possibly only a superficial, impression of the state of affairs. Before starting on my trip I had carefully studied the correspondence quoted in the margin and expected to find everywhere great misery and want and grave discontent.[16] My expectations were not realized. The explanation may perhaps be that circumstances have changed, and that the unfortunate victims of the outrages so ably depicted in the correspondence quoted are blessed with short memories. Since the disturbances which culminated in the outbreak of 1901, Dato di Gadong, who appears to have been at the bottom of the rebellion on Tutong River, has died, having sought an asylum in Limbang after the failure of his insurrection.[17] Other local Wat Tylers have also died or emigrated.[18] The cattle tax, which was the ostensible cause of the 1901 troubles in Tutong, has been allowed to lapse, the disturbance caused by its imposition having apparently deterred the Sultan from a second attempt. Further, His Highness' authority is growing weaker year by year, and since the wreck of his launch, the

Enterprise, on the Belait bar about three years ago,
he has had no easy means of communicating with or
sending any large body of men either to Tutong or
Belait.

Another possible explanation is that I was
unable to obtain reliable information of complaints
owing to the people being suspicious of a stranger.
This, however, does not seem to me probable. I
found the _Orang Bukit_ very unsophisticated. I
tried, in response to frequent enquiries, to explain
who I was and what the British Government was. I
was quite unsuccessful, and left them, I fear, both
in Belait and Tutong, under the impression that I
had something to do with Sarawak. This idea of the
Consul's _raison d'être_ is not confined to these two
rivers, but I am sure that in the case of them it is
due to ignorance of the world outside their own
districts. In the circumstances I should have
expected to hear at once of any definite grounds of
complaint. The only Governments of which they seem
to know anything are Brunei, Sarawak and the British
North Borneo Company, and their hopes are thus
naturally centered in Sarawak. Besides this, there
are in nearly every hamlet men from Sarawak who have
intermarried and settled down. They are continually
contrasting Sarawak and Brunei methods to the dis-
credit of the latter, and so increase the general
desire for Sarawak rule.

13. The lower part of the Belait is under the
Pengiran Pemancha, his claim being that he acquired
the _tulin_ rights by marriage. There is another
claimant, _Pengiran_ Asin, who appears to have justice
on his side. Naturally, however, this does not
commend his case to the authorities, and the Sultan
acquiesces in _Pengiran Pemancha_'s assumption of
ownership. The interior, known as Bukit Chawit, is
by Brunei constitution the _kuripan_ of _Pengiran
Bendahara_, but was transferred two years ago to
Pengiran Pemancha for ten years on payment of 8,000
dollars cash.[19] This transaction was discussed in
Mr. Hewett's letter, Confidential (apparently unnum-
bered) of the 16 April 1902. I gather from that
letter that Mr. Hewett thought the lease had been
cancelled, but inquiries on the spot, supported by
information obtained in Brunei, have satisfied me
that this is not the case, and that the _Pengiran
Pemancha_ exercises control over the whole of the
Belait. On that river I met at their respective
villages the headmen _Orang Kaya_ Lasip, _Orang Kaya
Pemancha_ Bugal, _Orang Kaya_ Antas and _Dato_ Bakong,

84

all of whom have been reported as having signed petitions asking to be taken under Sarawak rule. They all, except Orang Kaya Antas, denied having done so, and stated that they had no complaints to make, the Pengiran Pemancha's rule being fairly considerate, though he took more than his due in head tax. They are unable to read or write. I hesitate to attribute the comparative lenity of the Pengiran's rule to any generosity on his part. He is a Brunei Malay. The explanation lies rather, I think, in the fact that Belait is a long way from Brunei and very close to Baram, that the Pengiran is an old man in very bad health, suffering, as far as I can judge, from diabetes in advanced form, and that he has a wholesome fear of revolt, supported by the people of Baram, if his exactions are pushed too far.

14. On the Tutong the circumstances are somewhat different. The Sultan is at his wits' end for ready money, and makes continual demands on the natives of this river, which, being the kuripan of the Pengiran di Gadong, lapsed to him on the death, some six years ago, of that Minister.[20] The Sultan cannot afford to appoint a successor and so lose the revenues of the office. I find that he has this year collected head tax for three years in advance, is enforcing the fine of 2,000 dollars imposed on the river for the failure of the 1901 revolt, and is also collecting a further sum of 2 dol. 50c. a-head for the expenses of his son's funeral. Since my visit there have been other deaths in the Royal Family, and these will doubtless be the excuse for further demands. A Royal death undoubtedly causes great distress throughout the country. A further exaction, which affects, however, only the lower part of the river, must also be mentioned. This is a recent order for the building of a tongkang, to be delivered in Brunei in a fixed time, with a 12-fathom keel all in one piece and planks 3 inches thick, the draught to be 7 feet. The penalty for non-delivery is a fine of 500 dollars. Every effort is being made to comply with this demand, but it is difficult to find suitable material, and still more difficult to drag it to the river and build the tongkang. Even if it were built, I doubt is so unwieldy a craft could be sailed out of the Tutong River. The general impression is that the Sultan does not want the job completed, and that his only object is an excuse for the imposition of a fine. The headmen of the various hamlets all stated that

85

the Sultan's taxes were increasing yearly, and that they could not endure much more. I fear that if the present _regime_ continues it will not be long before their powers of endurance will be much more severely tried, for they now represent the only remaining source of revenue on which the Sultan can draw. At the same time, I must in fairness repeat that I saw no evidence of present poverty among the people. They are not, of course, rich, but they are certainly as well of as the average and more or less independent Brunei Malay. When analyzed, the frequent complaints heard resolve themselves into discontent at having to pay in a year sums varying from 10 to 20 dollars, when by custom, as followed in Sarawak, the only charge should be a poll-tax of two dollars each. It is of course scandalous that the taxes should be increased as much as tenfold simply to be squandered by the Sultan and his Court in reckless extravagance instead of being devoted to developing the country. I doubt, however, whether this point of view appeals strongly to the victim, and the conclusion which I have formed is, that the people of Belait and Tutong, to whom and to whose ancestors extortion is not a new thing, are really dissatisfied at having to pay more than their favoured relatives and friends in Sarawak territory. I am no admirer of Brunei methods, but I believe that even with a Government which had their interests at heart the collection of any tax beyond the recognized one of 2 dollars a-head would cause discontent. The greater the amount collected, no matter what results were shown, the louder would be the complaints.

I am also of opinion that the disturbances in 1901 were not altogether spontaneous, but were stirred up and fostered by intrigues, the headmen hoping to gain something by a change of allegiance. In this connection I may mention a conversation which I had with the Orang Kaya Kalan, the headman on the Sungei Abang, who took part in the rising. He informed me that he and his fellows were much disappointed at the inaction of the Government of Sarawak at the time of the disturbances. He said they were promised active assistance, and revolted relying on those promises, and all that they got were driblets of ammunition sent from time to time by secret agents, not enough to enable them to make a firm stand, and only sufficient to keep the revolt smouldering, and so lead to severe reprisals. I should hesitate to say that any reliance can be placed on these statements, but they were made to me uninvited, and greatly to my surprise, under the genial influence of borak and I repeat them for what they may be worth.

15. I have made no mention yet of the outrages described in detail in the correspondence quoted above. The accounts I received on the spot agree in the main with those reported, but do not give me so strong an impression of wanton cruelty. The so-called murder of the Birau men[21] is an admitted fact--admitted even by Pengiran Tajudin who was responsible for it.[22] It should, however, be remembered that the accounts given at the time were those of biased refugees to Limbang and Labuan, and that the other side of the question was not heard. The statement of Pengiran Tajudin is that the men in question were taken in open rebellion, that they tried to escape with the others and were summarily executed in consequence. If they were rebels they could hardly expect clemency from the authorities of a State such as Brunei, and any question of humanity in the method of their execution or murder would hardly appeal to any Malay. I mention this incident as I think that the statements made to known sympathizers by unsuccessful refugees in a time of rebellion should be considerably discounted.

16. A consideration of the information which I was able to collect, and which I have tried to put forward in a convenient form in the previous paragraphs, had led me to the conclusion that, though I cannot from personal inquiries endorse all the strongly-worded representations of my predecessors regarding the lamentable condition of the people of Belait and Tutong, yet they are undoubtedly taxed most unreasonably to support a Government which does nothing for them in return; that discontent is general; that various facts in the past have convinced the people that it is to Sarawak that they must look for delivery; and that with the increasing financial difficulties of the Sultan and his Ministers there is no security against a steady increase in oppression, which will at last overtax the patience of its victims.

[Signed] S. McArthur
July 14, 1904

PART THREE

DISPATCHES COVERING MCARTHUR'S

REPORT ON BRUNEI IN 1904

Source: CO 144/79 (10323)

SIR JOHN ANDERSON TO THE MARQUESS OF LANSDOWNE, NO. 3 (CONFIDENTIAL), 18 FEBRUARY 1905 (RECD. 18 MARCH 1905):

My Lord,

I have the honour to forward herewith Mr. McArthur's Report on Brunei.

2. I have not yet been able to find an opportunity of visiting Brunei, and it is unlikely that I shall be able to do so for some time to come, but I have every confidence in Mr. McArthur's ability and judgment, and it is unlikely that I should differ much from his conclusions if I made a personal examination of the condition of affairs there.

3. Though it is clear from this Report that the cruelty and oppression charged against the Government of Brunei has been greatly exaggerated, it is also clear that the country has, through the prodigal folly of its rulers, fallen into a condition of anarchy and bankruptcy which cannot continue indefinitely.

4. For this there are only two remedies: the establishment of a British Protectorate on the lines adopted in the Federated Malay States, or the absorption of the territory by Sarawak. Control by the British North Borneo Company is out of the question. It has already more territory on its hands than it can hope to administer efficiently, and is generally believed to be almost at the end of its resources.[1]

5. With regard to absorption by Sarawak, determined opposition by the Sultan and his chiefs appears to be certain, and unless the protection guaranteed the Sultan is nominal only, and the advantages of the Treaty are entirely confined to His Majesty's Government, it appears to me morally impossible for them to force it upon the Sultan, or even look on unconcerned and without interference while the Rajah of Sarawak continues his efforts towards absorption.

In these circumstances I think absorption by Sarawak ought to be regarded as out of the question.

6. There remains the question of British

protection with a Resident exercising similar powers to that exercised by the British Resident in the Federated Malay States.

Mr. McArthur states, paragraph 135, that in his opinion the Sultan would not be averse to this, and he informs me that the Sultan and his Chiefs have been quietly making inquiries as to the position of the native Rulers under British protection in the Federates Malay States.

7. One of the most important considerations in this connection is the state into which the neighbouring British Colony of Labuan has been allowed to lapse under the administration of the British North Borneo Company. I inclose copy of a letter which the local representative of the Labuan Coal-fields Company (Limited) has addressed to his London Directors on the subject of the present condition of that island.[2]

It will be observed that that gentleman refers to an interview which he had with me in September last, when he came to see me in regard to the currency of Labuan and other matters, accompanied by two of the local representatives of the Borneo Company (Limited), a company which is largely interested in the trade of Labuan, Borneo and Sarawak.

He wished me to exchange the old British and Mexican dollars current in Labuan for the new Straits dollar, then standing at a premium of 5 per cent.

That I could only refuse, and he then desired to make representations to me on the subject of the condition of affairs in Labuan, and I had to explain to him that the island was an independent British Colony, with the affairs of which I had absolutely nothing to do, and that if he had any representations to make he must make them to the Governor, or get his directors in London to make them direct to the Secretary of State for the Colonies in London.

8. In an unofficial manner the Manager of the Borneo Company (Limited) has more than once approached me on the same subject, and I have always had to give him the same answer, but the statements made to me appear to be fully supported by Mr. McArthur's observations during his brief stay in the island (paragraph 139).

I cannot think that His Majesty's Government will feel justified in allowing this neglect to continue. In spite of protests to the contrary, there can be no doubt that the British North Borneo Company draw a net revenue from the island, and there is therefore no excuse for the mismanagement and neglect of the trust confided to them by His Majesty's Government.

9. If it should be found impossible to terminate the connection of Labuan with British North Borneo and to resume its direct administration by the Crown, the head of the Administration, whether a Commissioner acting under the orders of the Governor of the Straits Settlements or independently, if that should be preferred, could also act as Resident in Brunei and be responsible for the Administration of that State in the name of the Sultan.

10. To start the Administration and redeem the mortgaged revenues a sum of, say, L20,000 would be required, but thereafter the Administration, which would be of a very simple character, should be self-supporting, and the amount now paid by His Majesty's Government for the Consulate would be saved.[3] There would be some advantage in working the Administration in connection with that of this Colony, but I see no insuperable difficulty, and in that event, the Governor of the Straits Settlements might be relieved of his functions as Consul General and the duties placed on the Administrator of Labuan.

11. I do not think that the sum mentioned would be an excessive amount for His Majesty's Government to pay to retrieve the condition of a country which has certainly not derived any benefit in the past from its position under British protection, and has, indeed, suffered, because its position and its regard for British protection and justice has rendered it easy for its neighbours to encroach on its territories, with serious results to its resources and revenues, as pointed out by Mr. McArthur, and I trust that His Majesty's Government will see their way to ask Parliament to vote the amount.

12. If the Administration of Labuan cannot be diverted from the British Borneo Company I think that the separate Administration of Brunei by a Resident should still be undertaken. It would, in that event, still be necessary for His Majesty's Government to provide the salary of the Consul or Resident and his office expenses, as at present, in addition to the grant of L20,000 which would be necessary to redeem the mortgaged revenues and to establish the buildings and other preliminaries necessary to start the Administration.

I have, &c
[Signed] JOHN ANDERSON

93

C.P. LUCAS TO UNDER SECRETARY OF STATE, FOREIGN
OFFICE, CONFIDENTIAL, 17 MAY 1905:[4]

Sir,

I am directed by Mr. Secretary Lyttelton to
acknowledge the receipt of your letter of the 31st
of March in which you forward a copy of a despatch
from Sir J. Anderson covering Mr. McArthur's report
on the state of Brunei.[5]
2. After giving careful consideration to the
question, Mr. Lyttelton has come to the conclusion
that the only satisfactory arrangement will be for
His Majesty's Government to induce the Sultan to
enter into a new Treaty under which a British
Resident can be appointed--in other words to adopt
in what is left of the State of Brunei the system
which has proved so successful in the States of the
Malay Peninsula.
3. If this course is adopted, it appears to
Mr. Lyttelton that it would be most desirable that
His Majesty's Government should resume the responsibility for the administration of the Colony of
Labuan. He would propose that the colony should be
placed under the administration of and possibly
annexed to the Straits Settlements and that the
officer who is placed in charge of it should perform
also the functions of Resident in Brunei and Consul
for Borneo, though possibly and even probably having
one Assistant who would actually live at Brunei.
This, however, and other details, will be for
further consideration.
4. In order to effect the transfer without
damaging the credit of the British North Borneo
Company, Mr. Lyttelton would propose to address a
confidential letter to the Managing Director of the
Company informing him of the intention to resume the
administration of Labuan and suggesting that the
Company should take the initiative by asking to be
relieved of the responsibility of governing that
Colony at the end of the present year. The interval
would afford time for the necessary negotiations
with the Sultan of Brunei for a new treaty. These
negotiations might possibly (?first) be conducted as
suggested by Sir F.A. Swettenham in the letter of
which a copy was sent to you on January 20th, with
the assistance of one or more Rulers or leading
Malay Chiefs of the Federated Malay States.[6]
5. As Sir J. Anderson points out in the last
paragraph of his dispatch, it will be necessary to
find a sum of money--estimated at L20,000--to redeem

the mortgaged revenues of Brunei and to provide some necessary buildings etc. Mr. Lyttelton is consulting Sir J. Anderson by telegraph as to the possibility of the F.M.S. advancing this sum on easy terms. Should this prove possible, it would seem that there is every possibility that the administration of Labuan and Brunei would be self-supporting or, at least, would become so after a few years. It would, however, be a great assistance if the Resident were allowed, at any rate for a few years, to draw the salary previously paid to the Consul for Borneo: this salary has, it is understood, recently been reduced but Mr. Lyttelton trusts that the Marquess of Lansdowne will invite the Lords of the Treasury to agree to its being restored to the original figure.[7] In view of the fact that it is suggested that the Resident should perform the duties of Consul for Borneo, Mr. Lyttelton considers that this payment would be a reasonable recognition of Imperial interests in Brunei--a country which, as Sir J. Anderson points out, has up to the present lost rather than gained by its connection with Great Britain.[8]

6.   I am to ask you to lay the foregoing suggestions before Lord Lansdowne and to say that Mr. Lyttelton would be glad to learn, at as early date as convenient, whether they meet with His Lordship's approval.[9]

I am, etc
C.P. Lucas

PART FOUR

REPORT ON BRUNEI IN 1904

by M.S.H. McArthur

Source: FO 572/39, pp. 4f-48.

GENERAL

1. All that is now left under the sovereignty of the Sultan of Brunei is a wedge of territory on the north-west coast of Borneo with an approximate area of 4,000 square miles and a probable population of 30,000 individuals. There is, as far as I know, no absolutely reliable map of the country; that published by Edward Stanford for the British North Borneo Company gives little or no information regarding Brunei except its position. The country is shown with greater detail and accuracy in a "Map of the Baram District" compiled by Dr. Hose, Resident of Baram, and published by the Royal Geographical Society. A glance at the accompanying schedules--Appendix I (a), (b) and (c)--will show how much of the State has been alienated, for how little consideration, and how comparatively small an extent of territory remains.* Brunei lies in latitude $4^\circ36'$ - $5^\circ5'$ N and in longitude $114^\circ4'$-$115^\circ22'$ east. It is practically surrounded by Sarawak territory. It comprises a coastline of about 100 miles, and lies between Lubok Pulai, the eastern boundary of Baram district, and Tanjong Puan, at the mouth of the River Trusan. The main districts in this territory are Belait, Tutong, Brunei, Temburong and Laboh. The very important River Limbang also lies within the limits I have given. It is under Sarawak control, but as it was seized by force and is occupied in the face of continued protests of the Brunei Government, who refuse to relinquish their claim to it, I do not know under that category it should come. On the further side of Trusan lies the territory now known as Province Clarke. The Sultan's sovereign rights over this tract of country have been recently sold to the British North Borneo Company, and the country can therefore no longer be considered part of his State.[1]

---

* The six appendices which accompany McArthur's **Report** are not included in the present volume.

2. It is an open secret that the Rajah of Sarawak is anxious to absorb the rest of Brunei. It is equally well known that the British North Borneo Company view his aspirations with disfavour and that both Governments have been for years endeavouring to increase their possessions at the expense of Brunei.[2] Appendix I shows what measure of success has so far attended their efforts.

3. As long ago as 1885 the Rajah of Sarawak obtained a perpetual lease of the River Trusan, the tulin or hereditary private property of the present Sultan, at the time Pengiran Temenggong, thus making the remainder of Brunei his "sphere of influence."[3] This view of the country is set out in Mr. Consul Hewett's dispatch, No. 9, Confidential, of the 10th May 1902. I cannot see what other object His Highness can have had in the acquisition of a district over 100 miles from the boundary of Sarawak proper. I understand that the revenues obtained from the river barely suffice to meet the expenses of its administration. Its isolation from the rest of Sarawak probably accounts for the disproportionate expense of governing it, for it has a rich and extensive ulu. The alienation of the outlying districts east of Trusan has been hastened by the establishment of Sarawak Government here. Brunei people, whose views are of course biased, state that the disturbances on the Limbang would never have reached sufficient proportions to afford a pretext for foreign intervention if the disaffected had not found encouragement from the presence of Sarawak officers on their borders. However this may be, the Rajah would certainly have found greater difficulty in defending his seizure of the Limbang if he had not acquired interests in the adjoining district. On the ground, I understand, that those interests were menaced by the disturbances on the Limbang, he obtained possession of that important district, "the life of Brunei," to quote a common native statement, which he could never have hoped to gain by negotiation.

CLIMATE

4. The climate of Brunei is similar to that of Sarawak or Labuan. Except for a certain amount of fever, only to be expected in a tropical country, it seems healthy for Europeans. The manager and assistants of the Island Trading Syndicate's cutch

100

Brunei Town about 1904. (Courtesy Public Record Office, Kew, United Kingdom)

factory, who live under rather adverse conditions in close proximity to the malodorous, if picturesque, town of Brunei, have always enjoyed immunity from sickness.[4] The country possesses two great recommendations, in that there are steady winds throughout the day which help to temper the heat of the sun, and that the nights are cool, the temperature falling sometimes as low as 68° Fahrenheit.

SOIL

5. The soil is fertile, except in places where the hills are precipitous or where salt water impregnates the ground, and, judging by the condition of the few plantations that exist, is well-adapted for the cultivation of rice, cocoa-nuts, fruit trees, gambier, pepper, and similar native products.[5] In the interior, there are almost unimpaired stores of jungle produce, such as getah, damar, rotan, sago and timber.

MINERALS

6. The country has never been systematically explored, but it is reported to be rich in minerals.[6] Coal is found in many places, more particularly throughout the length of the Brunei River, as is mineral oil. Antimony is said to be plentiful. I am told that traces of iron are also to be found, and that gold has been won by natives in the interior of Tamburong district. Various concessions for minerals have been from time to time obtained, but no success has as yet attended the efforts of concessionaires. I believe the explanation to lie in the weakness of the Government, which makes the investment of capital risky, and in the undeveloped state of the country, which makes the expense of winning minerals or bringing them on the market prohibitive. All the mineral concessions, except those held by the Rajah of Sarawak, are said to have lapsed.[7]

COMMUNICATIONS

7. The country possesses no roads, only rough tracks used chiefly by the Kadayans, an agricultural race, in bringing their goods to native markets, held periodically at convenient pengkalans, or

landing-places, near the centres of population. All travelling is in consequence done by water.[8] Fortunately there are numerous waterways and tributary streams which make access to most parts of Brunei fairly easy if time is no object. Brunei, the capital of the State, is distant 42 miles from Labuan. A local ship the steamship _Taganac_, 67 tons, calls twice a month, bringing in cargoes of sundries and taking out exports, chiefly cutch. Goods for the principal traders of Brunei, Belait and Tutong are also carried in their own _tongkangs_, which ply between the ports of the State and Labuan. The nature of the intervening country and the loss of the main waterway, the Limbang, make communication between the capital and the outlying districts tedious and difficult. As a result, their trade is independent of Brunei and is carried on directly with Labuan, which is the natural trading centre for the whole State.

CONSTITUTION

8. The Government of Brunei is despotic in theory, the Sultan being the sovereign of the whole territory.[9] As, however, the State is divided up into _negri_ and _hamba kerajaan_, or Crown property, _negri_ and _hamba kuripan_, or official property, and _negri_ and _hamba tulin_, or hereditary private property, it would, I think, be more accurate to describe the country as an aggregation of small and semi-independent fiefs acknowledging one head. The explanation of the terms given above is to be found in a document known as the will of Sultan Abdulmohmin, a duplicate of which, in the keeping of the _Pengiran Bendahara_, I have seen. It may perhaps be a convenience if I quote here the passages bearing on this system of tenure. They run as follows:

> _Tulin_. When a Chief inherits property from his ancestors, whether rivers or men, such property is called _sungei tulin_ or _hamba tulin_. The Sultan collects no revenue from such property. The owner collects the revenue, and is at liberty to bequeath the property to his heirs.
> _Kerajaan_. Those portions of Brunei, whether rivers or men, which are Crown property are called _negri kerajaan_ or

hamba kerajaan. The Sultan collects revenue therefrom, but he cannot bequeath them to his heirs. They must go to his successor on the throne.

Kuripan. Rivers or men belonging to a Minster in right of his office are called sungei kuripan or hamba kuripan. The Minister collects revenue therefrom, and if he dies the property reverts to the Crown until a successor in the office is appointed. The Minister cannot bequeath such property to his heirs.

As regards sungei tulin, the owners can do as they please. The Sultan can impress his wishes on the owner, and it is for him to give effect among his followers to the Royal commands.

Since we became Sultan we have observed the custom of former rulers. After our death those who succeed us should also follow these customs, so that no confusion may arise.

9. It will be seen from this that in many districts the Sultan possesses the shadow of power conferred by his so-called sovereign rights. The document also explains the present vacancies in the offices of the Pengirans di Gadong and Temenggong.[10] His Highness, to whom the revenues have reverted, is too poor to forego them.

10. The Sultan should, according to the ancient constitution of Brunei, be assisted by four Ministers of State, the Pengirans Bendahara, di Gadong, Pemancha and Temenggong. These offices are usually held by members of the Royal family as will be seen on reference to the attached Appendix II. It is from among them also that the Sultan's successor is usually chosen, it being left to them, and to the spokesmen of the people to nominate one of their number. Theoretically, each of these Ministers has separate functions to perform. In any matter affecting the State the Sultan is supposed to consult them, and their chops are necessary on any important State document.

11. The Pengiran Bendahara holds the highest position in the State next to the Sultan, and is supposed to be more or less responsible for the internal administration of the country. He acts as

103

Regent when necessary, keeps, or should keep, the
State Archives, and forms a Court of Appeal from the
decisions, in their respectives spheres, of the
other Ministers.

The Pengiran di Gadong is the Treasurer and
tax-collector. The idea of taxation being apparently inherently connected in Brunei minds with the
agricultural population, he is also in general
charge of the Kedayans and Bisayas.

The Pengiran Pemancha seems to be little more
than a deputy of the Pengiran di Gadong.[11]

The Pengiran Temenggong is in charge of the
forces of the State, leads expeditions, and carries
out executions.

There is another Minister, the Pengiran
Shahbandar, who is, I believe, a comparatively
recent innovation.[12] He deals, theoretically, with
all questions of commerce, port dues, and the like,
and is supposed to exercise a general control over
foreign traders.

12. The existing Ministers are the Pengirans
Bendahara, Pemancha and Shahbandar. Pengiran may be
translated "chief." Both the Bendahara and Pemancha
are now old men and take no interest in their
duties.[13] The Shahbandar lives at Brooketon, pro-
fesses, I understand to have left Brunei in disgust
at Brunei methods, and makes a point of being very
friendly with Europeans.[14] I understand that he
performs some ill-defined local functions in
Brooketon, the site of the Rajah of Sarawak's coal
mine, and that he is in receipt of a salary from the
Sarawak Government.

13. In all my interviews with the Sultan, of
which he has always had previous notice, it has been
the exception to meet any of these Ministers. The
excuse given is invariably that they are sick. It
is true that the Bendahara and Pemancha are always
ailing, but they seem well enough to attend the
mosque on Fridays. The real reason seems to be that
they are all working against the Sultan and each
other and only keep up a superficial show of
cordiality.[15] The result is unfortunate. His
Highness is surrounded by lesser chiefs and by
relations, all of whom have private interests to
serve in every matter that comes before him. The
advice he receives from them is generally against
the best interests of himself and of Brunei.[16]

14. The official revenues of the Ministers are

104

derived from their <u>kuripan</u> properties. These districts for annual payments are detailed in Appendix I. They are all, except the Tutong and the Limbang, either leased in perpetuity to Sarawak or British North Borneo or mortgaged for years to come to private speculators. The question whether the present holders of the offices have the power to dispose of the salaries attached thereto beyond the period of their own incumbency is not likely to occur to a Brunei Malay, but it seems open to argument. There would, of course, be no objection to the cession of these districts which would go to the holders of office, but in many cases these annual payments have been capitalized, and even where that has not been done cash advances have been obtained from private speculators who hold documents entitling them to draw the cession money annually as it falls due. The <u>hamba kuripan</u>, of course, remain in the districts not yet ceded, but even the right to collect taxes from these has in many cases been mortgaged to Chinese traders for cash for many years to come.

DISTRICTS

15. I have already given all the information at my disposal about the Belait and Tutong districts in the Report forwarded under cover of my letter No. 24 Confidential of 14th July last. [see above, Section II]. The other main districts which make up the present State of Brunei, are the Rivers Brunei, Tamburong, and Laboh, with their tributaries.

16. <u>Tamburong</u>. The Tamburong is a small and practically unexplored river inhabited chiefly by Muruts. It extends about five days' journey inland. I understand that it was at one time populous, but that it suffered severely in the cholera epidemic which swept over Brunei two years ago, and that the Murut population is now very sparse. The river is the official property or '<u>negri kerajaan</u>' of the Sultan. Its revenues from trade have been leased for ten years to a Chinese trader named Cheok Yu. The district is said to be rich in jungle produce, and <u>Pengiran</u> Tajudin, a son-in-law of the Sultan, tells me that gold has been won by native methods in the <u>ulu</u>.[17]

17. The Laboh, which joins the Tamburong at its mouth, is of about the same size and is the

105

private property or negri tulin of a relative of the Sultan, named Pengiran Muda Binjai Mohamed Tajudin, who is considered by his immediate adherents to be the rightful heir to the throne.[18] (He is an agreeable Chief, but weak and vain. He keeps up a pitiable travesty of State, and seems to hope that his pretensions to the throne will ultimately be supported by the Sarawak Government. I am unable to find any sound basis for his claims. A reference to Appendix II will show that he is a member of the younger branch of the Royal Family.) He has made an Agreement with a Company, represented by a Mr. Abrahamson, to let out the land on the Laboh for gambier cultivation for a period of ninety-nine years.[19] The soil is said to be well-suited for the purpose. No planting has yet been undertaken, but the rent, 500 dollars per annum, is paid regularly. The lease has been running for about eighteen years. I believe the company is connected with the Island Trading Syndicate.

18. The River Brunei has been often and fully described, but it is perhaps as well that I should make my Report as complete as I can by recording my own impressions of it. It seems to me that an erroneous idea is conveyed by describing it as a river. It is little more than a creek forming, in conjunction with the mouth of Limbang, an estuary broken up by a number of islands. It is, I think, the presence of these which has made its intimate connection with the important River Limbang less obvious; and this has been, for the Government of Brunei, a misfortune. The waters of the so-called River Brunei are salt throughout their entire length. They are connected by a number of terusans, or channels, with the Limbang and the main part of the town of Brunei itself is situated on an island thus formed. The direct mouth of the Limbang is spoilt by reefs and sand banks, and the channel is a long and devious one. In consequence of this, small boats, such as the launch kept for the use of the Resident at Pengkalan Tarap, find it convenient, as a rule, to enter and leave the river on the Brunei side of Pulau Berembang.[20] I cannot help thinking that, had the intimate connection of Brunei and Limbang been more fully appreciated in the past, the acquiescence of the British Government in the Rajah's seizure of the latter river would have been given with greater hesitation.[21]

19. The entrance to the Brunei River is most

picturesque, steep though low hills running down to the water on each side, fringed at their bases with narrow belts of mangrove. It possesses one great advantage over the other rivers of Brunei, or even of Brunei Bay, in that it has no bar. Unfortunately, however, a former Sultan, to secure himself and his country, as he hoped, for invasion, had a long and solid stone breakwater built across the channel in the neighbourhood of the small island of Pulau Chermin.[22] The top of the wall is almost awash at low tide, and is only covered by about seven feet of water at high tide. One end of it is now broken down, and there remains for those who know the natural bearings an easy channel past the obstruction. I have given the common account, but I do not know how far it is true. I believe that the greater part of this breakwater must be a natural reef, for the labour involved in its erection would otherwise have been enormous, in addition to which there is a lack of any stone, except a friable kind of sandstone, anywhere in the vicinity of Brunei and I have found no one able to explain whence the materials were obtained. Except for this obstruction, which is made more formidable by the absence of beacons and buoys, the channel is deep enough for any vessel which is ever likely to call at Brunei. His Majesty's Ship Phoenix and His Majesty's Ship Rosario have both been up to the town of recent years. It would, I imagine, be an easy matter to blow up the remains of this barrier, if it were considered necessary to do so, but it would present no difficulties to navigation were it properly buoyed.

20. Brooketon. At the end of the spit of land outside this breakwater and on the western side of the river is Muara Damit or Brooketon, the site of the only coal mine which is being worked in Brunei territory.[23] This was Mr. Cowie's original concession, purchased by the Rajah of Sarawak.[24] I have been unable to find in the archives of the Consulate any complete record of the concessions on which the Rajah's claims in Brunei are based; but I believe that these concessions (for coal only) were purchased by His Highness in a private capacity and not as Rajah of Sarawak and that he has since acquired rights of jurisdiction at Brooketon. Such rights are, at any rate, exercised, as are those of excise farming.[25] The place gives every appearance of prosperity, possessing good wharves and sheds, a stone sea-wall, a line of light railway running to

the mine about a mile inland, and heaps of coal. I
am told, however, that these appearances are decep-
tive and that the place does not pay. Even the
store of coal is said to give a misleading impression, for the greater part of it has been lying
there for months, or even years, unsold. The net
loss on the year's working is set down in the 1903
Report of the Treasurer of Sarawak as 108,747
dollars, an increase of 34,532 dollars over the
deficit of 1902.[26]

21. Buang Tawar. Above Pulau Chermin the
river opens out to a width of over half a mile, its
eastern bank for eight miles of its course being
formed by Palau Berembang, the island on which a
private speculator opened a coal mine about five
years ago. This incident was fully discussed in
official correspondence at the time,[27] and I need
only state here that, as a result of the decided
attitude of the Rajah, Mr. Crane was dispossessed,
the Rajah proceeding to Brunei in the Zahora[28] and
threatening to uphold his claim by force of arms
unless they were acceded to. In this case, again,
it appears that His Highness the Rajah fell into the
natural mistake of confusing his private rights as a
British subject in Brunei with his public rights as
Sovereign of a neighbouring State. On this island
is His Highness' settlement of Buang Tawar, ostensibly another coal mine. I have already described
this place in my Confidential letter to the 2nd of
June last.[29] Owing to the discovery of oil in the
process of running a lead for coal, all efforts to
extract the latter mineral have been discontinued,
and a fresh concession to work oil, the terms of
which are set out in the same letter, has been
obtained from the Sultan.[30] I may here add that the
works undertaken by His Highness the Rajah, and
referred to in my letter, were suddenly stopped at
the end of July. I am unable to say what led to
this decision.

22. Kota Batu.[31] Opposite the Island of
Berembang is Kota Batu, the so-called estate of
Inche Mohamed, at one time Consular Agent in Brunei.
This estate was recently purchased by the Sarawak
government. The transaction has formed the subject
of separate correspondence.[32]

23. Brunei Town.[33] Above the Island of
Berembang the river takes a sharp bend to the west,
and on rounding the point the first view is obtained
of the city of Brunei. It is distant about 12 miles

from the mouth of the river, and lies in the center of an ampitheatre of hills, the river--about half a mile wide at this point--having all the appearance of a lake. The town, which contains on a rough computation 1,000 houses, is built entirely over the water wherever mud banks make it possible to erect a dwelling. It is very picturesque--at a reasonable distance--and has been called the Venice of the East.[34] At low tide, the mud smells abominably, probably owing to the refuse it receives from the houses. It says much for the stamina of the Brunei people that they live and thrive under such conditions; but the rapid spread of cholera two years ago, and of the smallpox epidemic during my stay in Brunei, shows how really insanitary the place is.[35] The Sultan's house--for it is impossible to describe such a collection of hovels as a palace--lies at the junction of a tributary creek (the Sungei Kadayan) with the main river. Like all the houses of his subjects, it is in a shocking state of disrepair.[36] At the back of his house is an extensive tract of flat land, which would make an excellent site for a properly laid out town.[37] It has on it ruins of old brick shophouses, but they are only relics of former prosperity; and the trade, which is in the hands of Chinese, centres now round a small island in the middle of the town, on which are a number of disreputable-looking plank, tin and atap shops.

24. Cutch factory. Some way below the Sultan's house is an inlet called Subok, the site of the Island Trading Syndicate's cutch factory.[38] It is interesting to note that this was in the eighteenth century the site of an East India Company trading station. The remembrance still lingers in the name "Prigi Factor" by which the stream of water running down the hillside is known.

25. Consulates. Below Subok is the Consulate land, originally granted to Sir Spenser St. John, on which can still be traced the ruins of his house.[39] It is an excellent site for a European dwelling. On the opposite bank is the land granted to Mr. Lee Moses still known as the American Consulate site.[40]

26. Limau Manis.[41] The river extends inland about ten miles beyond the town of Brunei. The district at its head is called Limau Manis. Here, and at other places at the end of narrow and shallow tributaries, are various pengkalans, which are the common meeting ground of traders from Brunei and

109

Kadayans from surrounding settlements, and at which markets are periodically held. The trade revenues of Limau Manis have been recently leased for three years by their heirs of Pengiran di Gadong--whose tulin property it was--to a Chinaman named Chua Cheng Hee.

POPULATION

27. The inhabitants of the State are:
   1. Brunei Malays
   2. Kadayans
   3. Bisayas, or Orang Bukit
   4. Muruts and
   5. Chinese

28. Muruts. The Muruts may be dismissed in very few words. They are mere savages, and few in number in Brunei itself. They are serfs, and have by Brunei custom no more rights than domestic animals would have. They are to be found in the ulu of the Limbang, the Trusan, the Tamburong and Laboh. There are also a few in a district called Kargo, on the Belait, and these latter I tried to meet on my visit to that river. They seem very shy of strangers and some whom I met on the stream paddled away as soon as they caught sight of my boat. This is possibly the result of oppression. I had hoped to make the acquaintance of the race on the Tamburong, but they have retired far into the jungle in fear of small-pox, leaving their usual haunts deserted. They are, on the rivers where they live, the chief collectors of jungle produce, which they barter away in trade with Chinese, Bisayas or Malays. They are not Mahommedans, and are said to be an extremely dirty and depraved race, whose partiality to gin is rapidly destroying them. They are a more or less nomad race, and live too far off in the jungle to be the victims of any regular system of oppression.

29. Bisayas. I have already referred to the Bisayas in my notes on the Rivers Belait and Tutong. In these districts, like the Kadayans throughout the State, they form the agricultural element of the population, for the trifling amount of planting done by Malays is not worthy of serious mention. The Bisayas are "Kafirs" and serfs. They are allowed to plant as they please on the land of their owners-- tulin, kuripan or kerajaan--and it is they who

110

provide the ordinary revenues of the districts in which they live. Originally their payments were made in kind--so many bushels of rice and so many fowls being due every season. In most places their payments have now been commuted into a poll-tax. They claim that this should be only two dollars a household, which is, I understand, the amount charged them in Sarawak. It is hardly necessary to say that in Brunei it is anything their owners like to make it. Nor is this all. They are the victims of numerous other demands: <u>pertolongan</u> or benevolences on the occasion of a birth, death or marriage in the family of their Over-lord; <u>lapis kaki</u> on the occasion of a Chief's or underling's visit; <u>dagang serah</u> or forced trade, when their master is energetic enough to adopt that method; and, in fact, any contribution which can, reasonably or otherwise, be squeezed out of them.[42] In consequence of all these exactions they complain bitterly of poverty and distress. I have already stated in my notes on the Belait and Tutong, the chief homes in Brunei of these people, that the conditions under which they live do not seem to me to support their statements, and that they seem no worse off than the average Brunei Malay. I trust, however, that my remarks will not lead to the erroneous conclusion that these people are not the victims of very great extortion. Their houses are comfortable; they have cattle and ample stores of rice, and seem able to indulge in small luxuries beyond the reach of many Brunei Malays; and they are left very much to themselves under Headmen of their own race who are responsible for the collection of taxes. But a comparison with Brunei Malays is, perhaps, hardly fair. The Brunei Malay suffers from no direct oppression, and the apparent comfort of a Bisaya's house is no doubt chiefly due to his greater industry. The decrease in the population of the Tutong owing to emigration shows that the people have much to complain of, for they do not willingly leave their houses, and it is obvious that, with irresponsible power in the hands of their owners, they may suffer all the injustice that slaves on distant plantations would suffer in any country at the hands of agents of absent masters. There is every reason to fear that they will suffer more severely in the near future, for their labours represent the only available asset left to their impoverished masters, and they will doubtless be the first to feel the pinch of the absolute poverty into which the whole State is rapidly drifting. Their treatment varies, of

111

course, with the personal character of their owners, and, scandalous as are the exactions from which many of them suffer, they seem to me to have been the subject of some exaggeration in the past. It might certainly be urged, in answer to the accusations of wanton cruelty so often made against the Sultan in respect of these people, that the River Tutong was admittedly in revolt four years ago; that the revolt was quelled--or, rather, died a natural death--after disorganizing the whole district for a year; and that the fine imposed by the Government is only now being paid. A wantonly cruel and rapacious Ruler would surely have been less complaisant. Some of the complaints made to me were that innocent and guilty alike have to pay the fine. This is a breach of abstract justice, but I believe it has been found a useful expedient, even by His Majesty's Government, in dealing with recalcitrant native races elsewhere.

30. That the Bisayas are averse to Brunei Government, and that they are only kept peaceable by the idea which prevails among them that the country is soon to be merged in Sarawak, is patent. I am inclined to attribute their avowed anxiety for Sarawak rule to their ignorance of any other Governments, and to various influences which have been from time to time brought to bear on them. They are an industrious and peaceful race, and would, I think prove tractable and valuable subjects if governed reasonably. Their honesty is proverbial. Personally they are pleasant people to meet, hospitable and respectful, and free from that assumption of superiority which generally seems to accompany a mixture of Mahommedanism and ignorance, and which makes it difficult to more than tolerate a Brunei Malay or a Kadayan.

31. The Kadayans.[43] The Kadayans, who are apparently of Javanese origin, are frequently described as the most deserving race in Brunei. I am unable to say on what grounds. They are undoubtedly an industrious and thrifty race, and they seem to be successful, if wasteful, agriculturists. Their usual method is to burn down the jungle on a hillside, build some huts to live in, plant their padi, reap it, and then move off elsewhere and repeat the operation. The lalang-covered hillsides throughout the length of the Brunei River are examples of their method. I mention these because I have sometimes heard it asserted that they have been

112

deserted for places further afield owing to the
exactions of the Brunei Government. It is true that
numbers of Kadayans have left Brunei of late years
and have settled in Labuan, Sarawak and, in a few
instances, in British North Borneo. As they are,
like the Bisayas and Muruts, either tulin, kuripan
or kerajaan serfs, their treatment varies with the
character of their owners. Some of the Pengirans
who own such property are notoriously harsh and
cruel, but it seems hardly fair to make every
instance of private cruelty a direct accusation
against the really powerless Government of Brunei,
as is sometimes done. Nor would it be fair to
attribute all the emigration to actual cruelty or
oppression. It must be remembered that settlement
outside the boundaries of Brunei means to Kadayans
and Bisayas freedom from the obligations of slavery
--in itself a great gain--and that the Kadayans are
by nature a wandering tribe, who make no long stay
in any place. Besides this the Rajah of Sarawak has
been at some pains of late years to induce Kadayans
to move into Sarawak territory, free passages and
monetary assistance being frequently given to this
end. Many of the emigrants have, however, returned
to Brunei after a short experience of life in
Sarawak, finding probably, their surroundings too
strange in a new country peopled by different races
from those to which they are accustomed.

32. In some places--notably at Lugus, between
the Rivers Brunei and Tutong, where there are, I
should say, quite 1,000 Kadayans--permanent crops
have been planted; but these are the exception. In
the country districts of Labuan, where the Kadayans
are at least free from the extortions of a native
Government, their plantations are badly and care-
lessly kept.

33. They are Mahommedans of a sort, but their
prevailing characteristics appear to be stupidity
and petty avarice. Some of their Headmen are even
well enough off to adopt the role of money-lender.
The floating capital of the Headman of Lugus,
invested in this way among the Brunei pengirans, is
said to amount to thousands of dollars. An
unusually large number of them have made the
pilgrimage to Mecca, which argues a certain amount
of wealth. They are suspicious of strangers, and
show a singular lack of manners. They are, with it
all, honest workmen within their own limitations,
and make useful and energetic coolies or guides when

once they are satisfied that they will be fully paid. Those whom I have been able to engage in conversation have made no complaints of marked oppression. Those who are hamba kerajaan inform me that their yearly payments are two gantangs of rice and two fowls an adult.[44] This would not represent more than 1 dol. 50c per annum, and does not seem excessive. It must be remembered, however, that any Brunei Malay considers himself at liberty to steal from them, or abuse any power over them which circumstances may give them, and that, like the Bisayas, they have, theoretically, no rights. Their comparative freedom from gross oppression--for I do not think that as a race they suffer severely--is probably due to their solidarity. Instances are on record which show that injustice to individuals has often been the signal for a rising of the whole tribe and a consequent shortage of supplies. An instance of their independence and disregard of the orders of the Government came under my own notice during the small-pox epidemic. They were ordered to submit to vaccination, but they all refused to do so. The Sultan informed me that he had hesitated for some time to issue the order, fearing that it would be disregarded. His failure to take any steps to enforce it may fairly be attributed to his lack of interest in the well-being of his subjects, but I do not consider the Kadayans as a race intelligent enough to be able to judge when they may disregard orders without offence. From this and similar instances I conclude that they enjoy a considerable measure of independence.

34. Malays. The bulk of the population of the country is Malay, though they form a very small minority in some of the districts. Their numbers have been variously estimated, but in the absence of any reliable data it is impossible to make even a guess at their numbers throughout the State. I think, however, it would be no exaggeration to compute the population of Brunei town alone at about 12,000, including children.[45] This would give an adult male population of about 4,000. The first impression of absolute destitution conveyed by the squalor of the town and ruinous condition of the houses is considerably modified by further intimacy. I think that too much stress can be laid on these features, which might more fairly be taken as examples of the casual and shiftless way in which Malays seem to prefer to live.[46] The bulk of the people are undoubtedly poor. The large families

that they rear, the average household being well
over twelve, must be taken into account in any
consideration of their condition. Their poverty has
generally been attributed to the cruelty and
oppression of the Government. I do not know what
may have been the case in the past; I can only say
that the Sultan appears to exercise little or no
real power in Brunei at the present time. His
attempts to deal with individuals generally fail;
the intended victim generally curries favour with
some powerful Chief and defies the Sultan's
authority. The kampongs into which the town is
divided have Headmen of their own, who settle
matters without much reference to him. The only
direct control which His Highness and members of his
so-called Government exercise is over their own
uluns, or household slaves, many of whom have been
turned off owing to the poverty of their masters and
left to fend for themselves.[47] One cause of the
poverty that exists is, in my opinion, the Malay
aversion to regular work of any kind, even when it
means regular wages. The majority of people prefer
to live an independent life, earning their living by
fishing and petty trading. The loss of the Limbang,
with all its opportunities for trade (and, doubtless, rascality) has pressed severely on these. But
the principal cause is undoubtedly the heavy
indirect taxation from which the whole population
suffers. A reference to Appendices III and IV,
which are not exhaustive, will serve to show how
real a grievance this is. With all the necessaries
of life, except rice, imported either as monopolies
or under import duties amounting to 12 per cent. ad
valorem, and with no real trade competition to keep
down prices, distress is assured. Last year the
import duties were, on most articles, 7 per cent;
but it will be seen from Appendix III that the
Sultan has recently raised a few hundred dollars by
selling the 5% duties twice over. He gets personally a mere fraction of the proceeds, the real
profits going to the Chinese traders; but he is, I
understand, the originator of the system in Brunei,
and its existence and steady growth show, I fear,
how little he cares for the welfare of his people.
If it were not for the establishment of the cutch
factory in their midst the condition of the people
would be worse. It employs, either directly as
workmen, or indirectly as bark collectors and boat-
men under contractors, upwards of 400 Malays, and
pays locally in wages about 4,000 dollars a month.
What the people did before this factory was started

115

four years ago I do not know. There was one sago factory at work then which no doubt gave employment to some; but I have been frequently told, in answer to enquiries on this point, that the population of the town decreased considerably on the loss of Limbang, and that it is only recently, since the opening of the cutch works, that the people have begun to return to their homes from Sandakan, Labuan and other places along the coast.[48]

35. The Brunei Malays are usually described as a hopelessly dishonest and lazy race. The accusation has been supported in one Report which I have had the advantage of perusing by instancing the case of the Brunei Malay who cut down a cocoa-nut tree to get a cocoa-nut. Considering the labour this would involve, the evidence of laziness seems to me inconclusive. Mr. Birch, in his Report for 1902 on British North Borneo, gives a similar description of their character.[49] I think on consideration he would admit that this is a libel on the Brunei Malays settled in Sandakan and in other places round the coast. It is well known that all Malays are averse to the irksome obligations of regular employment, but I do not think a general charge of laziness can be supported in the case of Bruneis in the face of the work which they cheerfully perform in day and night shifts in the cutch factory and in their daily avocations, such as sea-fishing. Their pakarangans are heavy sea-boats, cumbered with nets and poles. The usual crew is four men. It is a point of honour to be first in the market, and it is a common sight to see them spurting up the last reach of the river after a 12-miles pull against a strong current.

36. I have no desire to dispute the charge of dishonesty. The petty thefts and pilferings that go on in Brunei are so frequent that they are looked upon as a matter of course, and I think they would probably rival those of any European sea-port town of the same size. Murder--generally the result of jealousy--is said to be common. During my stay in Brunei I have heard rumours of two such cases. The only wonder is that offences against person and property are not more frequent, when it is remembered that there is no police system, and that the public peace is allowed to look after itself.[50]

37. Pengirans. The Pengirans, or aristocracy of Brunei, deserve special mention, not for their

engaging qualities, but because they are largely responsible for the present hopeless condition of the country, and for most of the cruelty and rapine usually attributed to the Sultan. It is no exaggeration to describe them as a class as incorrigibly idle and constitutionally dishonest. Most of them were at one time the possessors of large estates of <u>tulin</u> property. Some of them possibly still have them, but I personally know of none of them, except <u>Pengiran Muda Binjai</u> and <u>Pengiran Pemancha</u>, who have not leased all their property to Sarawak or British North Borneo, or pawned it beyond the possibility of redemption by themselves to private speculators for cash. They have been living with increasing difficulty for years on the proceeds of this gradual disintegration of the State, being too lazy or too incompetent to do an honest stroke of work. They are now on the verge of destitution, and are eking out an unjustifiable existence by what they can extort from Kadayans or Bisayas subject to them, and by what they can raise from the sale of odds and ends of personal property and household goods. What they will do when these means are exhausted is merely a matter of surmise. They form the dangerous and discontented element in the population, and are always scheming and intriguing, being in the happy position of having now no stake in the country and nothing to lose whatever may happen. A very small minority of them seem anxious for Sarawak rule. The majority express anxiety for British control. All are probably insincere, but I think they have enough intelligence to realize that Brunei cannot remain independent much longer. With the exception of those who lost all their private property when Limbang was seized I cannot find that they have any grievances except poverty, and for that they have only themselves to blame.[51]

38. Border Raids. Complaints are frequently made by the Sarawak authorities as to the prevalence of cattle-lifting and raids on the Limbang. These cases are invariably attributed to Brunei Malays, probably with justice, but I am not sure that the accusations have ever been inquired into with marked impartiality, and I think that too much stress may easily be laid on such occurrences if they are used to prove the Sultan's encouragement or misrule.

39. A brief account of a case which came to my notice during my stay in Brunei may prove of interest in this connection. After the collapse of

the so-called Tutong rebellion in 1900,[52] three of
the instigators, Dato Kalam, Sahat and Merudin, fled
to the Limbang to avoid the vengeance of the Sultan,
who was anxious to put them to death; of these Dato
Kalam is, I believe, a Bisaya, while Sahat and
Merudin are Brunei Malays, hereditary uluns, or
vassals, of the Pengiran Bendahara. The Sultan
persuaded Mr. Roberts,[53] the Manager of the cutch
factory, to apply on his behalf to Mr. Ricketts, the
Resident of Limbang, for their rendition.[54] This
was refused, and they were allowed to settle at a
place called Awang up the Limbang River. The
Sarawak authorities soon found these men a menace to
the peace of the district, and, as a result of
continual robberies and acts of violence which kept
the people of Awang in a state of ferment, Dato
Kalam, a man named Sipak, Sahat and Merudin were
arrested and tried for a theft of buffaloes. They
were all convicted and punished, Dato Kalam and
Sipak being transported to Kuching. On leaving gaol
Sahat moved back into Brunei territory and settled
at Limau Manis, having obtained promise of protection from Pengiran Bendahara, whom he keeps supplied
with occasional buffaloes, raiding the upper waters
of the Limbang whenever opportunity offers. On 18
October last a man named Munggol, an ulun of the
Pengiran Bendahara, who had thrown off his Brunei
allegiance and settled in Limbang six years ago,
came to me and reported that three nights previously
Sahat had raided his farm in conjunction with one
Sahid and stolen two buffaloes, that he had traced
them to Brunei, and desired my help in recovering
his property. I at once took him before the Sultan.
The moment His Highness heard that Sahat was
implicated he expressed great pleasure at having at
last an excuse for punishing him, asking me whether
I thought that he deserved death. I, of course,
replied that the crime of cattle stealing was not
sufficiently heinous to demand such a penalty, and I
only report the conversation in view of the ultimate
result of the case, as I think it shows that the
Sultan was not anxious, whatever his motives may
have been, to screen Sahat. His Highness at once
sent messengers to find the two buffaloes and to
arrest Sahat. It was found that one of the beasts
had already been slaughtered, but Sahat and the
other buffalo were brought before the Sultan on the
evening of the same day. After a brief inquiry, His
Highness ordered the restitution of the buffalo to
Munggol and then asked Sahat and Sahid what defence
they had to offer. They both stated that they had

bought the buffaloes at Limau Manis. Pressed to say who sold them, they gave the name of one Si Untong, also a runaway <u>ulun</u> of <u>Pengiran Bendahara</u> now settled in the Limbang. The case was postponed, and I undertook to procure the presence of Si Untong as a witness. The Sultan ordered Sahat to be taken to the house of <u>Pengiran Bendahara</u>, and warned him that he would be put to death if he attempted to escape. On application to him, the Resident of Limbang sent Si Untong to Brunei, but at the same time requested me to apply to the Sultan for the rendition of Sahat. Though I had some doubt as to the wisdom of preferring such a request, seeing that the Sultan has consistently refused to recognize Sarawak rule in the Limbang, and that in any case Sahat is not actually a Sarawak subject, I applied accordingly to the Sultan. The Sultan refused to grant the request, stating that he alone had the right to try Brunei subjects, and that the Resident need not fear that Sahat would be allowed to escape. Meantime, however, the <u>Pengiran Bendahara</u> had been bestirring himself in the interests of his follower, and insisted on having the case tried by the five <u>hakim</u> or judges of Brunei. When the case was heard these <u>hakim</u>, two of whom by common repute receive part of the proceeds of all Sahat's raids, inquired whether Sahat and Sahid were willing to swear on the Koran to the truth of their allegation against Si Untong. This they agreed to do, and in spite of my pointing out that Si Untong was there ready to be cross-examined, or, if necessary to himself, swear a denial, the oath was administered. The <u>hakim</u> then reported to the Sultan that the oath must be accepted as a final answer to the accusation of theft. The Sultan told me he could do no more, but he insisted that Sahat and Sahid should pay to Munggol in my presence the price of the buffalo slaughtered. It is interesting to note that Sahid, who was not so case-hardened as Sahat, fell sick of diarrhoea two days after taking the oath, and died within five days, and that since this case the Sultan has issued a Proclamation warning all Brunei subjects that they buy or receive buffaloes from Sahat at their peril, thus making him practically an outlaw.[55] I have gone into this case in detail, because it seems to me to be a perfect epitome of the conditions now prevailing in Brunei and the Limbang. I have always found the Sultan perfectly willing to investigate any complaints which it has been my duty to bring before him but, as I have already explained, his efforts are generally nulli-

119

fied by the disloyalty of his leading Chiefs where
their own followers are concerned, and, though the
Sarawak authorities are very insistent in their
complaints against his subject when offences are
committed in Limbang, they make no allowances for
the difficulties of the Sultan's position, while
they allow the Limbang to be made an asylum by those
whom he desires to punish for offences committed
under his jurisdiction.

40. That settlement in the Limbang should be
sufficient to divest a Brunei Malay of his Brunei
nationality is, perhaps, a technically legitimate
result of the decision of His Majesty's Government
to approve the Rajah's occupation of the district,
but it is obvious that the Sultan's authority is
much weakened in consequence, and it is unfortunate
that cases should frequently occur which can only
intensify the resentment felt by him on account of
that decision. The murder of Si Ajak and Burok,
which formed the subject of official correspondence
in 1899, and, in respect of which the Sultan was
mulcted of an indemnity, are cases in point. His
Highness insists to this day, and common report in
Brunei confirms his contention, that the murdered
men were Brunei subjects born in Brunei and
subsequently settled in Limbang, and he resents
being forced to pay an indemnity to a usurping
government for them.[56]

41. Chinese. There are probably 500 Chinese
in the State.[57] Most of them are registered as
British subjects. Their claim to this status is
generally based on the payment of naturalization
fees in Labuan. Their numbers would hardly justify
their separate mention in this Report if it were not
for the fact that almost all the trade and practically all the revenues of the country are in their
hands, and will be, apparently, for years to come.
Great credit is doubtless due to them for their
thrift and industry, but their cupidity is, I
consider, one of the main causes of the distress and
poverty prevalent in Brunei.

42. The remarks which I offer in some later
paragraphs of this Report on the trade of the State
will show how cheaply they have won the power they
hold. I must admit that I have little sympathy with
their methods, though the seem unimpeachable from a
business point of view. It seems regrettable that
all the resources of the British Consul, including

in some cases the summoning of a man-of-war, should have had to be so frequently put at their disposal to extract, invariably from the Sultan, who is admittedly powerless to recover from his Ministers, the last farthing owed them. In one instance the Sultan was constrained by these means to pay, under protest, the balance of debts alleged to be due by his predecessor to a Malacca baba [Chinese born in Malaya] named Soh Eng Gin, in spite of the fact that he is not the late Sultan's heir, and has no hand in the disposal of the cession money, on the security of which the loan was said to have been given. In yet another instance a portion of the cession money due to His Highness by the Sarawak Government was deducted in a similar way to satisfy the claims of two Chinese traders against the Pengiran Pemancha for some rascality of his in regard to the lease of certain revenues in the Belait.[58] As far as I can understand the records of the case, the Chinese had been undoubtedly defrauded. The point, however, to which I invite attention is that the Sultan was made to pay because he failed to compel the Pengiran Pemancha to do so. The curious constitution of the country makes the Sultan only supreme in name, and his position is so much a matter of accommodation with Ministers as strong as himself that it seems unfair to expect him to risk, an open breach with them. The consequence was that in these cases the so-called British subjects obtained restitution at his expense, and not at that of the real culprits. Such cases only furnish him with a grievance, and serve to make him intractable in other matters. It seems to me that it would be better to warn British subjects, which would mean Chinese traders, that they advance money under the present regime entirely at their own risk, and that their transactions are of no interest to His Majesty's Government. They would probably refuse to lend on these terms, and the Sultan and his Ministers would find it less easy to anticipate their revenues. Many of the Chinese traders now hold documents giving them the right to collect cession-money and revenues for years to come. Such an arrangement seems unfair to the successors of the present holders of office, and should not, I think, be countenanced by the British Government.[59]

43. As far as I have been able to ascertain, the Chinese traders are averse to any change of Government in Brunei. This is only to be expected, for their profits are made out of the incompetency

121

and extravagance of the present titular Rulers, and
though they would have greater security for trade
investments under a settled Government they would
also lose their monopolies. Moreover, trading is
only the ostensible occupation of the more prosperous, who are really money-lenders, and a change
of Government would deprive them of the large
profits which they make on cash advances on the
security of cession money paid annually. Their
experience in regard to the Limbang makes them dread
the cession of Brunei to Sarawak. They state that
such of them as held monopolies in that district
were ignored on the taking over the reorganization
of affairs there. I do not suppose that they
suffered any substantial losses, for, at the prices
they pay, the holding of a monopoly for even a few
months ought to recoup them. The information given
in Appendix III may possibly be of interest in this
connection. There are, no doubt, many similar
documents which I have had no opportunity of
perusing. I must add in fairness to them that they
all express a great admiration for British methods
of administration and a fervent desire to see Brunei
taken under British control. The explanation of
their attitude is, in my opinion, to be sought in
the limited experience they have had. Their
admiration of the British Government is largely due
to the fact that their trust in it as the ultimate
means of recovering their numerous claims against
the Brunei Government has never yet been disappointed.

TRADE

44. No reliable data are available for the
present trade of Brunei, and I have had to depend on
the traders themselves for such figures as I can
offer. Appendices III and IV give a certain amount
of information regarding some of the imports. They
are obviously not exhaustive, and I only include
them in this Report because they held to show the
method of indirect taxation in vogue. The principal
traders of Brunei are two Chinamen named Chua Cheng
Hee and Cheok Yu. Appendix IV is in the main the
result of conversations with them, checked, where
possible, by personal enquiries among their rivals.
Appendix III is a summary of documents produced by
them from time to time for registration. The item
"sundries" in Appendix IV will serve to explain the
methods by which I have obtained my totals and their

probable worthlessness as trade statistics. Chua
Cheng Hee admits having received from others import
duties amounting to 3,230 dollars. At 5 per cent,
this represents 64,600 dollars. He states his shop
sold "sundries" to the value of 13,000 dollars. The
total on his showing is then 77,600 dollars. Brunei
town and district produces practically nothing at
present, and the people are dependent on the shops
for their food and clothing. As the population must
be at least 12,000, the figures given seem to me too
low. Besides the goods mentioned in the Schedule,
there is a considerable import trade in planks,
timber, hardware, nails, cutlery and crockery--the
latter chiefly of German manufacture. As Appendix
IV gives a total of 120,000 dollars, the total trade
of Brunei town must be worth, when sold at present
prices, very nearly 300,000 dollars annually. The
real value, if the goods were sold at reasonable
prices, would be far less; but I think the imports
might safely be put at 200,000 at fair prices. The
exports in 1903, reached nearly 200,000 dollars
also, made up as follows:
Cutch, 144,000 dollars; sago 50,000 dollars;
hides 1,500 dollars; getah 1,000 dollars.[60]

45. Taking these figures and those given
elsewhere for the Belait and Tutong, which are open
to the same charge of inaccuracy, the following
results are obtained:

Region	Imports	Exports (dollars)
Brunei	200,000	196,500
Belait	20,000	30,000
Tutong	11,000	20,000
Totals	236,000	246,500

46. I am much disappointed at my failure to
obtain a reliable estimate, but it is impossible to
do so in a country where all trade is in the hands
of irresponsible monopolists, whose statements
cannot be checked, and who have every interest in
concealing the real extent of their profits. Except
for the side light they throw on the condition of
Brunei, I must admit that the figures I offer are

123

not worth the time and trouble wasted in obtaining
them. I had hoped to be able to check them by the
help of the statistics of Labuan trade, but I have
had to give up that intention on finding that, in
the Returns for that Colony of recent years, the
trade of Western Borneo and Brunei is all classed
together.

47. The Brunei figures for 1884 and 1885 are,
however, available, and they seem of sufficient
interest to be recorded here.[61] There are as
follows:

Year	Imports	Exports	Total Trade (Straits dollars)
1884	131,054	158,311	294,365
1885	59,373	65,214	124,587

These are the actual amounts imported into,
and exported from, the Brunei River in those two
years. The decrease in 1885 was at the time
attributed to disturbances on the Limbang. The main
export was sago, which came to Brunei from the
Limbang. The total imports into the Limbang in 1903
amounted to 183,726 dollars and the exports to
199,397 dollars. The establishment of a settled
Government has probably doubled the trade of the
district, but a comparison of these figures seems to
me to show conclusively that the loss of the Limbang
has meant the loss to Brunei, and also to Labuan, of
imports and exports of an annual value of at least
200,000 dollars. I mention Labuan because it is the
distributing centre for all Brunei trade, and the
trade of the Limbang is now carried on by Sarawak
streamers directly with Kuching.

48. The value of the sago exported from Brunei
in 1903 was given me by Chua Cheng Hee, the owner of
the last sago factory there. He states that of late
years the works failed to pay their way, and that he
could not get sago from Limbang at a cost, when
export duties were paid at Pengkalan Tarap, which
would enable him to compete successfully with the
Sarawak traders. He has therefore closed down his
factory, and this item must be omitted in any
calculation of the trade of Brunei for the future.

49. I do not think it would serve any useful purpose to discuss the present trade in detail. Any conclusion drawn from the import figures would be vitiated by the fact that they are almost certainly inaccurate, and that the prices ruling in Brunei are fictitious owing to the monopolies held. In many cases the documents granting these are so loosely drawn up that there are no restrictions on price except the greed of the seller and the means of the purchaser.

50. At first sight an import duty of 5%, or even of 12% as in the case of "sundries," does not seem excessive for a native State, nor would it be if the goods were brought in under conditions of free competition, merely paying these charges to the Government or the Government's Representative. This, unfortunately for the people, is not the case. The transactions of the Sultan and his Chinese financiers in regard to sugar, kerosine and salt, shown in Appendix III, will serve as illustrations of the way in which the cost of living is increased. A trader obtains a monopoly for a cash payment. He sub-lets to other traders. Another financier then buys the right to charge a duty on their importations. In many cases the amount of duty to be charged is left to his discretion. The Sultan does not make much out of the transaction. The original monopolist possibly only makes a fair profit. The collector of import duties would claim that he only charges enough to recoup himself for his outlay with all its risks. By the time, however, that the goods are retailed these successive stages have enormously increased their price, and the customer has to pay enough to cover the profits of everyone concerned. The result is that all goods are of an inferior quality, and cost more than double what better kinds would fetch in Singapore. The monopoly ought theoretically to enable the holder to undersell others, but the conditions prevailing in Brunei do away with all incentives to free competition. It is to the interest of the original monopolist to sub-let the monopoly and so receive a fixed income from other traders, rather than go to the trouble and expense of maintaining a private preventive staff. He therefore sells at the same price as others, the cost of maintaining such a staff being shared by all, and the difference between his rivals' expenses and his own representing additional profit.[62]

51. I have taken no account in my figures of

125

the coal exported from Brooketon because that place
is to all intents and purposes part of Sarawak
territory.[63] I understand that about 14,000 tons
are exported annually, at an average price of 8
dollars a ton. The other items of export from
Brunei calls for little comment. Sago, as already
explained, may now be disregarded. So, strictly
speaking, might the cutch.[64] The presence of a
large native population is, I believe, the explanation of the choice of Brunei town as the site of the
factory. The greater part of the mangrove bark from
which the cutch is extracted now comes from the
Pandaruan, which is claimed as Sarawak territory and
from other creeks lying within the limits claimed by
Sarawak.[65] The Pandaruan is referred to in Appendix
I. The export duty is in consequence nearly all
paid to the Sarawak Government, and it is question-
able whether this item should appear as a Return of
Brunei trade.[66]

52. It is obvious that in a town like Brunei,
with a large native population dependent on outside
sources for all the necessaries of life, except a
certain amount of rice supplied by Kadayan and
Bisaya labour, the import trade must always be
considerable. In the case of the Belait and Tutong
the circumstances are different. The inhabitants
grow enough to supply themselves with necessaries.
There is an extensive ulu from which to draw jungle
produce, and the consequence is that the exports
more than balance the imports.

53. I have made no separate mention of the
Tamburong, because its trade is so small that, in a
rough computation, which is all that I can offer, it
may safely be disregarded. It is, moreover,
entirely in the hands of Brunei traders, and is
probably covered by their accounts.[67]

THE GOVERNMENT

54. Frequent complaints have been made of the
shameful misgovernment of the country. It would, I
think, be more accurate, in view of the conditions
prevailing, to say that there is no government in
the usual acceptance of the term--only ownership.
The Sultan has no real power except over his own
districts and people. Some of these he exploits or
oppresses by virtue of his tulin rights--which he
would possess if he were merely one Pengiran among

126

many--others by virtue of his _kerajaan_ rights. With the internal administration of other districts and people, whether _kuripan_ or _tulin_, he is unable by the Constitution or custom of Brunei to interfere. Were it only the power to check abuses that he lacked it would be possible to defend him from many of the charges brought against him as the ·Head of the so-called Government. Unfortunately, however, he shows no signs of a will to do so, and his treatment of his own subjects, though generally admitted to be free from gross personal tyranny or cruelty, shows how lightly he bears his responsibilities and how much he is imbued with the ideas of the class of which he is a member. Nominally he is supreme throughout Brunei. In practice _tulin_ or _kuripan_ holders do as they like in their own districts. They collect the revenues or farm them out as they please; they also sell or lease them wholesale when opportunity offers. The only thing to be said in favour of His Highness in this respect is that he seems more patriotic than others, for he has not sold or leased _kerajaan_ territory during his tenure of power, and has not even carried the alienation of _kuripan_ property to the extent that others have. The _Pengiran Bendahara_ is the chief offender against the State in this respect. By his actions he has no doubt furthered the cause of humanity, but the legality of these transfers of official appanages seems open to question. The only control which the Sultan has over _kuripan_ or _tulin_ owners lies in their relations with foreign Powers. These are theoretically subject to his sanction. That it is rarely withheld seems due to the fact that the alienation of these rights causes him no monetary loss, but, on the contrary, a gain. He is entitled to charge a fee for his "chops" in such transactions; I believe the customary sum is 2,000 dollars. Owing to the admitted poverty of would-be sellers and his own insatiable need of ready money, he has of late years considerably reduced his tariff; he now takes what he can get.

55. With no public expenditure and with a disreputable ruling class scrambling for cash advances from foreign Governments or private speculators, seizing all they dare from their luckless subjects, and valuing their position solely as a means of self-indulgence and extravagance, to talk of a Government seems ridiculous. There are no salaried officers--unless the _Pengirans Bendahara_ and _Pemancha_ can be so described--no forces, no

127

police, no public institutions, no coinage, no roads, no public buildings--except a wooden mosque, and--most crying need of all--no gaol.[68] There is the semblance of a Judicature, but little justice. Cases are sometimes tried before the Sultan or Pengiran Bendahara, but it is not often that the Brunei people have recourse to these Tribunals, for the fees--not so much for a hearing as for a verdict--are, in the Bendahara's Court at least, prohibitive; and, as a rule, cases are settled by a system of arbitration among the recognized, if unauthorized, Headmen of kampungs. British subjects are more fortunately situated, since by Treaty the Consul can claim the right to be present at trials before the Sultan.[69]

56. One such occasion presented itself during my stay in Brunei, a Chinese shopkeeper claiming sums amounting in the aggregate to some 400 dollars from a number of Brunei Malays. Here judgment was given for the plaintiff in each instance, after a somewhat irregular but apparently equitable trial, and the defendants were ordered to pay fixed sums every month until the debts were liquidated. This was done regularly during my stay in Brunei, the money being collected by the Sultan every month and handed over to me for distribution. I do not insist on this case as an instance of abstract justice, for the Chinaman had made previous unsuccessful attempts to get his cases settled. The judgment was the result of a certain amount of moral pressure, and may, perhaps, be attributed to the Sultan's fear that he would himself be held responsible for the debts.

57. Though I am anxious not to make my Report unduly long, it is, I think, only fair to the Sultan to record another case in which I had occasion to seek his assistance. Some seven years ago a Chinese-British subject, Teoh Ah Gau, leased the import and export duties of Bukit Sawat, on the Belait River, from Pengiran Bendahara. This Chinaman is, in my opinion, the most deserving of his class in Brunei, but his character quite unfits him for a successful career there, as he is too mild and timid to hold his own among his more pushing rivals. He is universally respected, and the Sultan has given him a seat at his council-table and the title Bendari (which means a "headman" in Brunei, and not, as in the Straits, a "sea-cook"). At the end of his lease, this man found himself devoid of

cash profits, but rich in book debts run up by
traders who took advantage of his lack of business
instincts to postpone payment of their dues. He has
managed since then to recover some proportion of the
debts, but he found it impossible to persuade a
Brunei Malay, named Si Radin, to pay anything on
account. He accordingly brought the matter before
the Pengiran Bendahara's Court five years ago,
claiming from Si Radin the sum of 177 dol. 88c. Si
Radin admitted that debt, paid 26 dollars on
account, and asked for three days' grace in which to
collect the balance. This was granted, and Si Radin
promptly retired to Singapore. Teoh Ah Gau then
obtained a copy of the judgment from the Pengiran
Bendahara, and a written request from him to Mr.
Little, at the time Resident of Labuan, asking him
to have Si Radin arrested on his return, as it was
rumoured that he intended to settle in Limbang. It
was, I suppose, quite impossible to accede to such a
request, and on his return Si Radin went unmolested
to Pengkalan Tarap, where he bought a row of
shophouses and began trading. His native kampong is
Burong Pingai, at the head of Brunei Town.[70] The
people of this kampong are very independent, and the
Government of Brunei seems afraid to deal with
offenders there. As soon as Teoh Ah Gau heard that
Si Radin had settled in the Limbang he interviewed
Mr.Consul Keyser and obtained a letter to the
Resident of Limbang.[71] The Resident refused to go
into his case, saying he could have nothing to do
with cases preferred against the inhabitants of
Limbang by inhabitants of Brunei. Teoh Ah Gau
returned and informed Mr. Keyser, and no further
action was taken for the time [sic]. During the
smallpox epidemic Si Radin committed some offence in
the Limbang and returned to Burong Pingai. Teoh Ah
Gau then brought his complaint to me. I laid it
before the Sultan, who said he remembered the facts
and that he would "persuade" Si Radin to pay his
debt. I asked him to insist on payment, but all he
would say was that it was a matter that required
patience, and that I must leave him to settle the
matter by arrangement with the Headmen of Burong
Pingai. Knowing how difficult the Sultan found it
to impress his wishes on the inhabitants of this
kampong, and being anxious to study Brunei methods,
I did not press for immediate action. The Sultan
sent continually for Si Radin, but he excused
himself from personal attendance on the plea of
sickness, and denied the debt, saying that the
Pengiran Bendahara's decision had been given ex

parte and demanding a fresh trial. This the Sultan refused, and at last Si Radin was ordered to pay the balance of his debt within three days. He promptly ran away to Brooketon. The Sultan found he had left behind him a set of brass gongs, worth about 60 dollars, and at once impounded them, paying their value to Teoh Ah Gau in part settlement of his claim. A few days before I left Brunei Si Radin returned. On hearing of his return I again went to the Sultan, and asked him to insist on the payment of the balance due. The Sultan said he would do his best, but pointed out that Si Radin lived in his boat on which he flew the Sarawak flag, and that in consequence he did not dare touch him. Up to the date of my departure nothing more had been done in the matter. This use--or, more correctly, abuse--of the Sarawak flag is very common. People who have run away from Brunei and settled in Limbang obtain Sarawak flags, and return under their protection when business or pleasure recall them to Brunei.

THE RULING CLASS

58. In the absence of any real Government it only remains to attempt to explain the present situation in Brunei by describing those who are in power. Space would not permit of a separate account of each tulin district and its owner, and I think these may fairly be treated in general terms. The irresponsible power possessed by the owners naturally lends itself to the gross acts of cruelty and oppression, and the only wonder is that the scandal is not greater. The explanation probably is that the owners are not only unscrupulous, they are also weak, inefficient and indolent, and leave all they can to local headmen, who, being of the same race as the rest of the serfs, are not invariably cruel. The real sufferings of the people occur when the chief or a follower takes a personal interest in the property. The extent of distress then depends on personal character, and the picture conjured up by my acquaintance with a number of Brunei Pengirans is not a pleasant one.

59. The Sultan. Sultan Hashim Jalil-ul-Alam Akamadin, the 25th Ruler of Brunei, is now an old man with all the failings that usually accompany extreme old age.[72] He claims to be 80. This would be an exceptional age for a Malay, but I believe him to be about 70.[73] As a result of a fall through the

130

rotten flooring of his <u>Astana</u> last year he is now
very decrepit. His lapses into what I can only
describe as senility, whether assumed or real, are
frequent, and I sometimes doubt whether he under-
stands the full import of all that is said to him.[74]
In spite of this, his bearing is dignified and
courteous and sometimes leads one to forget the
squalor of his surroundings. He is said to have
been at one time an able and intelligent chief, and
to have enjoyed the friendship of Sir Spenser St.
John, whose tenure of office as Consul is still
remembered as the Golden Age of Brunei, and whose
name is always mentioned with affection.

   60. His Highness seems now to have lost any
power of initiative or decision he may once have
possessed and to have substituted for it a double
measure of obstinacy, at least in his relations with
the British Government. His character has so often
formed the subject in recent years of the most
uncomplimentary reports that I feel bound in common
justice to him to point out how much his alleged
contumacy and disregard of his Treaty obligations is
the result of the unsympathetic way in which, in my
opinion, he has often been treated.[75] His attitude
is, in the main, the result of the Limbang episode,
the decision in regard to which has impoverished his
country, weakened his prestige among his subjects,
and destroyed his faith in His Majesty's Government.
The establishment of the Consulate in Labuan, 42
miles away across a stormy bay, has done much to
widen the breach. There is no direct or regular
means of communication between the two places and,
as a result, Consular visits have been few and far
between. The Consul has had to depend on interested
persons for his knowledge of what is going on in the
State in which his work ought principally to lie,
and his visits, made either in a man-of-war or in a
Sarawak steamer, have been undertaken as a rule
either to coerce the Brunei Government or to demand
the immediate payment of an indemnity or claim. It
does not seem to me possible that any satisfactory
relations with a Malay ruler can be maintained on
such lines, and it seems inevitable that the Sultan
should in such circumstances look upon the Consul as
his enemy.[76] I can only add that my personal
experience on the spot has led me to form a much
less unfavourable opinion of His Highness' character
than that recorded by my predecessors.

   61. His chief fault as a ruler is that he is

too weak and too prone to treat offenders, even
against his own laws, leniently. Nor is this
clemency extended only to his Malay subjects.
Foreign traders or settlers are similarly treated.
His treatment of his subject serfs in the matter of
taxation is of course indefensible, but it must be
remembered that by Brunei custom a serf has no
rights.

62. In the absence of any effort on his part
to assert his theoretical supremacy, his actual
power in the State is small; but I am sure that his
subjects generally would welcome a more energetic
attitude which would put a stop to the present
conflict of powers in Brunei. He is surrounded by
greedy descendants and unscrupulous parasites and
depends on them for the advice which ought to be
given by his Ministers. It is no credit to him, I
am afraid, that his administration has not caused
more widespread misery and distress, for, though he
bears a reputation for lenity among Brunei Malays,
he leaves everything to his followers and hangers-
on, and they are as disreputable as the system is
vicious. I have already described what I was able
in a brief visit to ascertain about his methods in
Tutong. Except that the people of Brunei are not
directly taxed very much the same system is pursued
there. It is kerajaan. Anything obtained from it
is the perquisite of the reigning Sultan. With such
an example before them it is not surprising that
other Pengirans adopt the same system in their own
districts, the evils being then intensified by the
fact that they are dealing with serfs and kafirs and
not with comparatively independent Malays. His
Highness' accession is stated to have been the
result of the popular choice, the Kadayans being
particularly insistent.[77] This seems to show that
his rule was considered comparatively lenient. It
is not, perhaps, a very great recommendation, for
the choice can only have been one of evils. I
cannot find that he has ever done anything to
justify his selection according to European ideas,
but it appears that in Malay eyes he has only lived
the natural life of a Rajah. Whatever he may have
been, he is now a weak man, trusting, indulgent to
those surrounding him, and only too willing to evade
responsibility and shelve unpleasant questions. I
must add that he is as proud as he is ignorant. He
rarely leaves the precincts of his Astana, and all
his knowledge of the world is derived from hearsay.
He seems unable to understand why he is not accorded

the same position in the estimation of the world as that to which ancient Sultans of the once powerful State of Brunei might perhaps have aspired.[78] His people sympathize with this attitude of mind, and the current explanation of the Sultan of Turkey's failure to accede to his request for assistance against the infidels is that his titles are greater than those of the Turkish Sovereign, who is popularly reported to have been amazed at finding he had so mighty a rival in the Far East.[79]

63. As far as I am able to ascertain, His Highness is most unwilling to part with the remainder of his territory, but I gather from hints which he has dropped from time to time that he would not be averse to a large measure of British protection so long as he was left nominally in supreme control. In the case of Sarawak his objections are strengthened by personal considerations and by resentment for the past. The records of the Consulate show that he has been deceitful and untrustworthy, but it must be remembered that throughout his reign the Limbang question has marred his relations with His Majesty's Government and left him distrustful and weakly hostile, and that he had not been very sympathetically treated by His Majesty's recent representatives in Brunei.[80]

64. He has frequently been accused of extravagance. It is hard to explain his continual penury considering what large sums have passed through his hands. I believe that all he gets is squandered by his followers, who trade on the supineness caused by his great age. He has apparently never spent much on himself. His Astana is a mere collection of ruinous hovels, his clothes are always poor and threadbare, and the furniture of his house is sordid and mean. He is said to have squandered thousands of dollars on the marriage of his favourite grandson, Pengiran Muda Tajudin, with the daughter of the Bendahara three years ago.[81] His excuse might be that it was a political alliance designed to do away with the long-standing estrangement between the Bendahara and himself, and that all his subjects benefited by a year of free feasting. The smallpox epidemic has made his waste of money in this respect futile, for husband, wife, and infant child all died within ten days of each other, and it is commonly asserted that "the rope between the two houses has been snapped."

133

65. However he may spend his money it is certain that he is now hopelessly poor. He has been dragging on for months on small advances from his creditors, but each successive one has been obtained with greater difficulty, and at greater sacrifice of the future, and he has little more to hope from them. He has just obtained a loan from the Rajah of Sarawak of 10,000 dollars, which ought to keep him in funds for a month or so, unless his creditors compel him to disgorge it immediately in payment of their claims. It is impossible to insist too strongly on the fact that no amount of money is of the slightest use to him. It goes as fast as it comes, and no one seems to know with any certainty where it goes.[82] The accounts I have received of his "necessary" expenditure vary between 300 dollars and 2,000 dollars a month. He maintains a household of 172 persons, and would probably require at least 1,500 dollars a month to support himself and them. Lately he has been dismissing uluns owing to his inability to feed them. Before his household was even larger.

66. Mr. Consul Hewett's energy and zeal in settling all outstanding complaints against the Sultan before proceeding on leave have left me little opportunity of judging of His Highness' character by an investigation of charges against him.[83] The only case during my stay in Brunei was a complaint by a Singhalese clerk at Brooketon colliery, who stated that he had been engaged as confidential clerk by the Sultan at 40 dollars a month, and after working for three months had been dismissed without ever receiving any pay. His Highness absolutely denied the allegation, saying that the man had lived for two months in the house of a Bengali in Brunei, and had frequently applied for the post and been refused. I therefore requested the complainant to give me some evidence in support of his claim. He was apparently unable to do so, and I had to allow the matter to drop. No other complaint against His Highness has been brought to my notice. The Chinese traders of Brunei stated that everything went smoothly in Brunei during my stay because the Sultan and his people were afraid to misbehave when there was a Consul on the spot to watch them.[84] Mr. Roberts, the Manager of the cutch factory, made the same statement. It appears, therefore, that the interests of British subjects in Brunei could be more successfully watched by a Consul permanently stationed in Brunei

than by one residing in Labuan with no regular means
of communication with the State. Whether, however,
their rights or wrongs are sufficiently important in
themselves to justify the existence of a Consul at
all appears to me doubtful. If it had not been for
the special duties intrusted to me I should not have
found enough to occupy my time.[85] The majority of
the "British subjects" in Brunei are Chinese. They
thrive on existing conditions, and too much
importance can I think be attached to their
occasional losses.

67. Pengiran Pemancha.[86] Owing to their
continual illnesses I have not been honoured with
more than a slight degree of intimacy with the
Pengirans Bendahara and Pemancha, and have therefore
been unable to make a close study of their charac-
ters. The Pemancha is by general reputation the
Gallio of Brunei. He takes no interest in affairs
of State and has little influence. He seems to be a
moderately fair ruler of the Belait district,
leaving everything to local headmen. Its distance
from headquarters probably saves it from gross
oppression. He is not so poor as his colleagues,
because he has been less reckless or more miserly,
and still has the remains of an assured income.
Being a Brunei Pengiran his main aims are the beg-
ging, stealing or borrowing of money, but he seems
as inefficient in these pursuits as in others. His
manners and bearing are pleasant, and create a
favourable impression. He has frequently been
proved guilty of acts of chicanery and dishonesty.

68. Pengiran Bendahara.[87] Of the Bendahara it
is difficult to find anything complimentary to say.
He seems greedy, cunning, unscrupulous and cruel.
He is also devoid of personal dignity. He was, with
Pengiran di Gadong deceased, an adopted son and heir
of the late Sultan Abdul Mohmin, and must have been
at one time the richest Pengiran in the State.[88] He
is now probably the poorest. He has sold, pawned or
mortgaged all that he can get people to take, and is
at present living on the proceeds of the sale of the
brass cannon which used to ornament his official
landing-stage, and of other household property. He
is continually scheming to sell the remains of his
territories to the British, Sarawak or British North
Borneo Governments. Any value they might possess is
discounted by the fact that their revenues are mortgaged or otherwise anticipated for years to come,
and that his demands have impoverished all his sub-

135

jects. His exactions in Bukit Sawat, a portion of
the Belait River, made his kuripan subjects there
unmanageable, and he found it wise to transfer his
rights to Pengiran Pemancha. His methods of taxation were the proximate cause, I am informed, of the
Tutong disturbances, and are also said to have been
one of the chief reasons for disaffection on the
Limbang. He seems to take no interest in his duties
except in so far as they offer means of raising
money, and he shows no loyalty to the Sultan.
During my stay in Brunei he offered to surrender all
his remaining territories in Brunei to the British
Government for 15,000 dollars. In forwarding his
letter he stated he had the Sultan's approval.
Thinking this improbable, I referred the matter to
His Highness, who disapproved of the proposal. It
appears that all the Sultan had approved was the
attempt, so congenial to the sympathies of all
Brunei chiefs, to borrow money. The rest of the
proposal was an inspiration of the Bendahara alone.
This instance serves to show the amount of loyalty
on which the Sultan can count, and also the amount
of confidence that can be reposed in the Bendahara's
word.

THE SUCCESSION

69. It has been suggested that he should
naturally be the next ruler of Brunei. Apart from
his age--he is about as old as the Sultan--I
consider from what I have seen of him that his
selection would be a calamity. He has himself every
hope of succeeding to the throne, and has a sufficiently strong following, his house being the centre
for all intrigues in Brunei, to seriously inconvenience any successful rival. It is to be hoped that
he may pre-decease the present Sultan. Should he do
so, the question of the succession, if it should
ever arise, will be made easier, and possibly the
Sultan's nominated heir would meet with little
opposition.

70. The nominated successor. Pengiran Muda
Omar Ali Saifudin, the Sultan's eldest son and
nominated successor, is generally said to be an
imbecile. He is kept very much in he background by
the Sultan, and certainly seems to be of weak
intellect. His son, Pengiran Muda Tajudin, showed
remarkable intelligence, and it seems probable
therefore that the father's mental failings have

been somewhat exaggerated. He has no power and no following. He flies a yellow silk flag, and is generally treated with the outward respect due to his position as heir to the throne, but it seems to be the general impression in Brunei that the Bendahara will never allow him to succeed, and is only waiting for the death of Sultan Hashim to have himself declared Sultan. His nomination by the Sultan was the result of pressure from the British Government, and it may be that the facts stated by Sir Charles Mitchell, in explanation of His Highness' reluctance to name a successor, disclose the reasons for the selection of the least capable of all possible aspirants. Pengiran Omar Ali has, at any rate, been given no opportunities of fitting himself for his destined position. The succeeding Sultan should be chosen from among the four principal Ministers of State. There have been for years two vacancies, to either of which he might have been appointed. This would, however, have reduced his father's income, and would also probably have made his incapacity too patent. The consequence is that he is a nonentity in Brunei politics, and his nomination seems, in the circumstances, to have been a mere farce. Should it, however, be the intention of His Majesty's Government to assume a greater control over Brunei affairs in the future, the Sultan's action in nominating so weak an heir merits approval for other reasons than those which probably prompted His Highness.[89]

71. Similar conditions might also have justified the selection of Pengiran Muda Binjai* Mohamed Tajudin, the owner of Laboh. He would be too weak to make a satisfactory independent ruler, but it is due to him to state that, unlike all other aspirants to the throne, he is of royal descent on both sides, and that, unlike the majority of Brunei chiefs, his treatment of his tulin subjects is marked by great forbearance and generosity. He is, however, an old man and very infirm. His followers are few and unimportant, and by his assumption of sovereign dignity he has made himself for years the butt of local wits. It says much for the Sultan's generosity that he has always refused to allow his pretensions to be interfered with, his comment always being that "Pengiran Muda Binjai is a good man and does no harm to any one." His selection

---

* "Binjai" is a nickname meaning "the idiot."

would, I fear, annoy all the influential chiefs in Brunei, and he is so extremely nebulous in character, that he would soon become a mere tool in the hands of petty intriguers.

THE LIMBANG QUESTION

72.   When I took up my duties in Brunei I was already aware that various attempts had been made from time to time to reopen the Limbang question, and that in every instance the Sultan had been informed that the decision of His Majesty's Government was final, and that the question did not admit of further discussion.   I have had frequent occasion to insist on this in my interviews with the Sultan and _Pengirans_ of Brunei, for such policy as exists among them hinges on this subject.   No interview seems complete without some reference to it, and I have heard every possible argument _ad nauseam_.   In the circumstances I had hoped to avoid all reference to the question in this _Report_.   I have, however, become so convinced of the importance of the district to Brunei, and so persuaded of the damage that its loss has caused to the inhabitants of the country, not all of whom are undeserving, that I find it impossible to deal with the present situation honestly without taking it into consideration, more especially as I am unable to agree with the remarkable statement recently made, in a letter from the Rajah of Sarawak to the Foreign Office, to the effect that the occupation of the district has conferred a benefit on the population of Brunei.

73.   A reference to any map of Brunei will show how much of the hinterland this river drains, and how large a portion of the country the district comprises.   Brunei itself is built on what may fairly be termed a delta at its mouth.   The river Brunei has practically no _ulu_, and is shut in almost throughout its length by low but steep hills, the soil of which is poor.[90]   In such circumstances, the resources of the fertile Limbang valley are of importance to a native community like that of Brunei, and its control by a foreign, even of professedly friendly, Government cannot fail to have adversely affected the population of the capital of Brunei, numbering at least 12,000 persons.   Sarawak offices claim that the Limbang is open to all, and that all traders are welcome.   I do not of course wish to imply that special pains are taken to

exclude Brunei trade, I am only concerned to point out that various restrictions and taxes, petty in themselves, but in combination important, have tended to destroy that trade with the Limbang and to accentuate the injury caused to Brunei by the alienation of the district.

74. There were at one time a number of sago factories in Brunei. They have all been abandoned, the last having been closed, after barely paying its way for years, during 1904.[91] The reason given by the owners, Chinese traders, is that they cannot work sago at a profit now that the only source of supply, the Limbang, is practically closed to them. Sago won in the Limbang has now to pay an export duty on leaving Pengkalan Tarap for Brunei.[92] When it is remembered that Sarawak steamers call at Pengkalan Tarap and carry produce free of tax to Kuching, it will be seen that the Brunei sago trade has naturally been unable to withstand the competition of Sarawak traders.

75. In the past it was the practice for Brunei Malays to take goods up the Limbang for barter with the native races there, and dispose of the proceeds, jungle produce or sago, to the Chinese traders of Brunei. There were also a number of Brunei Malays living for months at a time in the district, working sago, rotans and nibongs, and floating them downstream to Brunei. Sago workers from Brunei have now to report their arrival and to pay a tax of 1 dollar-a-head, or 2 dollars if they work for more than six months. Nibongs, bamboo, and rotans, which are extensively--almost, in fact, exclusively--used for house-building, fishing etc., in Brunei, are all obtained from the Limbang. Nibongs pay an export tax equal to about 15 per cent ad valorem, and bamboos and rotans one of 10 per cent. The result is that Brunei people find it does not pay them to live in Brunei and trade with the Limbang. They have therefore either to remain in Brunei and trust to wholesale traders to supply what they would in former years have obtained themselves from the Limbang, or to cut themselves adrift from Brunei and make their permanent homes in the Limbang. In the case of most of them--for, as a race, they are not less loyal to their Sultan than other Malays--sentiment prevents their adopting the latter alternative. There are, of course, a number of Brunei Malays settled now on the Limbang. Some of them are working permanently for Chinese traders at Pengkalan

139

Tarap, but most of them are men "wanted" for some offence or debt in Brunei.

76. The Limbang is also sometimes a convenient refuge from oppression or outrage, but the refugees are not always satisfied with the change, and it sometimes happens that a Brunei Malay, after a short experience of Sarawak rule, prefers to return to Brunei. In his monthly Report for April last the Resident of Limbang laid some stress on the emigration of forty blacksmiths, uluns of the Bendahara.[93] It appears that they ran away from Brunei in consequence of a rumour that the Bendahara intended to make the daughter of their Headman a concubine. On hearing of the matter the Sultan sent to recall them, promising them his protection, and they returned to Brunei and have not been molested. I have tried, unsuccessfully, to get from there definite reasons for their return. All they will say is that Sarawak rule is not easy for Malays, and that they prefer Brunei. It seems, therefore, that the only Brunei Malays who welcome Sarawak rule in the Limbang are the disaffected.

77. It is, of course, impossible now to form any true conception of the cruelty and extortion which were at one time considered sufficient justification for the Rajah's occupation of the Limbang: but for the reasons given above I venture to submit that His Highness'[*] intervention has punished innocent as well as guilty, and that the loss of the Limbang is a real loss to all Brunei, and not only to its unworthy owners.

78. As far as I know the Brunei side of the question has never yet been put before His Majesty's Government.[94] Mr. Trevenen, when making his inquiries on the Limbang, was accompanied by the Sarawak Resident, and even made his trip in the Sarawak launch.[95] In the circumstances it was hardly likely that he would hear anything except professions of admiration and gratitude for Sarawak intervention. The amount of cession money to be paid was fixed apparently without any reference to the Sultan, or to the numerous tulin owners whose rights were so summarily abrogated.[96] The account of the seizure of the river as given by the people of Brunei presents some points of interest, and

---

[*] Meaning the Rajah.

140

perhaps deserves, even at this late date, to be placed on record. According to native gossip, the Rajah entered Brunei in 1884 to depose the late Sultan Abdul Mohmin, and to put the present Sultan, then Pengiran Temenggong, on the throne. The intrigue was opposed by Pengirans Bendahara and di Gadong, and civil war would have resulted had it not been for the intervention of Sir W.H. Treacher, at the time Consul-General in Labuan. Hearing of the Rajah's action he hastened to Brunei, prevailed on the Rajah to retire, and pacified the rival Pengirans. It is stated--with what truth I cannot say-- that the lease of the Trusan district in perpetuity, for 4,500 dollars per annum, was the price of the Rajah's attempted assistance. The Bisayas on the lower reaches of the Limbang River were at the time in rebellion against the exactions of the Orang Kaya Burok--himself a Bisaya--and other local agents of Brunei Pengirans; and I have been told that in this fact lies the explanation of a special clause in the Trusan lease promising to Pengiran Temenggong Hashim, the present Sultan, the assistance of Sarawak if he were ever in difficulties. On the death of Sultan Abdul Mohmin in 1885 the Pengiran Temenggong, the most popular chief in Brunei at the time, was elected Sultan. Disturbances continued to break out in a spasmodic way on the Limbang, chiefly, apparently, because the Brunei Chiefs responsible for the government of the country were too busily engaged in intrigues among themselves to pay any attention to the matter; and ultimately, in 1890, the Rajah of Sarawak occupied the river, being persuaded to do so by Pengiran di Gadong, who was jealous of the Sultan, and only too willing to assist in any scheme which would humiliate him. The negotiations for the seizure of the river were commenced in Tutong, whither the Pengiran di Gadong proceeded to meet the Rajah, and were completed in Labuan. Mr. Everett, a concession hunter who had just joined the service of the Sarawak Government after transferring his lease of the River Pandaruan (cf. Appendix *) to the Rajah, was selected for the duty, and proceeded to Pengkalan Tarap with a force of Dayaks and hoisted the Sarawak flag.[97] On hearing of this Sultan Hashim at once sent a small force to demand his withdrawal. Mr. Everett pointed to the guns he had brought with him and to his hastily improvised fort, and dared the messengers to enforce their demands, stating that the Limbang was not Sarawak territory.[98]

141

79. The above is, of course, only the Brunei
account of the transaction, and may possibly be
considered unworthy of credence. I only mention it
because I cannot find from such records as are
available in the Consulate archives that the Brunei
side of the question has ever been considered. The
story, as current in Brunei, at any rate helps to
explain the animosity evinced by the Brunei people
as a whole against the Sarawak Government.

80. The Sultan claims that the facts of the
disaffection in the Limbang were much exaggerated,
and that if no interference had taken place the
district would have settled down in the same way
that Tutong has. In connection with this I may
point out that the disturbances first commenced when
the late Sultan Abdul Mohmin was on his death-bed;
that the present Sultan's accession roused the
enmity of all the other Wazirs; that he has never
loyally been served by them; and that, at least
during the first few years of his reign, intrigues
in Brunei were sufficient to absorb all his attention. The Batang Lupar expedition this year--
various, and doubtless garbled, reports of which
have reached him from native sources--has given him
an opportunity of pointing out that disaffection is
not unknown in Sarawak; and he asks with inconvenient insistence why, if rebellions are a proof of
misrule, the rivers in Sarawak on which they occur
are not forcibly taken from His Highness' control.[99]
His attitude with regard to the Limbang has hitherto
been remarkably consistent and dignified. From the
first he has obstinately refused to listen to any
terms, insisting that "Limbang is Brunei, and Brunei
Limbang," and that he could never agree to the
cession of the one, knowing how much the prosperity
of the other depends on its retention. When it is
remembered that he has been living for years on his
capital and his credit, that both have long been
exhausted, and that the cession money offered him
had grown to a considerable amount when he finally
refused it, his attitude is all the more striking.[100] The Bendahara and other Pengirans, who lost
private property in the district when the Rajah
seized it, have been exerting pressure on him for
years to induce him to agree to the surrender, and
so enable them to claim their shares. They are
becoming more insistent as their poverty increases,
and his resistance seems to be weakening owing to
his realization of the absolute destitution into
which he is drifting. It seems quite possible,

142

therefore, that in the end circumstances will prove too strong for his self-respect, and that he will ultimately allow himself to sink to their level and merely interest himself in obtaining compensation for his personal loss. It will be in many ways regrettable if his chief claim to respect should be thus abandoned. Hitherto the main effects on him of the Rajah's action have been to embitter his relations with the British Government and with Sarawak, and the question has overshadowed and ruined the whole of his reign.

81. The Brunei aristocracy are as vehement in their complaints on the subject as His Highness, but the insincerity of their lamentations over the consequent distress of the Brunei population is apparent when the invariable conclusion of their remarks is reached, and they proceed, with characteristic selfishness, to suggest that they would have no objections to offer to the Rajah's action if he would pay them for their personal right in the district. It is impossible to sympathize with them as a class, but it is generally admitted--even I believe, by the Sarawak authorities--that in the case of some of them (notably Pengiran Muda Binjai) their relations with their serfs in the district were not marred by any excesses on the one hand or disaffection on the other.

82. The boundary. Owing to the Sultan's refusal to admit that the Limbang is no longer Brunei territory the question of the boundary of Sarawak and Brunei administration is a constant source of friction, and it appears to me that, whatever is to be the future of Brunei, this at least is a question towards the settlement of which some effort should be made.[101] The Resident of Limbang has this year commenced collecting taxes from the inhabitants of two hamlets called Lisang and Batung, situated about five miles from the Limbang River and scarcely two from the town of Brunei. I have already reported this incident in my letter of 9th October last.[102] The reason given is that these places lie within the watershed of the Limbang, and this seems to be true. Unfortunately, however, for Brunei the contour of the country is such that the watershed of the Limbang comprises almost all the land between its banks and those of the Brunei, and all the Sultan's old resentment is aroused by this technically legitimate action of the Sarawak Government.

143

83. I have felt bound to record my opinion that for the reasons given above the loss of the Limbang has been the final step towards the ruin of Brunei. It has made life harder for the inhabitants of the capital, and by impoverishing a number of Pengirans has caused poverty and distress among the other inhabitants of the State; for, even granting that the exactions suffered by the people of the Limbang were sufficient reason for its seizure, it seems obvious that when the area of oppression is reduced its intensity over what remains must be increased, and most of the wrongs of which the people of Belait and Tutong complain may fairly be attributed to the increased poverty of their owners. At the same time it seems impossible, in view of the attitude hitherto adopted in regard to this question, to hope that the Limbang, or any part of it, can ever be handed back to Brunei rule.

THE LAWAS DISTRICT

84. I have already in a previous paragraph referred to the acquisition of Province Clarke by the British North Borneo Company, but the transaction has led to such a curious state of affairs in the territory taken over that some reference to it seems advisable in a report purporting to describe the present situation in Brunei. The rivers included in Province Clarke, the Marintaman, Mengalong, Lawas, Punong, Pelait, Siang Siang and Bumbun were the tulin property of various Brunei Pengirans. The sovereign rights over the territory were acquired first. As soon as they had been purchased negotiations were opened with the tulin owners for the cession of their rights. All have now been bought except those of Lawas and Merapok (the latter a tributary of the former). The question of the ownership of merapok has already been clearly explained by Mr. Consul Hewett, and it is only necessary here to record briefly more recent developments of the general situation created by the decision given in that matter by His Majesty's Government. When Pengiran Abubakar of the Lawas found that a rival claimant was supported by the Government of Brunei he invoked the assistance of the Rajah of Sarawak; the latter explained that he was unable to intervene on his behalf and refused his offer to hand over the country to him for 60,000 dollars. Failing to obtain the Rajah's protection, Pengiran Abubakar made overtures to Mr. H.C. Brooke

144

Johnson, a nephew of His Highness the Rajah, who was at one time in the service of the Sarawak Government, and who resigned owing to a disagreement with the Rajah and entered into partnership with a Chinese trader named, I believe, Ban Hok.[103] Pengiran Abubakar is now dead, but his heirs have shown me the Agreement made between him and Mr. Brooke Johnson, a translation of which I append to this Report (Appendix VI). Mr. Brooke Johnson has now been at work in the Lawas district for about seven months, and great credit is, I think, due to him and to the Pengirans on whom the government has devolved for the flourishing condition of the district. Monopolies, except for opium and spirits, have been abolished, their place being taken by the collection of import and export duties on a lower scale than that in force at Sarawak, roads are being made, special facilities are being offered to induce Chinese traders and planters to go into the country and open it up; Court is held regularly on more or less European lines, and the revenue for the year, only seven months of which have been under the new regime, already exceeds 7,000 dollars. The district is a rich one, and the revenue will probably be more than doubled next year.

85. In view of the excellent result achieved by Mr. Brooke Johnson, whose position in Lawas is practically that of adviser to the Government, and in the hope, no doubt, that he would assist them in overcoming the obstinacy of the Lawas Pengirans, the British North Borneo Company have this year appointed him Resident of Province Clarke. When he first went to Lawas he engaged in trade there in the name of his firm. His partner is still trading there, but I understand from what he has told me that Mr. Brooke Johnson is gradually divesting himself of all interest in the firm, as he admits that as a British subject trading in the country it is inadvisable that he should also have a voice in the Government. It was Mr. Brooke Johnson's curious position as a private trader, a Lawas officer and a British North Borneo officer which led Mr. Hewett to write his letter of 20 February last, as he had ascertained that Mr. Brooke Johnson was exercising rights of jurisdiction in Lawas. In consequence of Mr. Hewett's representations the principal representative of the British North Borneo Company undertook to instruct Mr. Brooke Johnson to desist from exercising jurisdiction in this district.[104] Since then, however, various efforts have been made by the

Company to persuade the Lawas Pengirans to authorize
Mr. Brooke Johnson to hold Court and exercise
jurisdiction there, as he does, naturally, in the
rest of Province Clarke. The heirs of Pengiran
Abubakar, who are jointly carrying on the Government, have twice consulted me on the subject and so
has Mr. Brooke Johnson. At their request I visited
Lawas and discussed the whole question with them.
They are greatly alarmed lest the Company's attempts
to obtain rights of jurisdiction may be supported by
the British Government and I ventured to assure them
that, as far as I knew, His Majesty's Government
would not countenance this except with their full
concurrence.

86. At the same time, the position is an
anomalous one which satisfies none of the parties
concerned. The presence of an independent State
(which is what the decision of His Majesty's
Government has to all intents and purposes made
Lawas) in the midst of their territory is unwelcome
to the British North Borneo Company. Taxation in
Province Clarke, as in the rest of their possessions, is inordinately high, whereas in Lawas the
people are more lightly taxed than in Brunei or
Sarawak. The consequence is that a steady stream of
emigration is being kept up from Province Clarke to
Lawas, while numerous opportunities are offered for
smuggling. Moreover, the Lawas district is the
largest and most valuable in Province Clarke, and
its exclusion from the control of the Company
renders their acquisition of the rest of the
province almost nugatory. The Pengirans of Lawas
are as little satisfied as the Company. It is true
that their scruples have hitherto been respected,
but they live in continual dread of some pretext
being found by the Company to force acceptance of
their terms. They refuse to recognize any sovereign
rights of the Company except those usually exercised
in the past by the Sultan of Brunei. Whatever the
sovereign rights may be theoretically it appears
that none have been exercised for decades in Lawas,
and were the Company now to endeavour to exercise
any, great friction would undoubtedly arise. Mr.
Brooke Johnson's position is still more awkward, as
he is endeavouring to serve two masters, whose aims
are diametrically opposed, and, incidentally, to
look after his own interests as a private trader.
It is only due to his great tact and ability that
matters have not yet reached an impasse, but his
acceptance of office under the British North Borneo

146

Company has aroused the suspicions of the <u>tulin</u> owners and rulers of the Lawas district, and I fear that he will very shortly find his position an impossible one.

In the meantime it is difficult, in their conflict of authorities, to ascertain what rights or powers the British Consul has in Lawas, or how the changes which have taken place affect the Treaty rights of the British Government.[105]

RESOURCES

87. As I have already stated, Brunei is said to be rich in minerals, but as the country has never been systematically explored its wealth in this respect is only a matter of surmise and native report. The presence of coal, at any rate, has been proved, and its existence is a valuable asset of the country. The only coal mine at present being worked is that at Brooketon.[106] His Highness apparently claims the sole monopoly of working coal throughout Brunei territory on the strength of his purchase of Mr. Cowie's concessions. I have been unable to find any complete record of them, but I gather from a copy of the Memorandum, which formed an inclosure to Sir Charles Mitchell's despatch of the 13th October 1899, that all that His Highness possesses is the sole right of exporting coal from the coast between Tanjong Nosong and the Tutong River up to the year 1922, and the first option merely on opening coal works in other localities up to the year 1962. This appears to fall very far short of a monopoly for it would be open to anyone with sufficient capital to force his hand by prospecting throughout the country and expressing, the intention of mining in various places. His Highness would then have either to exercise his right of option in each instance or relinquish it. If this interpretation is the correct one, it seems to me to have an important bearing on the terms offered by His Highness for the total surrender of Brunei.[107]

88. <u>Coal.</u> I have stated in a previous paragraph that the Brooketon mine does not pay. I understand that the coal obtained in Brunei is as good as, if not better than, Labuan coal. The various factors which have militated against the sale of Labuan coal, such as difficulties of approach to the port and absence of all facilities for loading, have operated still more strongly

147

against the Brooketon colliery. The coal won there
has to be taken across the bay to find a market; it
then comes into competition with Labuan coal carried
to the wharf at less expense and with less handling,
and, as few steamers care to attempt to make a
regular call at Labuan with all its difficulties of
access caused by the absence of lights, buoys, or
land marks, it is obvious that the Labuan output is
more than sufficient to meet outside demands. The
Brooketon coal then lies on the wharf, either at
Labuan or Brooketon, for months, and naturally
deteriorates from exposure. Then, when it is tried,
it is condemned as of inferior quality. The Rajah
of Sarawak has commenced a new venture this year,
having arranged for a ship called the _Dagmar_ to run
on a regular charter with coal from Brooketon to
Singapore. It will be interesting to learn what
measure of success attends this new departure.[108]

89. _Mineral Oil_. The discovery of mineral oil
at the Rajah's aborted coal mine at Buang Tawar has
already been reported by Mr. Consul Hewett.[109] So
far, the sanguine hopes expressed of the profits to
be obtained from it have not been realized. From
all that I have been able to learn on the subject
the oil is of a kind hitherto unknown, and its
usefulness or commercial value, is still apparently
a matter of conjecture. I am informed that, after
analysis of a sample, London experts have offered a
good price if they can be supplied with 1,000,000
gallons. It is estimated that at its present rate
of flow it will take two years to obtain this
amount, and it appears that any attempt to hasten
the output, which oozes out just as it was first
tapped by an accidental blow of a pick, would be
attended with considerable danger or at least great
expense, the gas from the oil being highly inflam-
mable and its fumes very dangerous. It seems,
therefore, that this oil cannot at present be
described as a valuable resource, and I believe that
the Rajah and his officers consider it a matter for
regret that its discovery should have interfered
with the working of coal on _Pulau_ Berembang.[110]

90. According to native reports there are
elsewhere in the country, notably at a place called
Kelakas in the Tutong district, large supplies of
first-class mineral oil fit for illuminating
purposes. Various concessions have been obtained or
sought for the right to work this, but nothing has
yet been done, and the Sultan states that they have

all lapsed. This being so it is impossible to say how much or how little truth there is in the native reports.

91. Antimony and jungle produce. There is said to be plenty of antimony on the Sungei Mangaris, one of the two rivers which unite to form the Belait, and it is certain that both the Belait and Tutong districts possess at present hardly impaired stores of jungle produce of their ulu. The soil of the country, abundantly watered by rivulets of very good water and almost universally fertile, is itself a valuable asset, and should produce a substantial revenue with a settled Government and an effective system of land administration.[111] I am informed that the Island Trading Syndicate are only prevented by the present hopeless state of the country from investing a very large sum in the planting of gambier for their tanning works in suitable localities in the neighbourhood of Brunei town.

92. Population. No enumeration of the resources of the country would be complete if it omitted all reference to the population. I know of no other Malay country which could boast, before European intrusion, a town of 12,000 native inhabitants. It was the presence of this large supply of raw labour which, I believe, determined the choice of Brunei as the site of the cutch factory, and it is evident that the population would be equally valuable if any real attempt were made to open up coal mines on the Brunei river. The agricultural element of the population would be an equally valuable asset in other parts of the country.

REVENUE

93. The circumstances being such as I have tried to explain, it is difficult to differentiate between personal perquisites, the results of ownership, and revenues which would, in a properly governed country, accrue to the Government. There is, for instance, no land administration or revenue. Land is occupied or cultivated by official or private hamba (serfs). But their contributions are not based on any consideration of the amount or even ownership of the land they occupy. The adult members of the Bisaya and Kadayan races pay an annual poll-tax to their owners, but it is a purely

149

personal form of revenue. The place of customs and licences is taken, throughout the country, by monopolies of trade. These afford no criterion of revenue, for they are sold, to satisfy temporary needs, at whatever they will fetch. The profits derived from them are equally misleading owing to the absence of restrictions as to price etc. There are no rates and taxes except the poll-tax. This should be two dollars for every adult hamba. In practice that is merely the irreducible minimum, and a convenient basis for every other kind of exaction that the ingenuity of the owners can conceive. There are no port or harbour dues, no fines or fees of office, except bribes, and, in fact, none of the items which generally go to make up a revenue to Government.

94. Sultan's receipts. If he had not sold or anticipated all his rights, the Sultan's annual revenue, other than that from poll-tax, would apparently amount under the present system to about 21,000 dollars, made up as follows:

	Dollars
Cession money from British North Borneo: (a) tulin	2,950
(b) kuripan	2,827*
Cession money from Sarawak: tulin	4,500
Coal revenue, Brooketon and Buang Tawar	3,200*
Approximate annual value of capitalized trade monopolies:	8,000*

To this must be added his receipts from poll-tax levied on official or private serfs. The Tutong district is kuripan di Gadong, though the river contains also small tracts of land held by others under tulin rights. The Bisaya population there is probably about 2,000.[112] Of these probably 1,500 would be hamba kuripan. About one-third of them would be adults. This would give a minimum Tutong poll-tax of 1,000 dollars. This goes to the Sultan, owing to the vacancy in the office of (Pengiran) di Gadong. The total number of Kadayans throughout the country is probably 8,000.[113] Possibly one-quarter of these are the property of the Sultan, but probably the hamba kerajaan or kuripan would not exceed 1,000. Allowing one-third of them to be adult, the Sultan's receipts from Kadayan poll-tax

---

* See reference in text.

150

would amount to about 1,500 dollars, of which about 750 dollars would be official. His Highness' annual revenue may then be set out as follows:

		Dollars
Cession Money, etc., as above		21,477
Poll-tax, Tutong (kuripan)		1,000*
Poll-tax, Kadayan (kuripan)		750*
Poll-tax, Kadayan (tulin)		750
	(Total)	23,977

But His Highness has various other casual and uncertain sources of revenue, as, for instance, receipts from fines, fees for affixing his "chop" to concessions, and also presents offered in advance by concession hunters. It may be said, therefore, that he can, theoretically, count upon a minimum annual revenue of about 25,000 dollars, and, that, if he chooses to extract more from his subjects in the way of poll-tax, his receipts might easily be swelled to 30,000 dollars per annum. As a matter of fact, his actual personal receipts are now a very small fraction of this. He had obtained cash advances from money-lenders in exchange for the right to collect the cession moneys for varying terms of years. The coal revenue due to him has been similarly disposed of, the trade monopolies are capitalized, and practically no fixed income remains to him except that derived from poll-tax. He has never yet had to live within these limits, for, hitherto, hardly a year has passed unmarked by the cession of an outlying district to one or other of his neighbours, and this year, when he was already beginning to feel the pinch of poverty, he obtained a loan of 10,000 dollars from the Rajah of Sarawak. Most of this has already been spent in redeeming cannon, jewellery and odds and ends of personal property which his straitened circumstances had forced him to pawn for ready money. From the figures given above it will be seen that the present official revenue of the Sultan should amount to about 15,500 dollars, made up of the items which I have marked with an asterisk.

95. Bendahara's receipts. Any estimate of the present revenue of Brunei must also include the receipts of the two surviving Ministers, Bendahara and Pemancha. There is no kuripan Shahbandar.

---

* See reference in text.

Omitting, for the present, poll-tax, which may be anything above 2 dollars an adult, the Bendahara's receipts appear to be:

	Dollars
Cession Money for the Baram (kuripan)	2,000*
Cession Money, British North Borneo (kuripan)	1,277*
Cession Money, Sarawak (tulin)	500
Cession Money British North Borneo (tulin)	1,250
(Total)	5,027

His kuripan slaves at Bukit Sawat on the Belait, now transferred to Pengiran Pemancha, apparently brought him in 800 dollars (*) per annum. He is the largest owner of tulin property in Brunei. His Kadayan hamba tulin probably number 4,000. Allowing one-third of these to be adult, his minimum receipts from them would be about 3,000 dollars. This would give him a total income of about 9,000 dollars per annum, of which 4,077 dollars, made up of the items marked with an asterisk, would be official. I do not think it is any exaggeration to say that he has forestalled all this for years to come, and that he has now nothing to live on except what he can extort as "presents" from his Kadayan serfs.

96. Pemancha's receipts. As far as I am able to ascertain, the Pengiran Pemancha's cession moneys are as follows:

	Dollars
Sarawak cession money (tulin)	500
British North Borneo cession money:	
(a) tulin	2,805
(b) kuripan	350

He is in possession of the Belait River, which he claims as his tulin property. There is another claimant, a nephew, but possession is ten points of the law in Brunei. The import and export duties bring him in 900 dollars per annum. He has probably at least 1,500 adult Bisaya hamba tulin, whose poll-tax would bring him in 3,000 dollars per annum, in addition to what he can get, probably 1,000 dollars per annum, from the hamba kuripan in Bukit Sawat, who are really the official property of the

---

* See reference in text.

152

<u>Bendahara</u>. His total income may thus be said to be about 8,000 dollars, of which only 350 dollars seems to be actually due to his office.

97. I much regret that I am unable to give any absolutely accurate statistics of Brunei, but it will I hope be understood that what figures I have been able to obtain are the result of very round-about inquiries, and that the nature of my mission, the necessity for secrecy, and the fact that the Consul is not supposed to take any interest in the internal affairs of the country, have made it impossible for me to apply directly to the persons interested. I cannot, therefore claim more than approximate accuracy for any of the figures which I offer, but I hope that they are sufficiently reliable to make them of use in considering the future of Brunei.[114]

GENERAL SUMMARY

98. I have endeavoured in the preceding pages to carry out the duty entrusted to me by making a full report upon the present condition of Brunei. I fear that my report is inordinately long, and possibly in many respects trivial. My excuse must be that nearly all my preconceived ideas of Brunei have been upset during my residence in the State, that the different conditions in each district and among each class of the population appear to require separate descriptions, that many of the reports submitted in the past appear to me to have been somewhat misleading, and that, though a residence of six months gives ample opportunity for collecting an inconvenient amount of detail about a strange country, it is hardly sufficient to enable one to sift the reliable from the inaccurate or the important from the trivial.

99. It is scarcely possible without the power of redress to win the complete confidence of a native race, and I fear that my description of the conditions under which the lower classes live must be to a large extent based on imperfect knowledge. The Bisayas and Kedayans, for instance, have been invariably described by others, whose experience perhaps exceeds mine, as the helpless victims of pitiless oppression. In the same way the Chinese become honest and thrifty subjects of His Majesty, whose lives and petty savings are in continual

jeopardy from the violence and rapine of a powerful and cruel tyrant, and the Brunei Malays become a worthless and lazy race whose extermination would be a matter for congratulation. I have explained that I have not found the universal signs of misery and distress which I expected. All the real inhabitants, for the Chinese are alien traders, are poor, some through their own criminal folly, others through oppression and in their own despite. All the cruelty to be expected from irresponsible owners is no doubt frequently practised; but the same conditions could probably be equalled in the records of other independent Malay countries.

100. At the same time I must express the hope that, in my endeavour to avoid the exaggerations which seem to me to characterize some of the accounts I have read, I have not fallen into the opposite error of minimizing the grave evils which undoubtedly exist. It must be remembered that, even if the actual condition of the country is not as bad as has sometimes been stated, there is nothing to prevent the possibility of the most ruthless cruelty and extortion becoming at any moment a fact. The state of affairs which I have tried to depict temperately in the preceding pages appears to me to be sufficiently hopeless to make all exaggeration unnecessary. When it is remembered that these evils flourish under nominal British protection, and that it is that protection alone which keeps Brunei in existence as a separate State, it seems obligatory on His Majesty's Government to take some steps to ameliorate them, either by insisting on internal reform or by withdrawing all semblance of suzerainty, when Brunei would rapidly be absorbed, piecemeal, by its neighbours.

101. However unfitted Malays may be as a race for the responsibilities of Government, and however exceptional the depravity of the Brunei aristocracy in this respect may be considered, it is only fair to them to remember that the decay of Brunei may be in great part attributed to purely natural causes. The opening of surrounding territories to European enterprise by the establishment of more or less civilized Governments in Labuan, Sarawak and British North Borneo has brought Brunei, a country in a condition somewhat analogous to that of England in the feudal age, into close contact with a shrewder and more energetic race, and the inevitable result has been to encourage the Malay's natural tendency

to live for the present only, taking no heed for the future. The consequence has been that the ruling classes have been living for years on the brink of bankruptcy, and that every year reduces the country to a more hopeless condition. The end of Brunei as an independent State is now in sight.[115] If no outside influences are brought to bear on it, its internal decay will be sufficient to destroy it. But it seems a pity that it was not finally disposed of years ago. Such a course would have obviated many of the difficulties of the situation, which time has only accentuated.

102. As a ruler, the Sultan has probably more means of finding money, at a pinch, than others, but it is certain that the majority of his Pengirans are at the end of their resources, and that they are not the kind of people to quietly await death by starvation. The Sultan refuses to allow any more of Brunei to be alienated, but it is to be feared that unless some means can be devised to assist the impoverished owners of tulin and kuripan property they will in the end disregard His Highness' displeasure and dispose of all that they have left for cash. Hitherto some surviving ideas of patriotism and pride have restrained them, but it is unfortunately impossible to credit them with sufficient strength of mind or loyalty to the wishes of their nominal ruler to withstand indefinitely the temptation to do so, and so delay for a few more years starvation or, what has apparently equal terrors for them, retrenchment and work.

THE FUTURE

103. If the present state of affairs is not considered sufficient to justify any intervention, the question of the immediate future of Brunei is a simple one. Things can of course be left as they are for the present. Unfortunately there would be nothing final about such a decision, and I do not think it could delay for more than a few years the final loss of Brunei independence, while the natural trend of circumstances might perhaps end in depriving His Majesty's Government of the opportunity now offered of moulding the ultimate future of this part of Borneo in accordance with their wishes or interests. The difficulties of the situation are certainly sufficient to daunt any would-be reformer, and in view of them it is not perhaps surprising

155

that matters should have been so long left to take their course. At the same time, it can hardly be said that the policy of _laissez-faire_ has proved a signal success, and matters seem now to have reached such a pass that strong remedies are required to arrest the decay of the country. The only result of inaction now will be to increase all the evils which are at present the subject of grave concern. Those who hold power in Brunei have been living for years on their capital and credit. Neither are inexhaustible. The first result of their poverty must, if they remain in power, be increased taxation and oppression. When the patience of their victims has been exhausted (and its limits in the case of the Bisayas are already almost reached), either the people will revolt and throw off their allegiance, or the rulers, realizing the hopelessness of their position, will come to terms with some other Government. To attempt to leave matters as they are is, therefore, only to postpone for a short time the final loss of Brunei independence, and in the meantime to increase the sufferings of the inhabitants of the State while encouraging the squandering of all its resources. The longer the delay the more difficult will be the ultimate task of evolving order out of chaos. It seems, therefore, that the time has arrived when some definite policy must be adopted with regard to the future, and the only possible alternatives seem to be the following:

(i) to support the present _regime_, trusting to the personal influence of a Consul on the spot to prevent or check abuses.

(ii) to encourage the British North Borneo Company to acquire what remains of Brunei.

(iii) to consent to the absorption of Brunei by Sarawak.

(iv) to establish British protection.[116]

104. _The first alternative_. I fear that such a proposal in such a country as Brunei must necessarily be foredoomed to failure. Even were it possible always to influence the Sultan, it is impossible for him, under the present _regime_, to exercise efficient control over districts where he has no real rights, and it would, I am sure, be equally impossible to evolve a consistent or efficient Government out of the material available under present conditions in Brunei. In any difference of opinion--and such differences would be frequent, owing to petty intrigues--the Consul's efforts would be nullified by the provisions of the

Treaty, which forbid interference in internal administration, and he would continually find himself in the unenviable position of having to withdraw his recommendations where they met with opposition, or to insist on them without any rights and in the absence of any recognized authority. The result would then merely depend on the personal character of the Consul, and matters would either continue as at present, or present something difficult to distinguish from "protection" would come into effect, in the face of the Sultan's Treaty rights and without any definite basis. Complete reorganization of some sort seems necessary if any satisfactory result is to be obtained. The right of oppression is a necessary corollary of the present system, and, while that system continues, there is no revenue available for public purposes. The virtual independence of the influential Chiefs increases the difficulties of the situation. They depend on oppression for their livelihood, and unless some compensation is offered them it would be merely Utopian to expect them to forego the only source of revenue which lies ready to their hands. In my opinion, therefore, this alternative may be dismissed as impracticable.

105. <u>Control by British North Borneo</u>. Though they have never, as far as I know, received any encouragement from His Majesty's Government the Chartered Company appear to be ambitious of acquiring further territory at the expense of Brunei, and their taking over of the whole country requires consideration as a possible alternative. I have not made a study of the administration of British North Borneo, all my energies having been devoted to the endeavour to discover the truth about Brunei. I doubt whether a residence of a few months in the country is sufficient even for this one purpose, and I am fully conscious of the limitations of my knowledge, but I can at least state that I have found the Brunei Chiefs on the whole favourably disposed towards British North Borneo. The Company has invariably treated them with fairness and has not found it necessary to invoke the assistance of the Consul to conduct its negotiations with them. Seeing how often the Company's administration has been made the subject of adverse comment, it is only fair to place this view on record. The Government being frankly commercial in its aims, taxation is naturally heavier than it would be in a British Colony, but taxation in Brunei is also heavy, and it

157

is possible that in this respect the change would not seriously trouble the inhabitants of the State. At the same time I must record the fact that on the rivers of Province Clarke which I have visited I have found far greater poverty and distress than in Brunei, that the people complain bitterly of the oppressive taxation introduced by the Chartered Company, and are full of regrets for the "happy-go-lucky" times of Brunei rule, when as they explain, though they might in some years have heavy calls made upon them, in others they were hardly molested at all. The Company would no doubt be willing to offer as good terms to the Government of Brunei as Sarawak, and they would have the advantage in their negotiations of having no rooted aversion to combat.

106. The misery of the subject races in Brunei has always been put forward as the main argument in favour of handing the country over to Sarawak. Presumably this argument would have equal force in favour of the Chartered Company, for though taxation is heavy in their territories, their rule is not cruel. The possession of Labuan--which, excepting the Limbang, is the only convenient centre for communicating with the outlying districts of Brunei --would make it easier for the Company to exercise efficient control over those districts than it is for the Brunei Government. Whether, however, they have sufficient capital to successfully develop and administer the country is another question.[117] Judging by the neglect everywhere apparent in Labuan, it would appear that they have not. They have yet to consolidate and open up the territories they already hold, and all the capital they can spare for years to come will hardly suffice for that purpose. Considering, also, how everything in the past, including the cession of Trusan and the occupation of the Limbang, has tended to earmark Brunei as the sphere of influence of Sarawak, and how fully the actions of the Rajah have been acquiesced in by Her Majesty's Government, it appears to me that it would require very much more forcible recommendations than any that I can think of to oust Sarawak in favour of the Chartered Company.

107. It seems, therefore, that if any action is to be taken with regard to the future of Brunei, the choice must lie between absorption by Sarawak and British protection somewhat on the lines of that which has proved so successful in the Federated

Malay States.

108. <u>Absorption by Sarawak</u>. The final absorption of Brunei by Sarawak seems to be generally looked upon as a foregone conclusion. There can be no doubt that His Highness the Rajah is anxious to make it a fact. This ambition must have prompted the purchase of Cowie's coal concessions, the acquisition of the Trusan and the seizure of the Limbang. The works undertaken at Buang Tawar and the purchase of the Kota Batu estate on the opposite side of the river have strengthened his hold on Brunei.[118] He has derived tacit encouragement from the attitude of His Majesty's Government and very active assistance from Consuls on the spot, and he would, I imagine, consider any change of policy a breach of faith.

109. The advantages which would accrue to His Highness [the Rajah] from the acquisition of all Brunei are many. His territories would be consolidated and increased by the cession of some 4,000 square miles of country, lying like a wedge between some of his districts, and he would gain an extra population of over 30,000 people.[119] His hold on the Limbang would be legalized.[120] He would obtain control over the trade of Brunei and the revenue to be derived from it. The trade must amount to about half a million dollars annually, even under present conditions. With a strong and settled Government these figures would probably be doubled in a few years.[121] He would gain a real instead of a limited monopoly of coal.[122] The Belait could be amalgamated with the Baram district at a very little extra expense, and I understand that it has already been settled that the administration of Brunei should be combined with that of the Limbang. The extra work would not demand any permanent strengthening of the European staff in either of these districts, and it is plain that, as far as expense goes, His Highness would be in a better position than others to undertake the administration of Brunei. Moreover, his occupation of the Limbang gives him easy access to all parts of the territory to be absorbed.

110. With all these inducements there is little wonder that His Highness should have made such continual attempts to realize his aims. In 1897-98 various negotiations were opened for the transfer to him of Belait and Tutong. His relations with the Sultan were, however, so strained that the proposals

159

came to nothing. The disturbances on the Tutong in 1900 gave him another opportunity.[123] From various admissions made to me by the people of that district, I believe that those disturbances were largely due to intrigue, and that the chief object of the rebels was to force a settlement which peaceful negotiations had failed to bring about. As a result of the revolt, Mr. Hewett endeavoured, with the consent of His Majesty's Government, to arrange for the surrender of Belait, Tutong and Muara (Brooketon) for an annual payment of 4,000 dollars. This scheme failed for the same reasons as before. (It is, perhaps, advisable to point out that the Secretary of State's letter of the 26th February, 1903 to the Sultan of Brunei appears to have been written under a misapprehension as to the nature of the Sultan's complaint against actions of the Consul. The Sultan referred in his complaint to the proposals for the cession of the whole of Brunei to the Rajah of Sarawak, and not to the already aborted negotiations for the transfer of Belait and Tutong.)[124]

111. The latest attempt has been the offer of 12,000 dollars per annum to the Sultan and 6,000 dollars each per annum to the Pengirans Bendahara and Pemancha for the surrender of all Brunei. It was to this proposal that the Sultan took such grave exception in his letter to His Majesty's Government.[125]

112. To the last Mr. Hewett seems to have hoped that his efforts would in the end be crowned with success, but I cannot believe from what I have learnt during my stay in Brunei that the Brunei Government has ever had the faintest intention of accepting the terms offered. They are influenced by many considerations apart from any question of the generosity of those terms. I fear that it is no exaggeration to say that His Highness the Rajah is generally disliked and distrusted in Brunei.[126] He has always been generous in lending money to the ruling class, but, unfortunately, the relations between lender and borrower, in other places than Brunei even, do not always make for real friendship. Brunei Pengirans will borrow from any one, and in the case of the Rajah they seem to look upon loans as a right.[127] They and the Sultan are never tired of pointing out that the first Rajah of Sarawak was a vassal of Brunei and, in their opinion, the present Ruler has won his position at the expense of

160

his Sovereign. It is most distasteful to have to repeat any opinion the reverse of complimentary regarding a Ruler so universally respected and admired as His Highness the Rajah of Sarawak, but it seems necessary, for a correct estimate of the Brunei point of view, to record as briefly as possible the grounds on which I find it upheld by my acquaintances in Brunei. Oppressors and oppressed combine, though from different standpoints, in bearing witness to His Highness' various attempts to obtain a predominant influence in Brunei affairs. Any sign of activity is, of course, welcomed by the oppressed, but it is resented by the oppressors, and it is with their sentiments that I am here concerned. They hold that since the seizure of the Limbang, His Highness has become their avowed enemy. They cannot be expected to realize how repugnant all their methods are to civilized minds, and they look upon the Rajah's interference as wanton aggression in the face of the rights of internal independence which they imagined they had secured by the Treaty of the 18th September, 1888.[128]

113. They also insist that of late years the Rajah has broken all his pledges. Their principal grievance is, of course, the occupation of the Limbang. I have already shown how greatly, in my opinion, this has damaged the owners of Brunei. In answer to their complaints that it would ruin Brunei trade and impoverish the people, His Highness authorized Mr. Consul Trevenen to assure them that no differential taxes or duties would ever be imposed there to the detriment of Brunei. This promise has not been kept. I am told that on acquiring Brooketon His Highness promised to treat the place as a mere private speculation. Jurisdiction is now exercised there by the Resident of Limbang and even the excise farms are leased out by the Sarawak Government. For this year they fetched 5,760 dollars. Since leaving Brunei I have been told that these excise rights were definitely ceded to His Highness years ago.[129] A similar promise was made with regard to Buang Tawar, His Highness' coal mine and oil concession on Pulau Berembang. It was agreed that the mine should be a purely commercial undertaking and that the Rajah's officers should have nothing to do with it. The Resident of Limbang visits the place periodically. Until I made representations to him the Brunei owners of cocoanut plantations on the island had even been forbidden to collect their crops. All the improvements made

161

there, roads, wharves, fort etc., have been carried out under his personal supervision, and the place is, like Brooketon, to all intents and purposes an outlying district of the Limbang. The last outrage (I am voicing Brunei sentiments) has been the purchase of the Kota Batu estate.[130] I have found it impossible to impress on Brunei minds the subtle distinction whereby His Highness is, in relation to Brunei, not only Rajah of a neighbouring country, but also a private British subject, and my failure to do so is not perhaps surprising considering how little the distinction seems to have been recognized in Sarawak and by His Majesty's Representatives in Brunei. The rancour of the Brunei people may perhaps be considered baseless and unreasonable, but it would be idle to deny that it exists and that it is an obstacle to any real friendship.

114. Mr. Hewett reported the refusal of the Brunei Government to entertain the Rajah's proposals in his dispatch No. 15 Confidential of the 10th July, 1902.[131] The letter from which he quotes is so uncompromising in tone that I think it advisable to append what is, I hope, a literal translation of it to this Report (Appendix V). This letter was the result of the deliberations of the whole Government of Brunei. I forwarded a similar communication from the Sultan personally, under cover of my letter of the 15th July last.[132] These letters seem to me to admit of no doubt as to the real nature of the sentiments of the ruling class in Brunei as regards the proposed transfer.

115. I believe that Mr. Consul Hewett was under the impression that the reluctance of the Brunei Chiefs to accede to the proposals which he so energetically pressed upon them was only simulated, and that they were standing out for higher terms. I can only report that frequent conversations with the leading men in Brunei have convinced me that this idea is quite erroneous. There might, perhaps, be room for doubt as to the real sentiments of the Pengiran Bendahara, for he is frankly venal, and has never, so far as I know, shown any but the most ignoble qualities. Even he has never discussed the amount offered him, and Mr. Consul Hewett's hope that he would assist in pressing the proposal on the Sultan and the other members of the Brunei Government was apparently based on his remark that he would agree if the Sultan would. Too much stress must not be laid on the fact that the Bendahara has

been for some time endeavouring to obtain money for his lost property on the Limbang. He has been told that the decision as to its occupation is irrevocable, and his point of view is that if he cannot get his property, he wants its value. He has persuaded other <u>tulin</u> owners to adopt the same line. Their willingness, if only the Sultan would allow them, to accept the Limbang cession money does not in any way argue a love of Sarawak or a desire to barter away the remainder of their possessions and powers to the Rajah. It is only the result of their increased poverty and their desire to obtain some compensation for what has forcibly been taken from them.

116. There is another consideration which I omitted to mention in dealing with the suggestion that Brunei should be handed over to the Chartered Company. It applies with equal force to that alternative or to the one now under discussion, and is that in either case, disguise it as one may, the Brunei Government would cease to exist, and the territory would become a mere district either of Sarawak or British North Borneo. In spite of his lamentable failure to live up to the dignity of his position, the Sultan is intensely proud of the past history of Brunei and so, apparently, are his people. They have sufficient acumen to realize that either change must mean the blotting out of an ancient dynasty; and this sentiment, however ridiculous it may appear to others in the present circumstances of Brunei, is sufficiently strong to mould their policy.

117. When I first took up my duties in Brunei it was with a great admiration for all that I had ever heard of the methods of government in force in Sarawak, and it has been an unpleasant surprise to find my preconceived notions in no way shared by the people of a race whose devoted friend I had always understood His Highness the Rajah to be. My ideas have become somewhat modified during my stay in Brunei, and it now seems to me that the very prevalent belief that His Highness has had great experience in the Government of Malays is based on insufficient premises. As far as I can learn the Rajah has never yet had an opportunity of controlling a really Malay population. His subjects seem to be mainly Dayaks, Kayans, Kenyahs, Bisayas, Muruts, and similar aboriginal tribes whose various religions, customs, and even language are widely

163

diverse from those of Malays.[133]   It is a mere
accident that all, or nearly all, speak Malay.   It
is the lingua franca of the Eastern Archipelago.

118. The Malay population of Brunei, at any
rate, seem as averse to Sarawak rule, as their
Government is.   They say the Sarawak Government is
benevolent to Dayaks and similar races on whose
support the Rajah depends, but that little or no
consideration is shown to Malays.   The free hand
which is apparently given to Dayaks in the suppression of disturbances certainly seems a great blemish
on the otherwise high reputation enjoyed by the
Sarawak Government.   No one could claim for them
that they are a civilized race.   To turn such a
people loose, without European control, to harry and
destroy in a disaffected district seems contrary to
European ideals, and must, one would imagine,
inevitably lead to much cruelty.   I can only hope
that some of the accounts which I have heard, not
only from the natives but also from Europeans, of
the actions of Dayaks on His Highness' punitive
expeditions are exaggerated.   That they are given a
great deal of licence is, however, plain from the
official account of the Batang Lupar expedition
published in the Sarawak Gazette of the 2nd August
last.   I am aware that European officers accompany
such expeditions, but I am informed that bands of
undisciplined Dayaks are sent on ahead of the main
force and that their actions are not controlled.[134]

119. Brunei Malays are, I am afraid, not
particularly courageous, and they seem to have a
great terror of Dayaks, and do not relish the idea
of being under an administration dependent on such
support.   From the erection of a fort at Buang Tawar
and his avowed intention of making that place,
rather than Brunei town, his centre of Government, I
gather that the Rajah himself does not expect to
occupy Brunei without some opposition.[135]   It would
no doubt be futile, and the presence of a force of
Dayaks would be sufficient to overawe resistance,
but it seems plain that the contingency has been
anticipated and provided for.

120. I have already stated that the Chinese
traders seem averse to the surrender of Brunei to
Sarawak.   They seem unable to view with equanimity
the almost inevitable substitution of Kuching for
Labuan as the centre for Brunei trade.   They are
connected, either by personal or monetary ties, with

164

the Chinese traders of Labuan and such a change
would disorganize their business. I do not lay much
stress on their views, for they seem to me to have
little claim to consideration in any case. They are
aliens, only kept in Brunei by self-interest, and it
is probable that their presence, or at least their
cupidity, has caused much of the poverty from which
the lower classes of the country are now suffering.
The probable effect of the change on the trade, and,
therefore, the prosperity of Labuan is, however, a
point which seems to deserve consideration.

121. The dependence of the Colony on Brunei, at
least as far as trade is concerned is, perhaps, too
obvious to require comment. The Chartered Company
are evidently anxious to open a port in their own
territory to serve their western districts, and if
their efforts are successful Labuan will lose all
but the Brunei trade. The bulk of the Limbang and
Baram trade already goes direct to Kuching in
Sarawak steamers. Similarly, most of the imports
into Muara (Brooketon) come from Sarawak. Labuan
is, under present conditions, the collecting and
distributing centre for the trade of Brunei, Belait,
Tutong, Tamburong and Lawas. Were Brunei and Labuan
both placed under the administration of the British
Government or of the Chartered Company no disturbance of trade channels would ensue. If, however,
Brunei is to be absorbed by Sarawak, it seems
probable that Brunei trade, with whatever advantages
it may bring, would, on the analogy of the Baram and
Limbang, be transferred from Labuan to Kuching.

122. The Sarawak Offer. My knowledge of the
exact nature of the terms offered by the Rajah of
Sarawak is so vague that I find any estimate of
their generosity difficult. All that I know
definitely of the Rajah's proposal is derived from
Mr. Hewett's dispatch, No. 12, Confidential of the
19th June 1902.[136] It appears that the Rajah offers
12,000 dollars per annum to the Sultan and 6,000
dollars each per annum to the Pengirans Bendahara
and Pemancha. Half these annuities are to be paid
to the "heirs" of the present holders of these
offices. If this means their families and not their
(problematical) successors, this proposal certainly
makes provision for the families which they would
lack, for the offices are not hereditary. It is all
the more surprising that the terms should have been
refused, and that refusal seems to show that even
self-interest is not enough to induce the ruling

class to welcome the total destruction of the Brunei constitution.

123. These Chiefs are to retain certain empty honours and to exercise jurisdiction over their own following. This does not include rights of taxation. Apparently, therefore, even if the Sultan only collected 2 dollars an adult head, he would lose poll-tax amounting to at least 2,500 dollars per annum and the value of trade monopolies worth perhaps 8,000 dollars per annum. I have already stated that the payments for these monopolies have all been capitalized and that His Highness no longer draws a regular yearly income from them. So long, however, as he remains in power he has the expectation of repeating his previous transactions at the close of each monopoly term, and the power to do so represents an asset of his present position. His gain on paper would not, therefore, be very obvious. His theoretical revenue would be as follows:

	Dollars
Cession Money: British North Borneo, tulin	2,950
Cession Money: British North Borneo, kuripan	2,827
Cession Money: Sarawak, tulin	4,500
Cession Money: Sarawak, for remainder of Brunei:	12,000
Coal and oil revenue (till 1922)	3,200
(Total)	25,477

It may of course be urged that, as he has capitalized his income for years to come and has already spent the proceeds, he would gain an immediate benefit by accepting the terms offered. This is no doubt true, but the transaction, even as a matter of business, does not offer any permanent advantages over his present position. It must be remembered that, hopelessly mis-managed as the country is, the sources of revenue he is asked to forego bring him in about as much, when calculated on a yearly basis, as the compensation offered him, and that, instead of provision being made to increase that compensation as the country develops under a more enlightened Government, the very reverse is the case.[137]

124. The figures which I have given in previous paragraphs for the equally theoretical annual incomes of the Sultan's Ministers will enable a

similar calculation to be made in their cases. Apparently the _Pengiran Bendahara_ would stand to gain about 2,000 dollars _per annum_, while the _Pengiran Pemancha_'s receipts would remain about the same.

125. One point appears to have been overlooked or disregarded in the draft agreement offered for the Sultan's acceptance, and that is the existence of _tulin_ rights, carrying with them a large measure of local government and power of taxation, throughout the country. If it is proposed that the Sultan and his two surviving Ministers should settle for these out of the annuities offered to them, their share of the price of Brunei will be considerably reduced. If this is not contemplated, injustice will be done to the holders, unless arrangements are made with them separately. Hitherto, in taking over a district, the Rajah has merely arranged to pay a lump sum, leaving it to the various owners to apportion the shares among themselves, and, I imagine, from the absence of any separate mention of these rights, that this is the intention in this instance. The _tulin_ rights in question have already been anticipated, in most cases, for cash payments covering years to come. It may be argued that the original owners have thus little claim for consideration, but it seems that the purchasers deserve some compensation. I do not suggest that the expectations of profit which may have led to the various transactions should be the measure of compensation to be paid, but it is plain that the rights have a money value and ought to be taken into account.[138]

126. From these remarks it will be gathered that I find myself unable to agree with Mr. Consul Hewett's reports on the extraordinary generosity of the terms offered by the Rajah of Sarawak. Setting aside the question of _tulin_ rights, they appear to me to deprive the present Rulers of Brunei of as much in money, while no account is taken of the loss of even nominal power which acceptance of them must inevitably involve. Nor do I think that the suggested settlement offers as satisfactory a safeguard against the future penury of the three families to be benefited as Mr. Hewett suggests. They would become mere pensioners with a crowd of relations and dependents to support, and the number of their descendants, coupled with the fact that the annuities will ultimately be reduced by half, would soon

make the provision inadequate, even if means could be devised to prevent them from anticipating it. From a monetary point of view, therefore, there seems little to induce the Sultan and his Ministers to accede to the terms pressed on them.

127. But even if the terms were more generous I am convinced that their reply would be exactly the same. Their absolute refusal to discuss the terms seems to me to show that they are sometimes actuated by less ignoble sentiments than mere greed and avarice. Though I should be prepared from what I know of him for any meanness or disloyalty on the part of the <u>Pengiran Bendahara</u>, the fact remains that even he has repudiated the Sarawak terms, and that he has recently preferred to offer to hand over the administration of all his private property to the British Government. These facts hardly seem to me to support the statement sometimes made that he is in favour of the Sarawak settlement.[139]

128. I understand that His Highness the Rajah considers the terms which he has offered more than generous and that he does not see his way to increasing them.[140] I regret that my own opinion of them does not coincide with that expressed by His Highness and Mr. Consul Hewett. The offer of ready money is no doubt a great temptation to a Brunei Chief, but to thus take advantage of their necessities or shortcomings need not necessarily be described as generous. Nor does it seem possible to resist the conclusion that Brunei, under a settled administration, would show a very substantial profit over the suggested cost, more especially as the additional expenses of that administration would not be heavy in the case of Sarawak.[141] Considering the advantages which would accrue to that Government from the absorption of Brunei and how easily the country can be amalgamated with existing districts, I am of opinion that His Highness might well have offered higher terms, even as a business investment. I am, in fact, inclined to think that the present necessities of the Rulers rather than the future prospects of the country have been the basis on which the price has been computed, and that many claims have been overlooked or disregarded. If the people were willing to treat on their terms proposed no exception could of course be taken to them, but if any compulsion has to be resorted to I consider that better terms should be given.

129. I do not, however, believe (and I have spent six months on terms of intimacy with Brunei _Pengirans_ on purpose to learn their real views) that any offer of the Rajah would ever be welcomed by the Brunei Government. The past is against any such possibility. It would, of course, be easy to ignore the wishes of objections of the Rulers of Brunei in this case as in the case of the Limbang; they are not in a position to offer any effective resistance, and, though I believe some disturbances would result from the forcible introduction of Sarawak rule, there is no doubt that the Rajah is sufficiently strong to quell them in a very short time. The Brunei Chiefs fully recognize this and I have often heard it admitted that the Rajah would only have to send one ship to Brunei to enforce the acceptance of any terms he chose to offer, unless His Majesty's Government intervened to stop his action. As far as I have been able to learn the only inducement which led the Brunei Government to enter into the Treaty of 1888 was the hope of thus saving their country from the aggression of Sarawak. Although the Treaty has never yet fulfilled their expectations, its existence, perhaps, justifies them in claiming sympathetic consideration of their views as to the future of their country.[142]

130. The arguments in favour of handing Brunei over to Sarawak would seem to be that His Majesty's Government would be relieved, without expense, of their present responsibility in the matter, that circumstances in the past have led His Highness the Rajah, whether rightly or wrongly, to count on the acquiescence of the British Government in his claims, that his rule would do away with the abuses that now exist and would be generally welcome to those who suffer most from them, that is to say, the Bisayas and many of the Kadayans, that His Highness is the only person who has shown any marked disposition to undertake the control of the country, and that he is financially, owing to its geographical situation, in a better position to do so than others. Against these arguments can only, apparently, be put the fact that this is the only solution of the question of which it can be said with certainty that it would not meet with the approval of the Rulers of Brunei. I do not think that much account need be taken of the unwillingness of the common people. It undoubtedly exists, but some of it is probably due to the influence of their Chiefs, and it is quite possible that as much is due

169

to the fact that they would not welcome any Government which would be unlikely to treat evil-doers with the leniency at present shown in Brunei.

131. From the Brunei point of view the position may perhaps be summed up by saying that surrender to either Sarawak or British North Borneo would be distasteful to the upper classes, since it must mean the loss of all their dignities, that they would dislike Sarawak rule more than that of British North Borneo, that the bulk of the Malay population would be more or less passive, acquiescing in anything that met the wishes of their Chiefs; that, though they do not seem to think it, they would probably find taxation easier under the rule of Sarawak than under the Chartered Company, and that the serfs, Kadayans, Bisayas, and Muruts, would certainly find themselves better off under Sarawak. It must not, however, be forgotten that these people are merely chattels without theoretical rights, that people in such a position are likely to welcome any change, and that, though the sympathies of at least the Bisayas are with Sarawak, any Government conducted on enlightened lines would relieve them from the distress which, they allege, the cruelty and heartlessness of their present owners impose upon them.

132. It is perhaps not irrelevant in this connection to invite attention to the fact that the Government of Sarawak is a personal despotism. That it has hitherto been exercised in such a way as to win universal admiration is no guarantee of its permanency, and the present Rajah has now reached an age when his retirement from active participation in the government of a tropical country cannot be indefinitely postponed. On leaving Sarawak a few months ago His Highness by Proclamation handed over the Government of the country to his son and heir, the <u>Rajah Muda</u>.[143] The general impression, though there is nothing official to support it, is that this act is by way of an experiment, and that if it succeeds His Highness will gradually withdraw from active control of the State. The task of establishing Sarawak rule in Brunei would be one of great delicacy, and it seems likely that His Highness' experience and reputation would be most necessary for its successful accomplishment.

133. <u>Objects of Interference</u>. The main <u>desiderata</u> to be sought in any arrangement for the future of Brunei appear to be the maximum of justice

to the oppressed with the minimum of interference with the rights and susceptibilities of those in power. I have tried to show how far in my opinion, the alternatives which I have already discussed meet those requirements. They have each of them the great recommendation of involving no extra expense to His Majesty's Government, while offering a fair prospect of the redress of the wrongs so long endured by the subject races of Brunei. In so far, however, as Sarawak or British North Borneo control is not compatible with any real continuance, even in name, of the present dynasty and constitution of Brunei, it cannot be said that either of the alternatives meet the second requirement. It has sometimes been urged that the Sultan and his Chiefs will agree to anything for money. In many instances this has, unfortunately, proved true; but it appears that, up to the present at least, they place a higher value on the remnants of their power than the price that others are disposed to offer, and that the question of the future of their country is complicated to their minds and to those of many of their subjects by considerations of sentiment as well.

134. <u>British Protection</u>. I do not know that Brunei people have ever seriously considered the advantages or disadvantages to them of such a measure of protection as is extended to the Rulers of the Federated Malay States. The proposal has never, so far as I know, been definitely been put before them and I have, of course, by the nature of my instructions, been precluded from ascertaining with any certainty their views on the subject.[144] It seems certain, however, that British protection would meet the case of the oppressed as fully as Sarawak or British North Borneo control, and as far as that requirement is concerned the question is only one of expediency and expense. I have been approached on two or three occasions during my stay in Brunei with tentative suggestions from members of the Sultan's and <u>Bendahara</u>'s <u>entourage</u> to the effect that a joint control, whereby His Highness and his Ministers received half the revenue, the other half going to meet the expenses of administration, would be welcome.[145] It is always made the basis of this suggestion that the Government should be carried on entirely in the name of the Sultan, British officers being appointed to do the work only. I cannot say how far these suggestions were authoritative or sincere, or how far they were mere attempts to

ascertain the intentions of His Majesty's Government with regard to Brunei.

135. My personal opinion is that the Sultan is not averse to British protection in its wider sense, and that he would infinitely prefer it to any other change, while I am convinced that Brunei people in general fully realize that matters have reached a crisis and that some change is inevitable. It is obvious to all of them that such a country cannot long retain its independence when the maximum of taxation has been reached without satisfying the wants of the ruling class. The Sultan and his Chiefs would undoubtedly prefer that the future should be a mere repetition of the past, but I believe from the many hints that I have received that British protection would be less obnoxious to them than loss of identity as a mere part of Sarawak or British North Borneo. The curiosity which has been evinced by the leading members of Brunei society in their inquiries of my followers as to the condition of Pahang and of the circumstances of its whilom rulers seems to me to show that, whether they desire or only fear a similar fate, at least they anticipate it as not improbable.

136. If, therefore, it were only Brunei that had to be considered I am of opinion that British protection has most to recommend it. There are, however, other considerations, involving questions of policy, into which it would be presumptuous of me to enter. I propose, therefore, only to offer a few remarks on certain aspects of the question which seem to fall more or less within the limitations of this Report.

137. Labuan and Brunei. It seems evident that were British protection to be established in Brunei, the administration of the State should be carried on conjointly with that of Labuan. Not only does Labuan depend to a large extent on Brunei for its trade, but communication also with the outlying districts of Brunei is easier from Labuan. Since the loss of the Limbang, the Government of Brunei has been greatly handicapped in exercising control over those districts. The configuration of the country is such that Brunei may be likened to a hand, the outstretched fingers of which represent more or less parallel ranges of hills, the spaces between them forming the basins of the rivers Belait, Tutong and Brunei. Travelling across

country from one river to another necessitates the crossing of these hills and the traversing of the swamps at their feet. In dry weather these present no great difficulties, but in wet weather the swamps are almost impassable the recourse is had to boat-shaped sledges drawn by buffaloes, and used by the Kadayans and Bisayas for the collection and removal of their padi crops. Communication by sea, at least in small boats, from Brunei is equally unsatisfactory. The hundred or so miles of coast between Brunei and Lubok Pulai are most exposed. There is no shelter except the rivers, and in a squall their boats render them impassable. Were the Limbang, or even one bank of it, still under Brunei control it would be easy, as in the past to go by boat up that river, cross a very narrow range of hills, and drop down at once upon the headwaters of the Tutong or the Belait. Failing this, the most convenient way is by ship from Labuan.

138. It appears, therefore, that the Government of Brunei, to be in any way satisfactory, should have control of Labuan or of the Limbang. The Limbang being apparently out of the question, it seems clear that if any Government except that of Sarawak undertakes the future administration of Brunei it should also have control over Labuan.

139. As far as I am able to judge from official reports of the Chartered Company and from my brief visits to Labuan, the island is looked upon as a mere burden upon the resources of the Company. Neglect and decay are everywhere apparent, and the people are full of complaints against the Administration under which they have been placed. Their grievances have been fully aired in Petitions to His Majesty's Government, and it is unnecessary to deal with them in detail here. A certain amount of "animus" seems inseparable from all petitions. Those from the inhabitants of Labuan have been marred by an excess of it, and it is a matter for regret that their case should have been thus weakened. That grievances do exist has been admitted by Mr. Birch in his Administration Report for 1901. The Colony has certainly a most neglected appearance. It is a frequent complaint that a larger staff is charged to the island than its Administration, as at present carried on, requires, that the time of officers stationed there is much occupied with business connected with the mainland, and that the excise farms, revenue apportioned to

173

Labuan, out of the total received for all the territories under the Company, is too small. I have not spent sufficient time in Labuan to venture to discuss the conditions prevailing there, but I can truthfully say that most of the officials seem, from what I have seen of them, either to have very little to do or to leave a great deal undone. Attendance in office is very lax, and I have myself found the transaction of business rendered difficult by apparent slackness and disregard of the interests of the public.

140. It seems that the island has never yet justified the expectations formed on its acquisition, yet it is difficult too see what it lacks to make it a valuable naval base. It has a good harbour, coal--not, perhaps, fit for war purposes, but presumably of good enough quality for use in time of peace--ample supplies of good water, a submarine cable, room for rifle ranges and manoeuvering grounds, and a soil fertile enough, were it only cultivated, to supply fresh fruit and vegetables to a fleet. With all these natural and potential advantages the neglect from which the Colony suffers is very regrettable. The harbour is, by all accounts, disgracefully lighted and buoyed, the country outside Victoria is a wilderness, the roads have become so over-grown with jungle that they are impassable, the people outside the limits of the town ar mere savages, allowed to live and die as they please, there is hardly a pretence at education, and, by the accounts of the Chartered Company, no revenue available to carry out necessary improvements. It seems, therefore, that in the interests of Labuan itself there is much to be said in favour of relieving the Chartered Company of this charge on their resources and energies.[146]

141. In any case, if British protection is decided upon as the most desirable end of Brunei, the resumption of Labuan by the Crown would eventually be the most reasonable arrangement possible and one the prospective advantages of which to both places should far outweigh any fear of injuring the amour propre of the Chartered Company, or, possibly, the value of its shares.[147]

142. Moreover, it seems impossible to resist the conclusion that the administration of the Chartered Company in British North Borneo has not hitherto been successful even from the point of view

of the shareholders of the Company, and this in spite of, or possibly, as some people say, because of the fact that everything is highly taxed. Signs are not wanting to show that before long the question of the future of British North Borneo will demand the serious consideration of His Majesty's Government.[148] It would, of course, be possible ultimately to hand the whole country over to the Sarawak Government for administration. If this is, by any chance, the intended end of British North Borneo, it is not to be expected that the very strong reluctance of the rulers of Brunei will be allowed to stand in the way of their prior assimilation. At the same time, seeing that the future of Labuan, a Crown Colony, is also involved, that the people of British North Borneo are of different races, customs, religions and languages from the majority of the present subjects of Sarawak, and that Brunei itself cannot be said to be willing to come under the sway of Sarawak, there are many objections to such a policy. The only alternative is for the British Government, if or when the occasion arises, to take over the territories of the British North Borneo Company. If this is to be done, the amalgamation of Labuan and Brunei under British administration would form a convenient nucleus for the future Colony or dependency.[149]

143. Expense. The undoubtedly heavy initial expense of establishing British protection in Brunei requires consideration. As the proposal has never yet, so far as I know, taken definite shape, it is impossible for me to deal with this aspect of the question in detail. The very apparent desire of Sarawak and British North Borneo to absorb the State would seem to show that the two Governments most competent, from previous experience of similar cases, to form an opinion have little fear of the result.[150] The cost of administration would, of course, depend on the arrangements made, but I have already stated that I do not consider the amount of compensation offered by His Highness the Rajah sufficient. It is, of course, easy to find reasons for the meagre offers made. It is no doubt true that all the possible revenues of Brunei have been recklessly anticipated and the proceeds spent. This has, of course, greatly reduced the present value of the country. It is also true that the original owners of the country, whether kerajaan, kuripan, or tulin would have to be bought out before any process or reorganization could be commenced, and this would

175

certainly require heavy initial expenditure. Similarly their various creditors and the financiers or money-lenders, who have acquired rights of taxation or the collection of revenue for years to come as security for loans advanced, would require some compensation, as also would the holders of trade monopolies. Having had no opportunities of seeing the documents on which the majority of these claims would be based, I am unable to say how large a sum of money would be involved, but in the case, at least, of official appanages it seems plain that the security depends mainly on the lives of the present holders of office, and that the creditors could not equitably claim from a successor yearly repayment of loans made for the benefit of his predecessor in office. No one presumably has the right to mortgage the salary of his post beyond the period of his own incumbency.

144. From the data available in Appendices III and IV it would appear that the buying out of the monopolists whose transactions are there shown would require at least 50,000 dollars, to which must be added reasonable interest. I have been unable to collect reliable data to enable an estimate to be formed of the amount which would be required to buy up <u>tulin</u> rights of taxation etc., but as financiers have been found willing to advance cash on the security of them, and as they are not likely to do so without the prospect of substantial profits, it does not seem unreasonable to suppose that it would ultimately pay any Government to buy them up.[151]

145. It would be purely a matter of arrangement how much of their present theoretical receipts should be left to the Sultan and his Ministers, but it is evident that rights of taxation and trade monopolies would have to be taken from them. The place of the latter would be taken, presumably, by moderate import and export duties, a system of taxation to which the people of Borneo are accustomed and one which, even if the present volume of trade were not enormously increased by a better system of Government, ought to produce about 15,000 dollars annually; while the poll-tax taken over from the Sultan and his Ministers ought to reach almost as much. The poll-tax may seem to be a barbarous system of collecting revenue, but it seems indigenous in Borneo, and, as worked in Sarawak and British North Borneo, it appears to suit the people better than a system of taxation based on land

176

tenure.[152]

146. These rough calculations are enough to
show that it could not be hoped that the country
wold prove self-supporting at first, but it does not
seem unreasonable to suppose that with a large and
on the whole peaceably inclined population, a
substantial volume of trade, a fertile soil, and
natural and mineral resources hitherto hardly
tapped, its future would ultimately be one of
prosperity were present abuses abolished. Whether
duty of expediency demand that the task of reformation should be undertaken by His Majesty's Government it is not for me to decide.

Singapore, 5 December 1904   [Signed] S.McArthur

NOTES

Preface

1. N. Tarling, <u>Britain, The Brookes and Brunei</u>
   (Kuala Lumpur: Oxford University Press, 1971),
   pp. 510-6.

2. Colonial Office 824/2 <u>Brunei Annual Report</u>
   <u>1938</u>, p. 2.

3. R. Nicholl, <u>Brunei Rediscovered: A Survey of</u>
   <u>Early Times</u> (Typescript of a paper delivered
   at the Eighth Conference of the International
   Association of Historians of Asia, Kuala
   Lumpur, August 1980), pp. 1-4.

4. T. and B. Harrisson, "Kota Batu in Brunei: An
   Introductory Report" in <u>Sarawak Museum Journal</u>
   (December 1956), p. 284. Kupang, the only
   other significant archaeological site yet discovered in Brunei, was clearly of lesser
   importance than Kota Batu. This does not rule
   out the possibility that the pre-Muslim
   capital was located outside the present boundaries of Brunei, perhaps in Lawas district.

5. Carrie C. Brown, "An Early Account of Brunei
   by Sung Lien" in <u>Brunei Museum Journal</u> (1972),
   p. 222.

6. R. Nicholl, <u>Brunei Rediscovered</u>, pp. 4, 10-12.

7. Ibid.; and R. Nicholl, "Brunei and Camphor" in
   <u>Brunei Museum Journal</u> (1979), pp. 52-68.

PART ONE

1. (a) CO 144/79 (1795) Sir F. Swettenham to C.P.
   Lucas (1853-1931), 17 January 1905; (b) CO
   273/300 (645) minute by R.E. Stubbs (1876-
   1947), 23 March 1905; and (c) Foreign Office

179

12/128 p. 408ff. memorandum by F.H. Villiers (1852-1925), 3 June 1905.

2. As note 1 (a). Sir Frank Swettenham (1850-1946). Legendary empire-builder in Malaya. Resident-General, FMS (1896-1901) and Governor of the Straits Settlements (1901-3). Retired 1903.

3. Foreign Office 12/127 pp. 1-4, FO to M.S.H. McArthur, 22 April 1904.

4. Ibid.

5. FO 12/126 p. 244, McArthur to Sir John Anderson (Governor of the Straits Settlements and ex-officio High Commissioner for Brunei, 1904-11), 9 May 1904, paragraph 2.

6. For example: (a) FO 12/69 p. 38ff. Consul P. Leys (1851-1922) to Marquess of Salisbury (1830-1903), No. 6 (Political), 6 February 1886, paragraph 16; also in CO 144/62 (9841); (b) CO 144/77 (27621) Consul G. Hewett (1858-1932) to Marquess of Lansdowne (1845-1927), No. 12 (Confidential), 7 May 1903, paragraph 6.

7. A.B. Ward, Rajah's Servant (Ithaca, New York: Cornell University Press, 1966), p. 20.

8. FO 12/127 (p. 95), Rajah to F.H. Villiers, 14 January 1904.

9. CO 144/81 (3460) Rajah to FO, 23 January 1906.

10. R. Pringle, Rajahs and Rebels: The Ibans of Sarawak Under Brooke Rule, 1841-1946 (London: MacMillan, 1970), p. 137.

11. As note 9.

12. FO 12/105 p. 40: Rajah to FO, 14 March 1899.

13. C.N. Crisswell, Rajah Charles Brooke: Monarch of All He Surveyed (Kuala Lumpur: Oxford University Press, 1978), p. 220.

14. FO 12/127 pp. 153-5, Rajah to Foreign Office, 20 May 1904.

15. FO 12/127 p. 160, Rajah to Colonial Office (enclosure in CO to FO, 21 September 1904).

16. FO 12/128 p. 408ff., memorandum by F.H. Villiers, 3 June 1905. Rt. Hon. Sir Francis Hyde Villiers, PC GCMG GCVO CB, 1852-1925. 1870: entered Foreign Office. Private Secretary at various times to Lord Tenterden, Sir J. Pauncefote, Lord Rosebery, and Lord Salisbury. 1894: Assistant Clerk. 1896: Senior Clerk. 1911-22: Ambassador at the Belgian Court. 1922 (Oct): retired. 1925 (18 November): died.

17. Crisswell, Rajah Charles Brooke, p. 197.

18. P. Blundell, The City of Many Waters (London: Arrowsmith, 1923), p. 215. See also, below, note 26.

19. A.L. Keyser, Trifles and Travels (London: John. Murray, 1927), pp. 126-7.

20. See below, p. 34.

21. FO 12/126, p. 78ff. McArthur to Anderson, No. 15, 2 June 1904, paragraph 9.

22. CO 531/4 (20919) minute by Mr. W.H. Lee-Warner (b. 1880; OBE 1928; d. ?), 2 July 1912.

23. FO 12/127, p. 231 report by Drs. Sheppard and Giddy, encl. in Anderson to CO, No. 292 (Straits), 7 September 1904. For further details see A.V.M. Horton, "The Brunei Smallpox Epidemic of 1904" in Sarawak Museum Journal 1984, pp. 89-99.

24. Blundell, The City of Many Waters, pp. 217-8. He added: "some of the wise men of Brunei said that the ghost of the smallpox had fled in alarm before the new consul and his Union Jack." See also, below, note 26.

25. CO 531/4 (26950) F.N. Butterworth to Anderson, 4 August 1912 (see also, note 26, following).

26. Frank Nestle Butterworth (1875-1952). Educated at University College, Nottingham and then spent some years at sea. 1901-1913: Engineer (1901-5) and Manager (1905-13) of

Island Trading Syndicate's cutch works in the Brunei capital. 1914-18: worked in Woolwich Arsenal. Author (using pen-name "Peter Blundell") of a book about Brunei (The City of Many Waters, 1923) and a long series of novels about Borneo and the sea. Source: The Times 8 November 1952, courtesy of P.W. Ellis, Area Librarian, Central Devon: letter to the author, 12 January 1984.

27. Blundell, The City of Many Waters, pp. 215-6.

28. CO 273/300 (645) Sir Frank Swettenham to C.P. Lucas, 11 January 1905.

29. CO 273/309 (27211) Sir John Anderson to C.P. Lucas, private, 6 July 1905.

30. FO 12/126 p. 244, McArthur to Anderson, No. 11, 9 May 1904, paragraph 2.

31. McArthur reported: I had the house hung with flags; prepared an enormous candle about six inches in diameter and nearly three feet high (a Brunei mark of respect) to place beside his seat; had the latter, a table and a smaller chair covered with yellow silk for His Highness and the heir to the throne, his eldest son [d. 1905]; and laid down a strip of white cloth from the jetty steps to the dais for His Highness to walk on. I borrowed four brass lelas (cannon) from the Pengiran Bendahara for a salute, obtained a supply of gunpowder from Buang Tawar, and also covered a chair with white cloth (his official colour) for the Pengiran Bendahara and one with black cloth for the Pengiran Pemancha." FO 12/126, p. 78ff. McArthur to Anderson, No. 15, 2 June 1904, paragraph 15.

32. For example FO 12/96, p. 7, Sultan Hashim to Sir Charles Mitchell, 2 Shaaban 1313 A.H. (16 January 1896) in which he complained about the appointment of F.R.O. Maxwell; or CO 144/77 (12955) Sultan Hashim to King Edward, 19 Jemadi/Awal 1322 AH (24 August 1902), in which he requested the removal of Consul Hewett and complaind that since the Protectorate Treaty of 1888 "not a single consul has done anything to help strengthen my country. They all seem to help Sarawak and to try to hand over my

country to Sarawak."

33. FO 12/126, p. 209, Sultan Hashim to high commissioner, 20 September 1904.

34. FO 12/126, p. 224, Sultan Hashim to high commissioner, 9 November 1904.

35. CO 1022/255 item 1: A.G. Morse to Sir G. Whiteley, confidential, 27 July 1955; Daily Telegraph 25 April 1983; and Telegraph Sunday Magazine 5 February 1984, p. 21 (latter courtesy of Mrs. D. Thomas).

36. CO 824/1 Brunei Annual Report 1918 p. 6; CO 531/12 (38835) Sir A. Young (1854-1938) to CO, No. 4 (Brunei), 10 June 1918, paragraph 1; and ibid., McArthur to secretary to high commissioner, 31 May 1918, paragraph 10.

37. CO 273/521 (12627), F.S. James to CO, 9 February 1923.

38. Sir A. Young, eg. CO 531/11 (10824).

39. CO 531/12 (38835).

40. British Malaya [the magazine of the Association of British Malaya] (March 1934).

41. D.E. Brown, Structure and History (1970), p. 157.

42. N. Tarling, Britain, The Brookes and Brunei (Kuala Lumpur: Oxford University Press, 1971).

43. D.E. Brown, Structure and History, pp. 66-7; and J.M. Gullick, Indigenous Political Systems of Western Malaya (London: Athlone Press, 1953), pp. 98, 125-31.

44. CO 144/77 (20118) G. Hewett to FO No. 9 (confidential) 10 April 1903, paragraph 4.

45. Ibid., paragraph 5.

46. CO 144/74 (17694), Consul A.L. Keyser to FO, No. 23, 30 April 1900. Also in FO 12/111 (p. 58).

47. As note 44 (above), paragraph 2.

48. Ibid., paragraph 9.

49. L.R. Wright, The Origins of British Borneo (Hong Kong, 1970).

50. CO 144/64 (16254), Sir F. Weld to CO, 20 June 1887, paragraph 12.

51. Colonial Office List 1940 p. 397.

52. FO 12/78, p. 165, minute by Sir R. Herbert, 31 January 1888. The 1888 UK-Brunei Protectorate Treaty was worded so as "not to stand in the way of such a consummation as the absorption, when the time arrives, of Brunei by Sarawak and the North Borneo Company. It would, in fact, enable the sultan to accept the inevitable on the best terms procurable." See also, ibid., p. 151: minute by Marquess of Salisbury.

53. CO 144/79 (1795) Swettenham to Lucas, 17 January 1905.

54. CO 144/73 (23569) Keyser to Rajah, 12 June 1899; and CO 144/73 (19517) Keyser to Mitchell, 7 June 1899, paragraph 8.

55. CO 144/73 (23569) Keyser to Rajah, 12 June 1899; and CO 144/73 (19517) Rajah to Keyser, 14 June 1899; also in FO 12/101, p. 216ff.

56. Godfrey Hewett (1859-1932). c. 1880-98: BNBC service. Participated in Kinabatangan massacre, 1890 (130 dead) and the devastation of the Inanam Valley in 1897. 1900-4: consul for "British" Borneo. 1904-14: consul at Rio Grande (1904), Pernambuco (1911). 1914: retired. See also Ward, Rajah's Servant, p. 85.

57. FO 12/114, p. 68, Hewett to Swettenham, 7 March 1901, paragraph 4; also in CO 144/75 (15738).

58. P.F. Cunynghame in Sarawak Gazette, 2 January 1900, p. 19; and Ward, Rajah's Servant, p. 78.

59. FO 12/114, p. 98ff. Hewett to Swettenham, No. 31, 10 April 1901, paragraph 9; also in CO 144/75 (24405).

184

60. CO 144/75 (33046) Hewett to Swettenham, 10 June 1901, No. 49 (confidential), paragraph 4.

61. FO 12/114, p. 133, Hewett to Swettenham, No. 36 (confidential), 19 April 1901, paragraph 2; also in CO 144/75 (24405).

62. Ibid.

63. FO 12/115 p. 102, Hewett to Lansdowne, No. 8 (confidential), 15 July 1901, paragraph 5; also in CO 144/75 (33046).

64. FO 12/115 p. 36ff. Hewett to Lansdowne, No. 7 (confidential), 2 July 1901, paragraph 4; also in CO 144/75 (33046).

65. Ibid.

66. FO 12/115 p. 115ff. Hewett to Lansdowne, No. 12 (confidential, 25 September 1902?, paragraph 1; also in CO 144/75 (41469).

67. CO 144/76 (20448) Hewett to Swettenham, NO. 13 (confidential), 28 March 1901 (encl. in FO to CO, 24 May 1902), paragraph 2.

68. Sarawak Gazette, 1 November 1901 (Baram Report for September).

69. Sarawak Gazette, 2 January 1902, p. 14.

70. Sarawak Gazette, 1 March 1902, p. 48.

71. In early 1899 Dato di Gadong killed three men; and in 1901 he shot several people "for refusing to join him."

72. Sarawak Gazette, 1 October 1902, p. 203.

73. Ward, Rajah's Servant, p. 79.

74. CO 144/78 (39970) M.S.H. McArthur to High Commissioner, No. 51/04, 8 October 1904, paragraphs 1-3 encl. in FO to CO, 23 November 1904.

75. CO 273/312 (691 05/06) McArthur and D.G. Campbell to High Commissioner, 6 December 1905, paragraph 14 (encl. in Anderson to Colonial Office, No. 480 (FMS), 14 December

1905).

76. FO 12/116 p. 34, Foreign Office to Colonial Office, 3 April 1901; also inn CO 144/75 (12121).

77. FO 12/115 p. 36, Hewett to Lansdowne, No. 7 (confidential), 2 July 1901, paragraphs 5-7; also in CO 144/75 (33046).

78. CO 144/75 (33046) Minute by C.P. Lucas, 21 September 1901.

79. FO 12/116 p. 87, Rajah to Lansdowne, 19 August 1901; also in CO 144/75 (37127).

80. FO 12/116 p. 117, Rajah to Foreign Office, 7 October 1901; also in CO 144/75 (37127).

81. CO 144/76 (36985) Hewett to Lansdowne, No. 12 (confidential), 19 June 1902.

82. See below, p. 161 (paragraph 114), and 254 (note 132).

83. FO 12/118 p. 73ff. Hewett to Lansdowne, No. 15 (confidential), 10 July 1902, paragraphs 3-5; also in CO 144/77 (40636). See also S. Baring-Gould and C.A. Bampfylde: A History of Sarawak under its Two White Rajahs (London: Southeran, 1909), p. 364.

84. FO 12/122 p. 47, Hewett to Swettenham (confidential), 24 June 1903, paragraphs 2-4; also in CO 144/77 (31599).

85. FO 12/122 p. 56ff. Swettenham to Lansdowne, No. 15 (Secret), 6 August 1903.

86. FO 12/124 p. 25, CO to FO, 23 March 1903 (plus minute thereon).

87. FO 12/127 ?c. p. 94-5 Rajah to Villiers, January 1904.

88. CO 273/300 (item 645 04/05) McArthur to Swettenham, (private), 13 December 1904.

89. CO 144/79 (1795) Swettenham to Lucas, 17 January 1905 (my italics).

90. As note 88 above.

91. CO 273/154 (21539) Sir H. Low to Sir C. Smith, 22 September 1888, paragraph 13; also in FO 12/78 p. 382ff.

92. See below, p. 153, Report, paragraph 100. In some respects a Brunei citizen appears to have been better off than his fellow in Malaya, who might have been required "to give his labour in making roads, bridges, drains and other works of public utility, to tend elephants, to pole boats, to carry letters and messages, to attend his chief when travelling, to cultivate his chief's fields as well as his own, and to serve as a soldier when required." Sir William Maxwell quoted by Sir R.O. Winstedt, The Malays: A Cultural History (London: Routledge and Kegan Paul, Revised Edition 1950), p. 55.

93. See below, Report paragraphs 42-3 and 120; and p. 212 (note 22).

94. FO 12/93 p. 105ff. Minute by Lord Rosebery, 22 September 1892; and FO 12/95 p. 21ff. Minute by Sir G. Dallas, February 1895; and ibid., (p. 50) minute by Sir P. Anderson, 11 July 1895.

95. FO 12/128 p. 449, H.C. Belfield (1855-1923) to Anderson, 5 June 1905, paragraph 32; also in CO 273/310 (33426).

96. CO 144/79 (10323) Anderson to Lansdowne, 18 February 1905, paragraphs 3-12.

97. Ibid., Minute by G.V. Fiddes (1858-1936), 15 April 1905.

98. As note 96, paragraph 11.

99. Ibid., Minutes by R.E. Stubbs, 14 April 1905, and Secretary of State, A. Lyttelton, 28 April 1905.

100. CO 144/81 (45446) Minute by C.P. Lucas, 12 December 1906.

101. CO 144/73 (24234) Minute by C.P. Lucas, 29 September 1899; and CO 144/70 (10680) Minute

by C.P. Lucas, 18 May 1896.

102. CO 273/309 (27211 and 43669), CO 144/79 (27763) and CO 273/310 (31745).

103. FO 12/128 p. 246ff. Anderson to McArthur and Campbell, 9 November 1905, (encl. in Anderson to Lansdowne, No. 23 Political, 7 December 1905).

104. CO 273/312 (691 05/06) Anderson to Colonial Office, No. 480 (F.M.S.), 14 December 1905.

105. CO 273/310 (43072) Anderson to Lyttelton, telegram, 5 December 1905. The Treaty had been signed two days earlier, on 3 December 1905.

106. FO 12/128 p. 9, FO to Anderson, No. 5, 24 July 1905; also in CO 144/79 (27763).

107. CO 273/312 (691) McArthur and Campbell to Anderson, 6 December 1905, plus enclosures "B" and "C."

108. CO 144/80 (5578) Anderson to CO, No. 1 (Labuan), 25 January 1906, paragraph 16.

109. CO 144/80 (36822) Sultan Muhammad Jemalul Alam to High Commissioner, August 1906, encl. in McArthur to Anderson, 10 August 1906.

110. Ibid., Anderson to Sultan, 7 September 1906, paragraph 5.

111. CO 273/317 (?1518) Anderson to Elgin, SS confidential, 25 January 1906, paragraph 2.

112. CO 144/81 (3460) Rajah to Foreign Office, 23 January 1906.

113. Ibid., Minute by R.E. Stubbs, 31 January 1906.

114. Bampfylde, A History of Sarawak, p. 367; Blundell, The City of Many Waters, p. 220; and Ward, op. cit., p. 102.

115. CO 144/81 (3460 and 4722).

116. CO 144/81 (16405) Anderson to Fiddes, private, 7 May 1906.

117. Quoted by C.N. Crisswell, <u>Rajah Charles Brooke</u>, p. 200.

118. CO 144/80 (26871) McArthur to Anderson, No. 133 (Brunei), 18 June 1906, paragraph 5.

119. In various dispatches in 1906 McArthur referred to Sultan Muhammad Jemal as aged 14, 15, and 16. J.F. Owen, the Resident, said that the new sultan himself did not know his age, but current report made him 17 (in 1908). Owen himself believed His Highness to be nearer nineteen.

120. CO 144/80 (26871) McArthur to Anderson, No. 133 (Brunei), 18 June 1906, paragraph 5.

121. CO 144/81 (27240) Sir Edward Sassoon, Bart. (1856-1912) to FO, July 1906, encl. in FO to CO, 25 July 1906.

122. Ibid., Pengiran Bendahara to O.F. Ricketts (Resident of Limbang, 1890-1909), 22 May 1906.

123. CO 144/80 (35280) McArthur to Anderson, 14 June 1906, paragraph 7 (encl. in Anderson to Elgin, No. 13 Brunei, 27 August 1906).

124. As note 128. Memorandum by C.A. Bampfylde, 22 July 1906. (C.A. Bampfylde 1856-1918. Sarawak Civil Service 1875-1903. Resident 1st Division 1896-1903. Retired 1903. 1903-12: Rajah's 'Political Agent' in the United Kingdom. 1912-18: Member, Sarawak State Advisory Council, Westminster).

125. CO 144/80 (40678) McArthur to Anderson, No. 228 (Brunei), 24 September 1906, paragraph v.

126. Ibid.

127. Ibid., paragraph i.

128. Op. cit., note 83 (above).

129. CO 144/64 (16254) Weld to Holland, 20 June 1887, paragraph 8; also in FO 12/75.

130. Blundell, <u>The City of Many Waters</u>, p. 68.

131. CO 824/1 <u>Brunei Annual Report 1911</u>, p. 11.

132. CO 604/4 <u>Sarawak Gazette</u>, 1 July 1913, p. 140.

133. See, for example, CO 943/1, File 5, item 30, Report by L.H.N. Davis, 5 March 1948.

134. CO 144/81 (27543). Sir Charles Dilke, among other things, was a historian and politician; Sir Charles Jessel was the Chairman of the BNBC, giving his name to its capital (Jesselton, now Kota Kinabalu).

135. CO 144/80 (29740) McArthur to Anderson, No. 148 (Brunei), 27 June 1906, paragraph 6.

136. Ibid., paragraphs 2-5.

137. CO 144/81 (45446).

138. CO 531/1 (34640) Rajah to Elgin, late September 1907.

139. Ibid., CO to Rajah, 7 October 1907.

140. CO 144/80 (10206) McArthur to Anderson, 13 February 1906.

141. Ibid., Minutes by Stubbs (30.3.1906) and Lucas (2.4.1906).

142. Ibid., CO to McArthur, 28 April 1906.

143. CO 144/80 (35282) Anderson to Elgin, 30 August 1906.

144. CO 537/839, Sir A. Young to Lord Milner, Borneo Secret, 19 February 1919 and enclosure, Rajah Vyner Brooke to Young, 26 December 1918.

145. CO 144/81 (23939) Bampfylde to Foreign Office, 25 June 1906, paragraph 4.

146. Ibid., Minute by R.E. Stubbs, 3 July 1906.

147. Ibid., CO to FO, 11 July 1906.

148. CO 144/81 (13408) McArthur to O.F. Ricketts, 14 February 1906.

149. Ibid., Rajah Charles Brooke to Earl of Elgin and Kincardine, 27 March 1906.

150. CO 144/80 (16405) Memo by Rajah Charles.

151. CO 144/80 (35281) Anderson to Elgin, 30 August 1906, paragraph 3.

152. Ibid., McArthur to Anderson, No. 151, 28 August 1906, paragraphs 4-7.

153. As note 151 (above), paragraphs 4-12.

154. Ibid., Minute by Stubbs, 29 September 1906.

155. CO 144/81 (41004) Rajah to Elgin, 6 November 1906.

156. CO 144/80 (45588) Minute by Stubbs, 11 December 1906, paragraph 5.

157. CO 531/1 (5130), Minute by Stubbs, 23 February 1907.

158. CO 531/1 (20553) McArthur to Anderson, No. 85, (confidential), 27 April 1907.

159. Ibid., Anderson to Elgin, 16 May 1907, paragraphs 2-3.

160. CO 531/1 (5866) McArthur to Anderson, 12 January 1907.

161. CO 531/1 (35898) and CO 531/7 (11155): Sir Frank Swettenham to Colonial Office, 7 October 1907 and 25 March 1914 respectively.

162. CO 531/1 (35898) Minute by Stubbs, October 1907.

163. CO 531/2 (11169) Memorandum by H. Chevalier, 9 February 1910.

164. CO 531/3 (9856) Memorandum by R.E. Stubbs, 25 March 1911.

165. As note 163 (above), Minute by Stubbs, 21 April 1910.

166. CO 824/1 Brunei Annual Report 1906, p. 15.

167. Ibid.

168. CO 144/80 (26871) McArthur to Anderson, No. 133 (Brunei), 18 June 1906, paragraph 12.

169. CO 824/1 Brunei Annual Report 1906, p. 7; and 1907, p. 3.

170. CO 824/1 Brunei Annual Report 1907, p. 3.

171. CO 824/1 Brunei Annual Report 1907, p. 3-4.

172. CO 824/1 Brunei Annual Report 1910, p. 12.

173. This figure represents loan expenditure only.

174. CO 824/1 Brunei Annual Report 1907, p. 2.

175. See below, p. 120.

176. See below, p. 125.

177. CO 824/1 Brunei Annual Report 1906, p. 7. Note: the term of years for which monopolies had been hypothecated was as at 5 December 1904; by January 1906, there may have been further extensions.

178. CO 824/1 Brunei Annual Report 1906, p. 8.

179. CO 824/1 Brunei Annual Report 1906, p. 11.

180. CO 824/1 Brunei Annual Report 1907, p. 6.

181. CO 824/1 Brunei Annual Report 1906, p. 5.

182. J.G. Butcher, "The Demise of the Revenue Farms Systems in the Federated Malay States" in Modern Asian Studies, 17, 3 (1983), pp. 387-412.

183. CO 824/1 Brunei Annual Report 1908, p. 1.

184. For details about Cheok Boon Seok's career, see Blundell, The City of Many Waters, pp. 122-6. There is a photograph of "Si Hock" facing page 122.

185. CO 824/1 Brunei Annual Report 1912, p. 1.

186. Cf. Straits Settlements, where opium revenue accounted for 45-50 percent of the total government income.

187. CO 824/1 Brunei Annual Report 1909, p. 2.

188. CO 824/1 Brunei Annual Report 1912, p. 3.

189. CO 824/1 Brunei Annual Report 1909, p. 2.

190. CO 824/1 Brunei Annual Report 1910, p. 8.

191. CO 824/1 Brunei Annual Report 1907, p. 7.

192. CO 604/7 Sarawak Gazette, 1 July 1920, p. 152.

193. CO 824/1 Brunei Annual Report 1907, p. 7 and 1908, p. 7.

194. CO 824/1 Brunei Annual Report 1908, p. 7.

195. Ibid., p. 10; R.H. Hickling, "Brunei Silver" in Corona (August 1955), pp. 294-6; and Blundell, The City of Many Waters, pp. 86-91.

196. Blundell, The City of Many Waters, p. 86.

197. Ibid., p. 91.

198. CO 824/1 Brunei Annual Report 1908, p. 10.

199. Table. Exports of brassware and silverware 1921-40. ($ Straits)

| | Exports of: | |
Year	(a) brassware	(b) silverware
1921	870	n.a.
1925	15,734	6,057
1930	9,104	13,560
1935	1,833	7,709
1940	5,795	4,019

Source: compiled by author from Brunei Annual Reports.

200. CO 824/2 Brunei Annual Report ?1938, pp. 20-2.

201. Borneo Bulletin, 19 March 1983, pp. 20-2.

202. See note 23 (above).

203. See below, p. 206 (note 5).

204. CO 824/1 Brunei Annual Report 1906, p. 10.

205. CO 824/1 Brunei Annual Report 1910, p. 16.

206. CO 824/1 Brunei Annual Report 1908, p. 6.

207. CO 824/1 Brunei Annual Report 1910, p. 11.

208. CO 824/1 Brunei Annual Report 1909, p. 8.

209. CO 824/1 Brunei Annual Report 1907, p. 5.

210. CO 824/1 Brunei Annual Report 1908, p. 4.

211. CO 824/1 Brunei Annual Report 1915, p. 12 and 1918, p. 6.

212. Eg. CO 824/1 Brunei Annual Report 1919, p. 7.

213. CO 531/11 (50598) G.E. Cator to High Commissioner, No. 2 (confidential), 30 April 1917, paragraph 6; and R.H. Hickling, Memorandum upon Brunei Constitutional History and Practice (2 January 1955, confidential, unpublished), paragraph 40 (Copy courtesy of Eussoff Agaki).

214. Ibid., (Hickling), paragraph 42.

215. CO 824/1 Brunei Annual Report 1909, p. 6.

216. CO 824/1 Brunei Annual Report 1908, p. 7.

217. CO 824/1 Brunei Annual Report 1906, p. 12.

218. Ibid., pp. 12-13.

219. Ibid., p. 14.

220. CO 824/1 Brunei Annual Report 1910, p. 15.

221. CO 824/1 Brunei Annual Report 1908, p. 8.

222. Dr. Adamson's initials are not available. He was a medical practitioner in Labuan who sometimes ministered to Europeans living in Brunei. In 1904 he also took charge of the

British consulate records in Labuan during the absence of the British consul.

223. Blundell, The City of Many Waters, p. 138. A.also pp. 171 and 174.

224. CO 824/1 Brunei Annual Report 1911, p. 10. (I discovered that the previous postmaster also carried the style "dresser"; but whether he fulfilled these functions I am unable to say. He was dismissed for embezzlement in 1910.)

225. CO 824/1 Brunei Annual Report 1916, p. (n.a.).

226. CO 824/1 Brunei Annual Report 1918, p. 4.

227. A.C. Watson, "Notes on the History of Bubongan Dua-Belas: The British High Commissioner's Residence in Brunei" in Brunei Museum Journal (1982), pp. 37-104.

228. G.E. Cator, "Brunei" in Asian Review, 1939, p. 744.

229. CO 531/12 (38835) Sir A. Young to CO, No. 4 (Brunei), 10 June 1918, paragraph 1.

230. Eg. D.E. Brown, "The Coronation of Sultan Jemalul Alam, 1918" in Brunei Museum Journal 1971, pp. 74-80; Cator, "Brunei," pp. 738-44; CO 604/6 Sarawak Gazette 4 June 1918, pp. 129-30; and C. Bruce (pen-name used by A.B.C. Francis) Twenty Years in Borneo (London: Cassell, 1924), pp. 221-3.

231. CO 531/12 (38835) McArthur to Secretary to High Commissioner, 31 May 1918, paragraph 7; and Cator, "Brunei," p. 742.

232. McArthur, as note 233, paragraph 10.

233. Ibid., paragraph 12.

234. Ibid., paragraph 17. Cator himself commented later that the Coronation had been the "high-spot of a long period of service in Brunei" (1916-21), which had provided many happy recollections and some friendships which still endured in 1939. Cator, "Brunei," p. 744.

PART TWO

1. Sir John Anderson (1858-1918) G.C.M.G. 1909,
    K.C.B. 1913. 1904-1911: Governor of the
    Straits Settlements and High Commissioner for
    Brunei. (1892-1903: Service in the Colonial
    Office, reaching rank of "Principal Clerk."
    1911-16: Permanent Under-Secretary, C.O.
    1916-18: Governor of Ceylon. 1918: died 24
    March).

2. Henry Petty Fitzmaurice, 5th Marquess of
    Lansdowne (1845-1927): British politician,
    Foreign Secretary 1900-1905. (1883: Gov-
    ernor-General of Canada. 1888-94: Viceroy of
    India. 1895: War Secretary. 1905-15:
    Leader of Conservative Opposition in the House
    of Lords. 1915-16: non-departmental office
    in Coalition Government. November 1917:
    letter to the Daily Telegraph appealing for a
    negotiated peace with Germany).

3. Mr. Oliver Marks (1866-1940) C.M.G. 1922.
    "Secretary to High Commissioner," Sir John
    Anderson, 1903-07.

4. The "Labuan authorities" at that time were
    officers of the British North Borneo (Char-
    tered) Company, which administered the island
    from 1890 until the end of 1905. (Labuan had
    been ceded by the Sultan of Brunei to Queen
    Victoria in 1846. 1846-1889: Crown Colony.
    1906-42: one of the Straits Settlements.
    1942-5: Japanese Occupation (Labuan renamed
    Maeda Island). 1945-6: Headquarters, British
    Military Administration, British Borneo.
    1946: handed to North Borneo rather than back
    to Brunei, an act which still rankles in the
    Sultanate. 1963: Independence as part of
    Sabah, Malaysia).

5. The actual distance is only about 70 miles.

6. Later renamed Marudi.

7. It was not until the 1950s that a serious
    attempt at river-clearing was made. In March
    1955--as part of Brunei's first Five Year
    Plan--a scheme was announced for the improve-
    ment of water communications, particularly the
    Tutong and Belait rivers. The objectives

included (a) assistance for those who depended
on water rather than roads for their highways,
and (b) encouragement of agricultural and
forestry production upstream by making the
rivers safe for navigation. The Belait was to
be cleared as far as Sukang (83 miles), the
Tutong for about half this distance. The
engineer in charge of the project was Captain
W.A. Doust, C.B.E.

Work commenced in Belait in mid-1956 and
in Tutong late the following year, when there
were said to be seventy labourers employed for
this duty. In January 1958 the Borneo
Bulletin reported that the stages in the
operation included felling trees along the
river banks, removing minor or medium-sized
snags by explosives, and burning the snags and
fallen trees. The task was far less onerous
in Tutong than in Belait, where one karangan
was 2,200 feet long, and several others were
between 900 and 1,600 feet long; in Tutong the
obstacles were much smaller.

Three months later it was announced that
the $300,000 Belait river scheme had been
abandoned because no more funds were forth-
coming. Ibans in the Sukang area were
reportedly "bitterly disappointed." (Borneo
Bulletin: 18 August 1956, 18 January 1958,
and 5 April 1958). One of my informants,
however, declares that the Sultan was somewhat
reluctant to spend money on his non-Muslim
subjects, such as the Ibans and Orang Bukit of
ulu Belait and ulu Tutong.

8. Before 1928 district administration head-
    quarters was at Kuala Balai (Pengkalan Balei).
    Until the British Malayan Petroleum Company
    began serious oil exploration in the district,
    i.e. from 1923, "Kuala Belait" consisted of "a
    swamp with a few fishing huts dotted along the
    banks of the Belait River" in an area "infest-
    ed with mosquitoes, wild beasts and reptiles."
    In 1928, however, (Sir) P.A.B. McKerron (1896-
    1964; British Resident 1928-31), "realizing
    the difficulties of having his headquarters
    accessible only by river," transferred the
    administrative centre of Belait district from
    Kuala Balai (then some hours upstream) to
    Kuala Belait (at the mouth of the river). He
    was responsible for the planning and layout of
    the original roads of the oilfield towns

197

(Kuala Belait and Seria) and his name was given to the most prominent. The BMPC, which had been established in Labi, also moved its head offices to Kuala Belait about this time.

After the discovery of oil (1929), the population of Kuala Belait expanded rapidly: from 1,193 in 1931 to an estimated 5,000 by 1938 and approaching 9,000 by 1960. The growth of Seria, built originally on a site known as Padang Berawa (Wild Pigeon's Field), was even more marked: too insignificant to be listed in the 1931 census, the town contained 17,595 inhabitants in 1960. During the 1950s the garden coastal township of Kuala Belait, Panaga, Seria, orderly and pleasant looking, was presented as a model of modern industrial town planning. Electricity and piped water--unknown in McArthur's time--were almost universal in these towns by the end of the Residency Era (1959).

9. In 1954 Tutong Village was said to have 700 inhabitants, including 200 Chinese, and seventeen shops. But there was only one cinema for the "entertainment-starved" population; and water and electricity supplies at that time were inadequate (Borneo Bulletin, 27 November, 1954). The 1960 Housing Census, however, revealed that there were 112 houses with 580 occupants in the village at that time. One-third of the dwellings were owner-occupied (compared with only 12% in Seria); and 86 percent of them were supplied with electricity.

The writer of the Brunei Annual Report for 1911 refers to a tradition which ascribed the founding of the settlement at Kuala Patani (Tutong Village), the chief kampong on the Tutong River, to an immigration from Patani (S. Thailand). The writer thought this legend might find confirmations through the retention, in the existing "conglomerate dialect" of words actually Patani, or traceable to Patani roots. The salt workings along the coast, moreover, resembled the Patani methods. The writer added that Tutongs "collectively and individually, are more industrious than any other native inhabitants of the territory still left to the Sultan of Brunei" (CO 824/1 Brunei Annual Report for 1910, p. 17).

10. The 1911 Census (CO 531/3: 34002), the first
     taken in modern Brunei, disclosed that Tutong
     district had 3,423 of the country's 21,718
     inhabitants; whereas Belait, despite having
     the largest area, was the least populous
     "river," with a mere 1,126 people. By 1931,
     just before the first consignment of Seria oil
     was exported, the numbers in Belait had risen
     to 3,897 (12.93% of the total population, then
     31,135), while Tutong was still ahead with
     5,651 (18.75%). At the time of the 1960
     Census, however, Belait accounted for 31,708
     of the sultanate's total population of 83,877,
     Tutong for only 10,718. Hence, while Tutong's
     proportion of the total (12.8%) had remained
     fairly stable, Belait's share had jumped to
     37.8%.

11. These remained the staples of trade for
     several years after the beginning of the
     British Residency (1906). There was, however,
     a rapid expansion in annual exports of
     jelutong (rubber), the value of which from
     Tutong alone jumped from only $753 in 1908 to
     $12,597 two years later.

12. Expansion of agricultural production was
     delayed by the need to settle land claims
     after 1906. Land administration had still not
     commenced in Belait as late as 1913, although
     400 land applications had been demarcated in
     Tutong by that date. The outbreak of war in
     1914 "disclosed the fact that most of the rice
     consumed in Brunei Town and the Belait River
     [was] imported" and the "Native Magistrates"
     were urged to induce people living in their
     districts to plant padi in order to minimize
     possible shortages due to war. Despite the
     discouragement of successive droughts which
     ruined the harvests, the Dusuns of Tutong and
     Bisayas of Belait responded well to the
     Government's call and, by 1920, "the out-
     districts were self-supporting in rice
     throughout the year and Tutong and Belait had
     a surplus for export." It is unlikely that
     Belait remained self-sufficient for long,
     because of the inflow population after the
     discovery of oil. During the 1930s Brunei
     produced around one-third or less of its
     domestic rice requirements, and, in 1934, only
     one-sixth. After the Japanese Occupation, a

"Grow More Food" campaign resulted in three-quarters of demand being produced at home (83.9% in 1950), but this level of output could not be maintained, partly because the Sultanate's population more than doubled between 1947 and 1960, and partly because of the lack of suitable agricultural land.

13. In 1960 Dr. G.E. Wilford, who published the first comprehensive geological survey of Brunei, commented: "Reports of antimony, gold and diamonds occurring in the area have yet to be substantiated." Surface mineral oil has never been of much commercial significance, although small quantities were exported from the Rajah's coal mine at Buang Tawar (on Berembang Island in the Brunei River).

14. Goh Ah Lai (Lye), b. 1851: Chinese British subject (see McArthur's Report, paragraph 42).

15. McArthur appears to have been not unjustified in doubting the honesty of Chinese traders. During 1910 two of the largest Brunei importers were fined on the prosecution of the Assistant Resident for declaring false values on dutiable articles; while the leading Chinese trader at Tutong was convicted of smuggling dutiable imports. It was also found, after a full examination of the outlying districts, "that Chinese traders were declaring entirely false values on among other things the jelutong and getah exports. Thus, while jelutong from Baram (Sarawak) was valued at $9.00 per picul (90 cents duty) that at Belait, the neighbouring river, was declared at $4.00 per picul." (CO 824/1 Brunei Annual Report for 1910, p. 6).
     With regard to the volume of trade, it is regrettable that complete returns were not kept in the early years of the British Residency, apparently because only a slender customs staff was available (CO 824/1 B.A.R. (1911), p. 3; and B.A.R. 1906, p. 9).
     McArthur estimated the value of imports into Belait in 1904 at $25,000 (see paragraph 45 of his Report).
     The value of imports in 1912, however, was given at only $14,797 and in 1913 only $18,135; so McArthur may have been exaggerating somewhat. He gave the value of

imports into Tutong in 1904 at $11,000; subsequent figures were $19,841 in 1908; $16,368 in 1912 and $14,380 in 1913.

One might also present subsequent customs receipts to compare with the figures presented by McArthur:

Year	Belait District Imports(1)	Exports	Tutong District Imports(1)	Exports
1908	n.a.	n.a.	1,122	850
1909	n.a.	n.a.	1,321	1,308
1910	n.a.	n.a.	2,819	3,208
1911	2,054	3,394	2,405	2,212(2)
1912	3,711	5,508	5,014	3,018

(1) Duties in Straits dollars.
(2) or 2,218.

Source: Compiled by author from Annual Reports. These figures are of doubtful accuracy; indeed, in different places in the same series of reports, different figures are given under the same heading. The increase in export duties was accounted for almost wholly by the rapid expansion of jelutong shipments.

16. The correspondence listed in the margin was: (a) Secretary of State, No. 23 of 1899 (ref. n.a.), (b) ditto, No. 12, of 1901 (CO 144/75 item 41469), (c) High Commissioners No. 14 of 1901 (FO 12/114 and CO 144/75 item 12266), (d) ditto, No. 31 (Confidential), of 1901 (FO 12/114, p. 98 and CO 144/75 item 24405), (e) ditto, No. 37 (ref. n.a.), (f) ditto, No. 39 (FO 12/115, p. 102ff. and CO 144/75: 33046), (g) ditto, No. 34 (CO 144/75: 33046), and (h) ditto, No. 49 (Confidential), of 1901 (CO 144/75: 33046).

17. In November 1901 the Tutong rebels agreed to pay a fine to the Sultan after the failure of their revolt. Most of the chiefs surrendered "not having arms or ammunition to continue the struggle," while others were moving into Limbang as they did not intend to pay the fine. Dato di Gadong and Dato Kalam, co-

201

leader of rebels, were excepted from this fine and were to be put to death if caught' in Brunei territory; as a result, they sought sanctuary from the Sarawak authorities in Limbang. This was granted; but a little later Dato di Gadong "stupidly returned to Tutong," where, in about July 1902, he was "murdered by order of the Sultan of Brunei" (Sarawak Gazette, 1 March 1902 and 1 October 1902; and A.B. Ward Rajah's Servant (Ithaca, NY: Cornell University Press, 1966), p. 79).

18.   Wat (Walter) Tyler (d. 1381), apparently a tiler of Dartford (Kent). Leader of the English "Peasants' Revolt" (1381). The immediate cause of the uprising was the imposition of poll-tax in order to raise revenue for the prosecution of the Hundred Years' War. Richard II, the boy King, met the advancing rebels at Mile End, conceding all their demands. The following day, after the peasants had dispersed, Wat Tyler was murdered by the Lord Mayor of London; thereafter, with their leader slain, the revolt was easily crushed.

Of the other Tutong "Wat Tylers" mentioned by McArthur, the most important was Dato Kalam, who fled to Sarawak, where he proved equally unmanageable to the authorities. In 1904 he was arrested for continual buffalo theft and for terrorizing part of Limbang district. He ended his "adventurous career" with three years' imprisonment in Kuching (Ward, Rajah's Servant, p. 79).

19.   (a) Pengiran Bendahara, chief minister, first-ranking of the four wazirs, from whose ranks was usually chosen the successor to the throne.

(b) Pengiran Pemancha: third-ranking wazir.

(c) tulin and kuripan: respectively private hereditary property (land and serfs) and property, likewise, belonging to successive holders of particular offices. (Further particulars may be found in McArthur's main Report.)

(d) Godfrey Hewett (1859-1932): British Consul to Brunei, 1900 to 1904. (BNBC officer, c. 1880-c. 1898: responsible for Kinabatangan massacre, 1890 (130 dead). 1900-

1914: British ^onsular Service. 1914:
retired. 1932: died).

20. Pengiran di Gadong, Muhammad Hassan, died in
January 1900 rather than in 1898, which would
be suggested by McArthur's "about six years
ago."
     The office of Pengiran di Gadong (not to
be confused with Dato di Gadong) was second in
rank of the four wazirs. His duties, Professor Brown states, "were variously stated, but
frequently contained three elements. He was
in charge of finance or the treasury. He was
in charge of the Sultan's household. He was
in charge of the Sultanate's dominions especially with regard to taxation. I believe the
latter should be interpreted to mean that he
was in charge of the Sultan's appanages. . . .
There is no sound evidence from the
nineteenth century that the Pengiran di Gadong
discharged such duties by virtue of the office
he held" (Brunei: The Structure and History
of a Bornean Malay Sultanate, Special Monograph of the Brunei Museum Journal, Vol. 2,
No. 2, 1970, p. 109).
     Pengiran Muhammad Hassan himself was a
nephew of Sultan Abdul Mumin (r. 1852-1885)
and a brother of Pengiran Bendahara, Pengiran
Anak Besar (c. 1829-1917; Bendahara 1883-
1917), with whom he quarrelled over the
division of the property inherited from their
uncle. Pengiran Muhammad opposed any extension of British influence in Brunei. In 1887
Sir Frederick Weld described him as "at once
the Sultan's second Minister and leader of the
opposition." In 1899 Consul Keyser reported
that the Pengiran was "a man of no intelligence and stone deaf" who took "no part in any
matter of State." Allowance must be made,
however, for the fact that at this time the
noble was close to death; and Keyser admitted
he had only once met the man (CO 144/73,
34409).
     The office of Pengiran di Gadong remained
vacant--principally for financial reasons
originally--from 1900 up to 1968.

21. On 15 July 1901 Consul Hewett reported that he
had received information that Pengiran
Tajudin, leader of the sultan's forces, with
about 350 followers had attacked and killed

four people in Birau (a tributary of Tutong) "probably because they had refused to fight the rebels, who were of their own blood." The Birau people (100 families) were robbed of everything and then fled, destitute, into Limbang (FO 12/115, p. 102ff. Hewett to Lansdowne, No. 8 (Confidential), 15 July 1901; also in CO 144/75: 33046).

22. Pengiran Tajudin: McArthur did not see in him the monster described by Hewett. During the smallpox epidemic in 1904 the noble vaccinated a large number of Tutong people, leading McArthur to comment that "if the previous account of Pengiran Tajudin's misdoings . . . are true, he is evidently now appearing in a new role there" (CO 144/78: 39970, McArthur to Sir John Anderson, No. 51, 8 October 1904, paragraph 3).

PART THREE

1. For BNBC's finances, see below, p. 250 (note 117).

2. Labuan Coalfields, Ltd., founded 1902, con- tinued coal-mining until 1911, and went into liquidation five years later. This company was actually a restructured version of the Central Borneo Company (1887-98), retitled Labuan and Borneo Company (1898-1902), which had acquired exclusive coal rights in Labuan for the ninety-nine years following 1889.

3. The United Kingdom continued paying the Resident's salary until the end of 1927, when it was abolished "in view of improved finances of Brunei and pressing need for economy in imperial expenditure" (CO 717/58, file 29220, item 1: CO to High Commissioner, telegram, 17 October 1927). The Resident declared that the withdrawal of the subsidy (L600 annually) came "as a distinct blow to this struggling State, where every cent is doubly precious" (CO 717/59, file 52345, memorandum by E.E.F. Pretty, 4 January 1928).

4. Sir Charles Prestwood Lucas (1853-1931) K.C.B. 1912, K.C.M.G. 1907. Assistant Under-Secre- tary of State, Colonial Office, 1897-1907.

Educated at Winchester and Balliol (Oxford).
1877: first in the Civil Service List. 1907:
first head of the Dominions Dept. Author of a
number of works about the British
Commonwealth.

5. Rt. Hon. Alfred Lyttelton, PC, MA (1857-
1913). British sportsman and Conservative
politician, Secretary of State for the
Colonies, 1903-05. Educated Eton and Trinity
College, Cambridge. 1880-4: International
cricketer (4 Test Matches vs. Australia).
1882-6: Private Secretary to the Attorney-
General, Sir H. James. 1895: MP for
Leamington, 1900-1: Chairman, Transvaal
concessions commission.

6. CO 144/79 (1795) Swettenham to Lucas, 17
January 1905.

7. In 1903 the consul was paid, according to one
source, L400 annually, plus an office allowance of L200 (CO 144/77, item 7692, minute by
R.E. Stubbs, 26 February 1903. By 1905,
however, the post had been reduced in status
to that of a vice-consul, and the salary cut
"from L450 to L350-L450" (FO 12/128, p.
408ff.: memorandum by F.H. Villiers, 3 June
1905).

8. The consul's duties, principally, were to
relay to the sultan British decisions on
Brunei's foreign policy and to protect the
interests of British subjects in the sultanate. The consul had no right to intervene in
Brunei's internal administration (except in
certain specific cases). See below, p. 253
(note 128).

9. FO 12/128, p. 424, Villiers to CO, 10 June
1905. Concurred in the course of action
proposed by the Colonial Office (also in CO
144/79, item 20058).

PART FOUR

1. A number of points arise out of this opening
paragraph. Sarawak annexed Limbang in 1890
and has retained the district ever since. The
Brunei Government has never recognized this

usurpation, and has made several unsuccessful diplomatic attempts to recover the lost province, the latest being a claim published in 1970, which was rejected by Malaysia. Although some doubt remains about the real intentions of the Limbang people in 1890, they have since revealed little or no inclination to be handed back to Brunei. This is inconvenient for the sultanate, whose territory is split into two detached wings by the Limbang.

The actual area of modern Brunei--Belait, Tutong, Brunei-Muara and Temburong (including "Laboh," sic Labu)--is only 2,226 square miles; its population at the time of the first Census (1911) was 21,718; and its correct geographical limits are $4^O2'$ - $5^O3'$ N and $114^O4'$ - $115^O22'$ East.

The lack of a proper map of Brunei mentioned by McArthur had a significant impact on the history of the sultanate. The acquisition of Trusan by the Brooke State (1884-5), for example, was approved in Whitehall in the belief that it would result only in the advance of the Sarawak frontier from Baram towards Brunei Town. Had it been known that, in fact, Sarawak rule was being established on the far side of Brunei, the cession of the district would not have been countenanced. For further details, and other instances, see D.E. Brown, "Maps and the History of Brunei" in Brunei Museum Journal, 1973, pp. 88-90. I understand that it was not until 1914 that a map of the State, principally based on the survey work of H.M.S. Merlin, was compiled for the first time (CO 824/1 Brunei Annual Report, p. 6). The result showed "that the sketch maps forming part of those of British North Borneo or Sarawak were very incorrect. The Temburong Valley proves to be larger than was imagined, while those of Limbang and Trusan are much smaller" (ibid.).

2. McArthur appears to be mistaken here. Whatever may have been the case in the 1880s, by 1904--and certainly by 1906--the BNBC had lost all interest in acquiring further portions of Brunei's territory. In CO 144/81 (item 3460), for example, there is a letter from Mr. Cowie, Managing-Director of the BNBC, to Sir Charles Brooke (dated 6 January 1906) it which he says: "Personally I think it is to be

regretted that His Majesty's Government did not agree to let you take in hand the civilization of that so long mis-governed territory" (Brunei). In CO 144/81 (item 27543) there is another letter from Sir Charles Jessel to the Foreign Office in which he writes: "I am sure it would save time, trouble and probably bloodshed to the Foreign Office to simply hand over Brunei to Sarawak. Speaking for my company (Sir Charles was Chairman of the BNBC), we would welcome such a policy as tending to relieve us from any anxiety" (my emphasis added). Furthermore, Governor E.W. Birch of North Borneo (1901-3) was one of the most persistent advocates of a British Residency in Brunei; and this idea had also been suggested by Governor W.H. Treacher during his term (1881-7), when he also acted for a time as Consul for Brunei (1884-5).

3.   The background to the Trusan cession was as follows: in 1884 twenty-one Sarawak subjects had been murdered in the district and their property stolen. F.R.O. Maxwell (1849-1897), Resident of the Sarawak First Division, went to Brunei demanding compensation of $1,000 for each of those killed, plus $2,000 for the property lost. Pengiran Temenggong Hashim, acting--though not yet installed--as Regent, found it impossible to pay; so Sarawak demanded the cession of Trusan instead. Later the Pengiran claimed that he had had no desire to lease the river, but had had no alternative.
     At this time there was a power struggle in progress in Brunei for the succession to Sultan Abdul Mumin (r. 1852-1885), who was non compos mentis in 1884-5. One party was led by Pengiran di Gadong Muhammad Hassan (d. 1900) who, along with his brother, the Pengiran Bendahara (c. 1829-1917), was due to inherit Sultan Abdul Mumin's private wealth; and another led by Temenggong Hashim, son of the previous Sultan, Omar Ali Saifuddin II (r. c. 1824-1852). In order to support his claim to the throne, Pengiran Hashim sought the support of Sir Charles Brooke. In December 1884 they signed an agreement whereby the Temenggong agreed to transfer Trusan to Sarawak in return for the Rajah's help should he be threatened with internal revolt in Brunei.

207

The Pengiran di Gadong, acting in the name of his uncle, Sultan Abdul Mumin, protested to Acting Consul Treacher that the transfer of Trusan had been made without his knowledge or consent. On May 6 or 7 1885, the Rajah unilaterally raised the Sarawak flag in Trusan; and it was not until 15 July 1885, by which time Pengiran Hashim had succeeded to the throne, that the sovereign rights over Trusan, were formally transferred to the Brooke State. For many years thereafter the Muruts of the district gave considerable trouble to the Sarawak authorities, culminating in the great expedition of 1900, one of the largest even mounted by the Rajah Brooke.

4. This is an important point because the alleged unhealthiness of Brunei for Europeans was one of the factors which had made the British Government reluctant to appoint a Resident (eg. CO 144/74, item 9036, minute by T.C. McNaghten, 4 April 1900).

Opinions on the subject differed. On the one hand, Messrs. Keyser (CO 144/73, item 5120), McClelland (CO 273/331, item 33045), Douglas (CO 531/8, item 19347) and Dickson (CO 717/20, item 19334) complained about the unhealthiness of the place; whereas Consul-General Sir Spenser St. John was said to have lived in Brunei without any difficulty, and Treacher recalled in 1903: "I have resided for considerable periods of time in Brunei and found it a perfectly healthy place. My recollection is that when Sir Henry Bulwer (1836-1914) was Governor of Labuan (1871-5) he used to go over to Brunei for the benefit of his health." (FO 12/122, p. 56ff, Treacher to Sir F. Swettenham, 6 July 1903).

McArthur himself was continually ill during his service in Brunei (1904-8) and, on one occasion, was recalled to Singapore for several days in order to recuperate (CO 144/80, item 35280).

5. McArthur was being somewhat over-optimistic here, perhaps. Very little of Brunei's soil is suitable for agriculture because of the intense leaching of nutrients caused by heavy tropical rainfall. Dr. G.E. Wilford described Brunei's soils as "mostly thin and poor in assimilable bases and many are highly acid"

(G.E. Wilford, The Geology and Mineral Resources of Brunei and Adjacent parts of Sarawak (Brunei 1961, p. 261). Similarly see Borneo Bulletin, 4 October 1958; Brunei Annual Report 1970 pp. 73-6; and D.E. Brown, Brunei: Structure and History, p. 2. As late as the 1930s, scarcely 30,000 acres in Brunei were under cultivation.

6.   The pre-Islamic Brunei Empires--Srivijaya (c. seventh to ninth centuries) and P'o-ni (tenth to fifteenth centuries)--depended for their prosperity on gold and camphor derived from the west coast of Sabah and the Philippines.
     In the twentieth century the only minerals to have figured in Brunei's export lists are (a) coal--from the Rajah of Sarawak's mines at Brooketon (1888-1924 worked before 1888, periodically, by other companies) and Buang Tawar (1900/1--1917); (b) petroleum (exported since 1932); and (c) natural gas, (exported since the 1930s and since 1972 in liquified form). Reports of antimony, gold and diamonds occurring in the area "have yet to be substantiated" (Wilford). Iron minerals are common, but not in commercial quantities. In the 1950s, however, production of construction materials--gravel, clay, sand--increased rapidly. Wilford advised that there was scope for cement and glass-making industries.

7.   Sir Charles Brooke held a concession to mine coal throughout Brunei east of the River Tutong until 1962 (cf. note 107, below); and another for mineral oil, obtained from a spring issuing gently into his coal mine at Buang Tawar on Berembang Island.
     In December 1904 the Rajah, in the name of his youngest son, H.K. Brooke (1879-1926), bought from W.C. Cowie (see note 24 below for a biography of W.C. Cowie) concessions to all minerals in Brunei (or, so he thought).
     The first concession, originally granted to A.H. Everett (see below, note 97) in 1883, had been transferred to the Central Borneo Company (CBC) in 1887. Three years later the CBC acquired a further concession. The rights lapsed in 1895 and were finally cancelled in 1897, the delay being caused by representations from the British Government. After the cancellation, the defunct leases changed hands

several times, finally being bought by the Rajah. In 1914 Sir Charles advanced a claim, based on these lapsed concessions, to all minerals in Brunei. The Colonial Office had some difficulty in convincing Sir Charles of his mistake. (In 1890 the Rajah himself, in a letter to the Foreign Office, had declared that he could prove that the CBC's new lease was illegal according to the law of Brunei.)

8. This remained the situation for much of the Residential Era (1906-59). A road to Tutong was eventually completed in 1927, after several false starts, but a section of beach had to be used between Tutong and Seria until as late as 1958, when a proper highway was finally opened. In the 1930s the capital was linked by road with Bangar (via Limbang and Pandaruan), Kuala Abang and the coast to the due north of the capital. But, as McArthur pointed out (Report 137), in wet weather the swamps were almost impassable and rendered very difficult the construction of roads.

9. See also P. Leys, "Observations on the Brunei Political System 1883-5" in JMBRAS, Vol, 41, Part 2 (1968), pp. 117-30; for a modern analysis, see D.E. Brown, Structure and History, pp. 86-118.

10. The office of Pengiran Temenggong remained vacant until 1967, that of Pengiran di Gadong until 1968 (D.E. Brown, Structure, p. 109). For most of the Residential Era, Brunei was too poor to finance such office-holders.

11. D.E. Brown (Structure, p. 109) comments as follows: "The Pengiran Pemancha has nearly always been described as the mediator of the State Council. There is (however) little if any nineteenth or twentieth century evidence of his performance of that role."

12. This is quite erroneous. The office of Pengiran Shahbandar is mentioned in sixteenth century Iberian accounts of Brunei (D.E. Brown, Structure, p. 86; and J.S. Carroll, "Berunai in the Boxer Codex" in JMBRAS 1982, Part II, p. 6. Although strictly only a cheteria (order of noble officials ranking below the wazirs), the Pengiran Shahbandar in

210

practice was subordinate only to the Sultan;
hence, he enjoyed the same status de facto as
one of the wazirs. For the functions of his
office, see D.E. Brown, Structure, p. 111-2.

13. (a) Pengiran Bendahara, Pengiran Anak Besar:
born c. 1829 (?); died 3 July 1917 "said to be
88." Nephew and adopted son of Sultan Abdul
Mumin (r. 1852-1885). Installed as Pengiran
Bendahara in 1883. Illiterate. (See also,
below, note 88; and Report paragraphs 68-9).
   (b) Pengiran Pemancha, Pengiran Muhammad
Salleh (died 2 December 1912). Installed
?1898. Likewise illiterate. (See also,
below, note 87; and Report, paragraph 67).

14. Pengiran Shahbandar, Pengiran Sahibul bin
Ismail (d. 1912). Tulin-owner of Padas Damit
River. Famous for his role in the "Shahbandar
War" (1888-1890) against the Chartered Company
(see I.D. Black, A Gambling Style of Government: The Establishment of Chartered Company
Rule in Sabah 1878-1915 (Kuala Lumpur: O.U.P.,
1983, pp. 84-89). 1889: sought refuge in
Labuan. Later Rajah Brooke's magistrate in
Brooketon (Muara)?. 1906-1912: Brunei State
councillor. 1912: died of cholera in Mecca.
   Consul Keyser's comment that this Pengiran
was "intelligent and of better manners and
education than any Malay I have yet seen in
this country" (CO 144/73: 5120: paragraph 32)
is fairly typical (see also CO 144/67: 18177;
and Black, op. cit., p. 85).
   The Pengiran's son, Pengiran Anak Hashim
(b. ?1864; d. 1949) had a distinguished career
as a Brunei district officer (1907-1932) and
was also Pengiran Shahbandar, 1918-1949, with
a seat on the State Council.

15. Since the 1840s at least the Brunei Royal
Family was divided into two factions. In 1845
members of the pro-British, pro-Sarawak faction led by Pengiran Bendahara Muda Hassim and
Pengiran Budrudin were murdered (or committed
suicide before they could be murdered) by a
rival faction led by Pengiran Yusof.
   These divisions persisted during the reign
of Sultan Hashim. For, among the murdered
brothers, was Pengiran Tajudin, father of the
Pengiran Bendahara, Pengiran Anak Besar (1829-
1917) (mentioned above, note 13) and the

Pengiran Di Gadong, Muhammad Hassan (d. 1900).
Sultan Hashim, a young man in the 1840s, was the son-in-law of Pengiran Yusof and had participated in the massacre. He found, therefore, that the leading ministers would not participate in his State Council. Hence he turned for advice to two non-nobles, Inche Buyong and Inche Mohsin, which exasperated the wazirs still further. By 1905, when Inche Buyong and Inche Mohsin had passed from the scene, Sultan Hashim relied for advice almost exclusively on Edmund Roberts (see below, note 53), manager of the cutch factory. Indeed, there is a curious clause in the Island Trading Syndicate's (cutch lease, which runs as follows:

> 13. In consideration of the privilege for carrying on the above said work, the said Island Trading Syndicate professes good friendship to the said Sultan of Brunei . . . and also the said Syndicate shall render the said Sultan . . . all lawful assistance when required" (emphasis added). (Source: FO 12/116, p. 150ff.

This appears to suggest that Sultan Hashim looked to the ITS to bolster his position. F.N. Butterworth, who succeeded Roberts as the manager of the cutch factory, also acted as an adviser to Sultan Hashim.

16. See note 15 (above).

17. Temburong district was kerajaan (apart from Labu) and so was the most easily developed during the first years of the British Residency. It was here that most of the European rubber estates were established after tulin claims had been settled (1906-11).
The district contains three main rivers: Temburong itself, the Labu, and the Batu Apoi. In 1907 Temburong was reported to be a district "rich in timber and jungle produce," but undeveloped. Labu was tulin, leased to E.E. Abrahamson (see note 19 below), who had formed a company for planting rubber on an area originally destined for tobacco. His

212

company also worked jelutong, "but the methods of tapping were so bad that many of the trees . . . have died." The lower reaches of the Batu Apoi (south of the Labu) comprised "the major portion of the sago plantations in Brunei territory." (For further details: see note 67.)

18. Pengiran Muda Binjai Muhammad Tajudin (d. 1916), son of Pengiran Muda Hassim (see above, note 15). Cousin therefore of Pengiran (Bendahara) Anak Besar (note 13 above) and Pengiran Di Gadong Muhammad Hassan (d. 1900). Butterworth (1875-1952) remembered that many considered him to be the rightful heir to the throne (on Sultan Hashim's death in 1906) but described him as an "elderly, dull-witted man who lived in a state of great poverty in a small hut on the outskirts of the town" (Blundell, The City of Many Waters (London: Arrowsmith, 1923, p. 84). Died mid 1916 (Sarawak Gazette, 2 October 1916, p. 217).

19. E.E. Abrahamson. Secretary of the Island Trading Syndicate (Island Trading Company from 1914). Formerly, during W.H. Treacher's term as Governor, he had been a magistrate (J.P.) in South Sandakan (Sabah). Died during the First World War, probably in 1915.

20. Pengkalan Tarap, that is, Limbang Village. After the annexation of the district in 1890, the Sarawak Government station was established about fifteen miles from the river's mouth; and in 1909 it was described by Bampfylde as "a flourishing little place . . . the prettiest outstation in Sarawak" (Baring-Gould, and Bampfylde, A History of Sarawak, pp. 355-6). McArthur, in 1904, was also favourably impressed by Pengkalan Tarap, in particular its neatness, cleanliness and prosperity which formed a sharp contrast with the squalor and filth of the town of Brunei (FO 12/126, p. 78ff. M.S.H. McArthur to Sir John Anderson, No. 15, 2 June 1904).

21. This is very true. Consul Trevenen, in 1891, (when he had been asked to report on the Limbang annexation, which had not yet been approved by the British Government), had given no indication of the true importance of

Limbang to Brunei.

But, in 1887, Sir Frederick Weld (1923-91, Governor of the Straits Settlements (1881-7), had spelled out clearly the Limbang's crucial significance to the sultanate:

> The true Brunei River is the Limbang. The arm of the sea called the Brunei River is a mere nothing in itself, but is part of the Limbang estuary, and to convey a real idea of the politico-geographical position . . . it would be as correct as say that Brunei is on the Limbang as to say that Alexandria is on the Nile . . . The valley of the Limbang is about as essential to the life of Brunei as the valley of the Nile is to that of Alexandria (CO 144/64, item 16254).

22. According to H.R. Hughes-Hallett, "A Sketch of the History of Brunei" in JMBRAS, Vol. XVIII, Part 2 (1940) (p. 27) Sultan Berkat, the third Muslim Ruler of Brunei (?1520s) caused forty junks to be sunk at the mouth of the Brunei River. This strategy, however, "is also attributed to a later Sultan."

R. Nicholl of the Brunei Museum comments:

> I think (the artificial barrier) was most probably made by Sultan Berkat when he assumed power shortly after Pigafetta's departure. It may have been one of the elements which enabled him to quell the rebellion of "the pagan city" across the bay, Kuala Lawas, the old capital. . . . The object was to compel vessels to hug the true left bank and so expose them to artillery . . ." (letter to author, 25 January 1984).

With regard to the British warships mentioned by McArthur later in this paragraph of his Report:

(a) H.M.S. Rosario visited Brunei in late May 1901 and achieved the settlement of certain debts owing to certain Chinese British subjects and various other matters. "No undue pressure was put on the Sultan beyond the mere presence of H.M.S. Rosario" (CO 144/75, item 26341, G. Hewett to Sir Frank Swettenham, No. 37?, 1 June 1901).

(b) H.M.S. Phoenix visited Brunei Town on 1 June 1903 with instructions "to obtain proper settlement of any claims or grievances of British subjects, and to prevent the improper [sic] granting of oil concessions" (CO 144/77, items 27621, 20180, and 24152).

Earlier, in October 1900, H.M.S. Bramble had also gone up to the Brunei capital. On this occasion the "unsettled claims" of British subjects were brought up and the Kuala Lama issue settled. The Consul commented: "I have no doubt . . . that the presence of H.M.S. Bramble contributed largely to this satisfactory settlement as without her the Pengirans would undoubtedly have interposed the given trouble, as they were all present at the interview" [between the consul and the Sultan, presumably] (CO 144/74, 914/01; and CO 144/75: 1227). Hewett urged that every gunboat that called at Labuan should also visit Brunei as part of the general routine of the cruise, the mere presence of a gunboat in Brunei being always attended by a beneficial result (CO 144/74: 41242: FO to CO, 17 December 1900). The Admiralty, however, ruled this out because difficulties of navigation made it impossible (CO 144/75, 16881).

23. McArthur states here that Brooketon was the only mine in Brunei. In fact, there was another at Buang Tawar on Berembang Island, also owned by the Rajah, where coal production continued from about 1900 until 1917. Approximately 1000 to 1500 tons were turned out annually.

Coal at Muara (Brooketon) was worked by four different companies between 1848 and 1880 (G. Irwin, Nineteenth Century Borneo: A Study in Diplomatic Rivalry (Singapore: Moore, 1965, p. 177). In March 1882 W.C. Cowie (see note 24 below) obtained a concession to work coal in Muara Damit. Modifications were made to his lease in 1884 and 1887 by which he obtained the monopoly of coal working through-out Brunei east of the River Tutong. On 6 September 1888 these rights were purchased by Sir Charles Brooke for L25,000, the colliery site having been renamed "Brooketon" in honour of the Rajah by Cowie. The Sarawak Government kept this colliery open until 1924, seven years after the death of Sir Charles.

G.E. Wilford records that during the years 1891 to 1924 650,000 tons of coal were turned out, exports after 1906 totalling 315,396 tons valued at $2,688,400. All the coal, Wilford adds, was mined by opencast methods until the removal of overburden became prohibitively expensive. After 1909 only about ten percent of the coal in the seams could be extracted because large coal barriers had to be left to prevent the spread of fires (Wilford, op. cit., pp. 160 and 164).

24. William Clarke Cowie (b. ?1847; d. 1910). 1870s: petty trader operating out of Labuan. 1882-88: coal-mining at Muara. 1888: sold his rights to Sir Charles Brooke for L25,000, investing L3,000 in the British North Borneo Company. Director (1894-), Managing Director (1897-1910) and Chairman (1909-10) of the BNBC. 1910: died "aged about 63" at Bad Nauheim, 14 September. Left estate L53,759 (gross), L53,270 (net). Sources: The Times 19.9.1910, p. 11; 21.9.1910, p. 11; 24.9.1910, p. 11; 27.9.1910; and 5.12.1910, p. 15. See also: I.D. Black, A Gambling Style of Government: The Establishment of Chartered Company Rule in Sabah, 1878-1915 (Kuala Lumpur: Oxford University Press, 1983). O. Rutter, British North Borneo: An Account of its History, Resources and Native Tribes (London: Constable, 1922).

25. Certain excise rights were held by lease separate from the coal mining leases. Under the terms of a lease dated 12 January 1887 granted by Sultan Hashim to Cowie and later transferred to the Rajah, Sir Charles was entitled, for so long as he should continue to pay the Sultan $500 annually, to collect land rents in Muara Damit and the revenue from excise farms there. He was specifically excluded from exercising judicial powers, but he had a right to one half of fines imposed on those convicted of infringing his revenue farms.

Sir Charles Brooke, however, on his own authority, appointed and paid the salary of a

Malay Magistrate (?the <u>Pengiran Shahbandar</u>), introduced Sarawak police, opened a post office, and permitted the Resident of Limbang to style himself "Civil Administrator of Brooketon." One British official suggested that one of the first tasks of the proposed British Resident in Brunei would be "to harry Rajah Brooke out of the position he has usurped at Brooketon." The rights were recovered, piecemeal, between 1906 and 1932.

Sultan Hashim's attitude is summed up by this extract from a letter written by Consul Keyser:

> The Sultan of Brunei has frequently asked if I go to Brooketon, and when I reply, "yes," he asked to be informed where I live when there. On my stating that I rent a Malay house and do not occupy that of the Rajah <u>he expresses content</u>, though asking why I go to Brooketon at all" (FO 12/111, p. 212ff. Keyser to Secretary of State, No. 16, 28 February 1900, paragraph 26).

26. The Brooketon colliery incurred heavy losses from the outset and it was not until 1917 that even a miniscule surplus ($1,527) was shown on a year's trading. In the interim the deficit (including purchase price) amounted to approximately $1,500,000. Good profits were made in the years 1918-1920, but the colliery lapsed into the red in 1922, and, despite small surpluses in 1923 and 1924, Rajah Vyner closed the mine in November of the latter year.

Sir Charles Brooke's mine at Buang Tawar also ran consistently at a loss.

These losses were borne by the Sarawak Treasury, not by Sir Charles Brooke personally.

27. Correspondence relating to the Crane incident includes the following:

   (a) FO 12/102, pp. 60ff and 127ff.
   (b) FO 12/108, p. 31
   (c) FO 12/111, p. 58ff.
   (d) CO 144/73, items 31524 and 34409
   (e) CO 144/74, items 17691, 12756 and 15399

To give a brief summary, in November 1898 H.A. Crane, a merchant of Singapore, reported that he had acquired from Pengiran Jeludin (Sultan Hashim's son-in-law) a concession to mine for coal on Berembang Island. On 26 September 1899 Sir Charles Brooke, who pointed out that this island fell within the area covered by his own existing lease, informed Consul Keyser that he was determined to defend his rights and "failing to do so by fair means, I shall be obliged to resort to force of arms, and bloodshed, it is to be feared, will be the consequence." The act of repudiation, he added, showed that "all honour, reliance, truth and everything else is entirely gone from those who rule Brunei." A British gunboat was despatched to the Sultanate to preserve the peace between Sarawak and Brunei; but Sultan Hashim was obliged to cancel the concession granted by Pengiran Jeludin to Crane.

Sir Charles Brooke began mining on Berembang Island not later than 1901 (until 1917). He intended to make Buang Tawar his administrative capital when, as he expected, Brunei was incorporated within Sarawak.

It is noteworthy, also, that a petition dated 11 May 1906 requesting the removal of the British Resident from Brunei was signed by a Pengiran Jeludin.

28. The Zahora (1894-1927), Sir Charles Brooke's armed yacht, mean speed 15.255 knots. 1894: built by Lobnitz and Company of Renfrew. 1896: Purchased by the Rajah. 1917: lent to His Majesty's Government "for the duration." 1925: last voyage. 1927: scuttled (CO 604/13 Sarawak Gazette, 3 January 1928, p. 4).

"Perhaps it is not generally known," McArthur commented in 1906, "that the Zahora is armed, carrying a quick-firing gun prominently-mounted in her bow, that she carries a force of uniformed and armed Sarawak Rangers . . . and that she is run on regular man-of-war lines when his Highness (the Rajah) is on board her, with armed sentries at the gangway etc . . . Consequently she is looked upon as a man-of-war by the (people) of Brunei . . ." (CO 144/80: 40678, M.H.S. McArthur to Sir John Anderson, No. 228, 24 September 1906, paragraph v). See also, A.B. Ward, Rajah's

Servant, p. 13.

29.	In the letter under reference, McArthur pointed out that, under the supervision of Sarawak officials, a road was being laid out, jungle was being cleared, and a substantial blockhouse and a wharf were being built on Berembang. The place, indeed, promised to be "as neat and pleasant as Pengkalan Tarap" (see above, note 20). Yet McArthur was curious that Sir Charles should have cared to spend so much money on the island, since the sovereign rights were not held by Sarawak. The Acting Consul feared that "with their usual supineness" the Brunei Government would allow Sir Charles "to establish a station there and eventually exercise jurisdiction as if it were a part of Sarawak territory." Although the Rajah had promised that his coal and oil works should be carried on purely as a private business, McArthur noted that "the (Sarawak) Resident of Limbang visits the place (Berembang) periodically, the place is being opened up under his instructions, the buildings are under his charge" and that the public works under construction were not required for the coal mine, from which they were a long way off (FO 12/126, p. 78, Sir J. Anderson to Marquess of Lansdowne, 17 June 1904, enclosing McArthur to Anderson, No. 15, 2 June 1904, paragraph 12).

	In fact, the Rajah, who assumed that Brunei would fall to Sarawak, was intending to make Buang Tawar his administrative and commercial centre, leaving Brunei Town to those who wished to remain there (see Sarawak Gazette, October 1983, p. 29).

30.	The suspension of coal-mining can have been only temporary, since operations continued until 1917. Production averaged about 1,000 to 1,500 tons annually (see above, note 23).

31.	Kota Batu (Stone Fort), situated about one mile downstream from Bandar Seri Begawan (Brunei Town), is the only substantial archaeological site in Brunei (apart, perhaps, from Kupang). The settlement was in occupation for a millennium from the seventh century and again in more recent times. An enormous amount of Chinese and indigenous pottery has been unearthed, along with a number of coins. Kota Batu also contains the tombs of several former Sultans of Brunei; and, nowadays is the home of the Brunei Museum.

32. The Inche Muhammad Estate. For further details see A.V.M. Horton, "Brunei, Sarawak and the Kota Batu Lands 1903-17" in Brunei Museum Journal 1985, pp. 62-74.

33. See D.E. Brown, Structure, Chapter Five; and Abdul Latif bin Haji Ibrahim, "Variations and Changes in the Names and Locations of the Wards of Brunei's Kampung Ayer Over the Last Century" in Brunei Museum Journal (1971, p. 56-73.

34. In 1909 Bampfylde quoted one Italian, Beccari, who took exception to this comparison: "I admit that Brunei has its points, but what irony to compare for a moment the city of marble palaces (Venice) with the mass of miserable huts, which a single match could easily reduce to ashes." Nowadays, Brunei has marble palaces of its own, so this comparison may no longer be so fanciful.
    Butterworth, writing in 1923 using the pen-name of Blundell, considered that Vienna would have provided a better comparison, i.e. a capital of a monarchy having only a little bit of country left on which to support its dignity (The City of Many Waters, p. 68).
    Brunei Malays, of course, declare that Venice is the "Brunei of Europe."

35. The cholera epidemic of 1902, according to one eye witness, left few huts without one or two dead, whereas the smallpox epidemic, two years later, resulted in the deaths of perhaps one-tenth of the people of Brunei Town, and spread, also, to the outer districts (For further details, see A.V.M. Horton, "The Brunei Smallpox Epidemic of 1904" in Sarawak Museum Journal (1984, pp. 89-99).
    With regard to the alleged "unhealthiness" of Brunei Town River Village, opinion remained divided. One school, represented by Messrs. McArthur, Lee-Warner and Butterworth, favoured the construction of a "clean, dry village with suburbs of kampung houses" on neighbouring dry land along with the discouragement of further

building in Kampung Ayer. Another opinion,
supported by Dr. Hoops (Principal Medical
Officer, Straits Settlements, who visited the
Sultanate in 1921), argued that there was "no
justification" for removing people from the
River Village on health grounds. "The
question of scavenging is inexpensively and
suitably solved. The river is tidal and
dejecta are speedily washed away."
Meanwhile, life in Kampung Ayer continues
much as it has done for centuries. Fortunately, there has been no repetition of the
disasters of 1902 and 1904.

36. See also McArthur, Report, paragraph 634.
Sultan Muhammad Jemalul Alam and his household
removed to dry land in 1922 (CO 824/1, Brunei
Annual Report 1922, p. ?15). Sultan Hashim's
great-grandson, for his part, has just moved
into a palace, complete with escape tunnels,
costing perhaps $350,000,000 (Asia Week, 6
January 1984, p. 33).

37. In 1909, when Dato W.H. Doughty (1886-1971)
first arrived in Brunei, he saw only five
buildings on dry land: the Residency, the
cutch factory and three bungalows (Borneo
Bulletin, 23 May 1959). In the Brunei Annual
Report 1910 it is recorded that during that
year a number of Chinese established their
shops on the mainland. The following year,
1911, "four fine shophouses with stone walls
were added to the (land) town." In all there
were 26 shop houses on land. A number of
street lamps were added and the filling and
levelling out of the swampy land in the town
was continued. Much had still to be done to
make the place clean and healthy and the want
of money was sorely felt in this direction. A
short road was made from the shops past the
mosque to a point on dry land opposite the
Sultan's palace over the water. A small atap
market was built, but it was discovered not to
be large enough even for existing needs.
The population of the land town reached
10,619 by 1947, but at the time of the 1960
census had fallen back to 9,702 (D.E. Brown,
Structure, p. 41).

38. ITS cutch factory (1900/1-1952). Destroyed by
Allied bombing in 1945. Rebuilt by 1949.

Dismantled in 1952, when the company transferred its operation to New Guinea.
Island Trading Syndicate: founded 1900.
Reformed as Island Trading Company, 31 October
1911. Went into voluntary liquidation in 1957
(The Stock Exchange Official Year-Book 1957,
pp. 1432-3). (See below, note 48, p. 224).

39. Sir Spenser St. John (1825-1910), GCMG 1894.
1848: Private Secretary (later biographer) of
Rajah Sir James Brooke, KCB DCL. 1855-61:
Consul-General to Brunei. 1861-96: further
appointments in British diplomatic service,
including envoy to Mexico (1884-93) and
Stockholm (1893-6).

40. Charles Lee Moses (d. 1867). Discarded member
of the U.S. Navy, an adventurer of dubious
character. American consul to Brunei 1865-7.
The "American consulate" was an atap hut which
the penniless Moses himself fired in the hope
of obtaining "compensation" from the Sultan.
The latter refused to pay a penny. An
American gunboat was despatched to the scene;
but, after investigation, its captain upheld
the Sultan. Moses drowned in 1867 while on
his way back to the United States. During his
tenure of office, he obtained the cession of
North Borneo, which he resold to Messrs.
Torrey and Harris. No American consul was
appointed after 1868 (K.G. Treggoning, History
of Modern Sabah (Singapore: University of
Malaya Press, 1965, pp. 5-8; and Tarling,
Britain, the Brookes, and Brunei, pp. 169-71).

41. In the early days of the British Residency, a
customs official was stationed at Limau Manis.
In 1907, however, this clerk was dismissed
because of "extortion and criminal misappro-
priation" and, by 1908, Limau Manis had been
incorporated with Brunei district. The former
tulin owners, presumably, had been bought out
by the Government.

42. Other taxes included chukei bongkar-sauh,
levied when the owner took his departure; and
chop bibas, a permission granted by a sultan
to a needy favourite to levy a contribution
for his own use anywhere he thought he could
most easily enforce it (W.H. Treacher, British
Borneo" in JSBRAS ?1890, pp. 33-4).

43. For further information see P.M. Shariffudin, "The Kedayans" in Brunei Museum Journal 1969 pp. 15-23, which contains a bibliography. (See also, above, pp. 59-60).

44. One gantang is equivalent to about 8 lbs.

45. Doctors sent to Brunei in August 1904, at the time of the smallpox epidemic, estimated that there were 900 houses in the River Village, with an average of fourteen occupants per house. This would indicate a population of 12,600. Only 9,767 people were enumerated in the 1911 Census, however; and, although people had begun to settle on dry land after the establishment of the British Residency, I am inclined to believe that the figure of 12,600 for 1904 is an exaggeration. D.E. Brown, on the other hand, considers it to be "trust-worthy" (Structure, p. 41); and he points out that the trend of population was downwards, for in 1921 only 7,623 people lived in Kampung Ayer.

46. Cf. Report, paragraph 23 (above, p. 108) and note 35 (p. 218). In 1899 Keyser reported that Brunei Town consisted of "rows of miserable hovels surrounded by accumulations of floating filth and rubbish. The streets are approached by broken ladders and the flooring or footway consists of a single plank on rotten poles. There is no attempt to improve, clean or repair." (CO 144/73: 5120). One year later the situation was even worse. Through "natural decay consequent on bankruptcy and misrule, this town of Brunei has dwindled and is perceptibly disappearing." During the year 1899-1900 "some hundreds of houses [had] gone" and "hundreds more are in ruins or empty." The town appeared to be populated disproportionately by women and children, the men being absent for long periods in search of work and food (CO 144/74: 17694. See also The Times 23 December 1905, letter to the editor from--?the Rajah of-- 'Sarawak').
    In the 1950s E.R. Bevington, like McArthur, argued that appearances were decep-tive. The houses over the water were "cool-- the wind blows all round, all over and under- neath"; and, although to European eyes an

223

unpainted house looked shabby, "to Malay eyes it does not" (E.R. Bevington, The Economic and Development of the State of Brunei, June 1956, pp. 46-7). [Unpublished manuscript, copy courtesy of E.R. Bevington, CMG, chartered engineer.]

47. Slavery. British policy at the outset of the Residential Era was to let slavery die a natural death, rather than to attempt prohibition at a stroke (CO 144/80, 36822: McArthur to Anderson, 10 August 1906). In 1932 a Mui Tsai Enactment was passed in order to prevent the treatment of Chinese women as chattels. In fact, however, there was only one such slave in Brunei, who ended up in a Singapore lunatic asylum (CO 273/598, file 33069/34, item 16, Caldecott to Cunliffe-Lister, No. 503, 30 August 1934).

48. See above, note 46, and below, p. 233 (note 64). The cutch factory remained an important employer. Wages amounted to $102,000 in 1915, $28,000 in 1916, and $50,000 in 1921. See Blundell, The City of Many Waters, pp. 103-4.
Cutch, a khaki dye from mangrove, was used in the leather and fishing industries for tanning and for the treating of nets and sails. The process of manufacture, briefly, was as follows:

> The raw bark is crushed and placed in vats, to which water is added for leaching purposes. The liquid is then evaporated to dryness in vacuum pans, leaving a solid residue. The finished product is a hard, brittle substance, not unlike pitch, but reddish-brown in colour. (CO 824/2 Brunei Annual Report 1937, p. 26).

The Island Trading Company (ITS) obtained its concession in 1900. A payment of $500 was made to Sultan Hashim for signing the agreement. Annual rent of $300 was to be paid in advance, and a duty of five cents for each pikul (133 1/3 lbs.) of manufactured bark exported was charged. Stubbs noted that "the syndicate got it cheap, but, unlike most Brunei concessionaires, they seem quite honest workers" (CO 531/2 (28140) minute by R.E.

Stubbs, 26 August 1909). The factory was built on a site previously occupied by a sago works.

Features of the cutch industry included incompetent British management and fluctuations in the world market. The Island Trading Company (as it became in 1911, with an authorized capital of L100,000), suffered from its own short-sighted policy in the early years of the Residential Era, when the mangrove areas near Brunei Town were recklessly wasted, with no attempt at conservation or reforestation, so that by the mid-1920s, most of the bark consumed came from outside Brunei, at great extra expense and trouble. From an employee's point of view, moreover, the company was unreliable: in 1907, 1938 and 1939-40, for example, the factory was practically closed; and in 1917-18 wartime shipping restrictions resulted in a sharp cutback in production and the redundancy of bark collecting gangs, who were difficult to reassemble thereafter.

The whole of the production was exported, mainly to the United States, France and Argentine until World War I (1914-18) when demand grew in the United Kingdom, Japan and China.

Cutch was Brunei's most valuable single export from 1906 to 1922 (except 1918 and 1921). Output averaged at around 2,000 tons annually, except during the Great Depression, when almost 3,000 tons were exported annually. The slump in the price of rubber after 1929 gave cutch renewed comparative importance and in 1931 it was once again at the top of the export list ($194,457 or 38.77% of total exports). In 1937 even more cutch by value ($212,239) was exported, but this then represented less than four percent of total exports.

The cutch factory was a most important employer of labour, particularly during the Great Depression. The number of employees rose from 500 in 1926-8 to 700 and over during the years 1930-2.

Dividends on the paid-up capital of L86,216 amounted to:

1929	5%	1939	
1930-1	nil	1940	7 1/2%
1933	6%	1941-7	nil
1934	6%	1948	5%
1935	3%	1949-51	5% + 5% bonus/year
1936	7 1/2%	1952	5% + 2 1/2% bonus
1937	2 1/2%	1953-4	nil

The ITC also owned a cutch factory in Sarawak and a rubber estate of 1,419 acres in Brunei. The latter was sold for $400,000 in September 1955. These dividends, therefore, were not derived solely from cutch operations in Brunei.

As mentioned earlier, (p. 220), the cutch factory closed in 1952; and the ITC went into liquidation five years later. At the time of liquidation the directors were as follows:

A. Parker-Smith (Chairman)
H.C. Backway
Charles Reid DSO CA
T.H. Kay

The "local director in Borneo" was one R.T. Lloyd-Dolbey. See note 64, p. 233 (below).

49. Sir Ernest Woodford Birch (1857-1929) K.C.M.G. 1876-1910 Malayan Civil Service. 1900-1903: seconded to North Borneo as Governor.

Son of J.W.W. Birch, murdered first British Resident of Perak (1875). Educated at Harrow. 1897-1900: Resident of Negri Sembilan. 1904-10: Resident of Perak. 1910: retired. 1929: died 17 December.

50. D.E. Brown comments that in the pre-Residency era to enforce the law the sultan had basically two alternatives: "he could commission a segment of the population to take up arms on his behalf, or he could give a permit to an aggrieved party which allowed that party to seek its own retribution" (Structure, p. 98-9).

It must be pointed out here that during the Residential Era the Brunei people constantly were complimented on their law-abiding nature. In 1913, for example, there was no serious crime in Brunei Town, apart from an infringement of the Revenue Farms Enactment. The Resident thought this was not

226

a bad record for a town of 10,000 souls. Again, in 1919, the capital was described as "completely clear of serious "crime." Indeed, the most difficult police problem immediately after 1906 was cattle rustling, especially in Tutong district. Even following the Second World War, the crime rate remained impressively low, the main offences being housebreaking and breaches of traffic regulations. Even housebreaking and petty pilfering from the oil company were considered negligible "in relation to the size of the (oilfield), the opportunities presented and the number of labourers employed." The Brunei Police Force numbered only thirty-nine in 1921, eighty-five in 1936-8 and 328 by 1959.

W.M. Johnson, one of the Shell staff in the 1930s, stated as follows:

> Never did I have anything stolen when I was in the jungle or in the oilfields. Nor do I recollect had any of my friends. At times I had quite large sums of money. I did not even have it locked up, although such a sum for any of the locals was a real fortune. That money was collected from the oilfield head-quarters by one man travelling alone and staying in whatever dwelling he found on his way and where he enjoyed hospitality. . . . (Letter to author, 27 January 1984).

51. See below, p. 244 (note 96).

52. Sic, 1901.

53. Edmund Roberts (c. 1866-1948). Described by F.N. Butterworth (referring to 1901) as "a sallow-complexioned man in the thirties with deep-sunken eyes" (Blundell, The City of Many Waters, p. 37).
1900-1905: Manager of the ITS cutch factory and adviser to Sultan Hashim, who appointed him Dato with a seat on the State Council. 1906-1921: Director of Public Works, Brunei and Labuan. 1921: retired. 1948: died. Dato Roberts exercised an influence beyond his official title. At times of crisis (such as the succession in 1906 and the murder

of the British Resident, Maundrell, in 1916)
his influence ensured calmness and continuity.

54. O.F. Ricketts (1855-1942/3), first Resident of
Limbang (1890-1909) and founder of the
Government station at Pengkalan Tarap (see
above, note 20).   Son of G.T. Ricketts,
soldier and diplomat, first British Consul in
Kuching (1964).
     1877-81: tea planter in Ceylon.   1881-
1909: Sarawak Civil Service.   1885: Assistant
Resident Trusan.   1890-1909: first Resident of
Limbang--concurrently Resident of Brooketon
(1900-6), Trusan (from 1906) and Lawas (from
1905).   Leader of 1900 Trusan expeditionary
force.   1909: retired, but continued to hold
various posts (eg. 1921 he became Acting Head
of the P.W.D.).   Died a prisoner of the
Japanese.   (Sources: CO 604/2 Sarawak
Gazette, 16 March 1909; and CO 604/22 Sarawak
Gazette, 4 January 1937, p. ?24.)   Described
by A.B. Ward, his understudy at Limbang, as
"kindness itself," a "perfect host," and a
keen shot (op. cit., pp. 69-70).

55. Sahat was evidently captured not long afterwards, for in the Sarawak Gazette, dated 1
June 1905, it is recorded that "Sahat,
imprisoned by His Highness the Sultan, has
since escaped" (CO 604/1).

56. The official correspondence may be found in
the following references: (a) FO 12/99, p.
104ff. and p. 115; FO 12/100, p. 12; and FO
12/105, pp. 7-8.
     (b) CO 144/73, items 14878, 16317, 20104
and 34409.
     (c) Sarawak Gazette, 1 December 1897, p.
210.
     Summary: In October 1897 two Brunei
Malays, Si Ajak and Si Burok, who had settled
in Limbang, were murdered in Brunei territory
after a dispute arose "as to the capture of
some buffaloes."   Si Ajak was a hereditary
serf of the Pengiran Bendahara; Si Burut,
likewise, of Pengiran Jambol.   The deceased
men, at the time of their death, "claimed to
be acting under the authority of the Pengiran
Bendahara."   The murderers included one Haji
Asim, a Brunei subject.
     Sir Charles Brooke applied to the British

Consul asking that compensation should be obtained from the Sultan of Brunei for the murders. Sultan Hashim, on the other hand, declined to make any payment until he had conducted an enquiry into the matter. To this end, he invited the claimants, Limbang chiefs, to give evidence in Brunei; but they were forbidden to come by the Sarawak authorities who claimed that the sultan's summons was "an act of discourtesy as an assertion of his jurisdiction over Limbang district." Sultan Hashim then asked the consul to help to get them to come and, through the consul, sent a conciliatory message to the Sarawak authorities; but he refused to deal directly with the Resident of Limbang, because that would be an admission that Sarawak was the legal government there. The consul, however, failed to pass on the sultan's message to the Sarawak authorities, who decided that, as the sultan paid no attention to the consul's representations, it was useless to make further requests to Brunei. The Rajah paid $1,000 in compensation to relatives, intending to deduct the amount from the next installment of Trusan cession money when it fell due.

The Foreign Office agreed that Sarawak "appear on their own responsibility to have behaved in a very high-handed manner" and requested the High Commissioner to see that a proper enquiry was conducted into "the circumstances in which the unfortunate men met their deaths." This was in February 1899.

Sultan Hashim, however, refused any further enquiry; and so, after warning had been given, $1,000 was deducted from the Trusan cession money in order that the Sarawak Government might be reimbursed for the money they had paid to the relatives of the murdered men.

Sultan Hashim's attitude was that Si Burut and Si Ajak were his own subjects; they had committed crimes in Brunei territory "which makes it not right to demand from us an indemnity of $1,000 . . . and it will never be agreed to by us; for it is very unfair and not at all right in any way to deal with us in this manner." His Highness wondered "that all matters and doings of the Rajah of Sarawak's side were so completely approved and justified (by the British Government)."

The presence of a British gunboat--sent to Brunei, in fact, to prevent potential Sarawak aggression, arising out of another dispute (see above, note 27)--ensured that Sultan Hashim accepted the reduced amount of Trusan cession money; but Consul Keyser felt that, if it were not for the presence of HMS Redpole, he would not have done so.

57. The 1911 Census disclosed that there were 736 Chinese living in Brunei, or just over 3% of the total population (21,718). Shopkeepers, it was reported, tended to be Hokkiens, while tailors and timber workmen were Khehs (CO 824/1 Brunei Annual Report 1911, p. 11).
    There was a rapid influx of Chinese into Brunei from the 1930s, when the Seria oilfield came into production. They dominated the business community and commercial farming. Today they comprise around one-quarter of the population.

58. The only case of this type of which I am aware involved not two, but only one, Chinese trader, Goh Ah Lye (see Notes, paragraph 10).
    If this is the case to which McArthur was referring, then the issue would not appear to be quite as clear-cut as he suggests.
    In October 1899 Consul A.L. Keyser reported that the Pengiran Pemancha "was in open revolt of the Sultan and (cared) nothing for his orders." Keyser quoted the example of a Chinese trader, Goh Ah Lye, who had paid $600 to Sultan Hashim for the right to trade on the Belait River and to take his goods in and out free of duty. The Sultan had issued him with a duly sealed authority to be exempt from duty. Notwithstanding this, the Pengiran Pemancha (Pengiran Muhammad Salleh) continued to levy toll on all goods belonging to the named Chinese trader and "cared nothing" for the Sultan's remonstrances, if, indeed, such remonstrances were made. Keyser had been endeavouring for six months to have this matter settled.
    If, however, McArthur was correct that the sultan did not have the right, constitution-ally, to interfere with the internal adminis-tration of kuripan property, then it was the sultan who was at fault. Hence if this inter-pretation is correct, McArthur's contention

would fall to the ground, that is, the sultan should have been obliged to pay up.

59. Nor were they. The procedure adopted by the Resident after 1906 was to cancel all such concessions and, in compensation, to return the purchase money less a sum proportionate to the number of years the concession had already been held.

The resumption of such monopoly rights, as well as of tulin and cession monies, was extremely costly, necessitating a loan of $439,750 from the FMS during the years 1906 to 1914. This was expensive but essential if a revenue for the Government were to be obtained.

The Rajah of Sarawak, needless to say, was permitted to retain intact the monopolies he held in Muara district. The reasons were (a) consideration for the Rajah's great age and (b) a desire not to upset him further after his bitter disappointment at not being allowed to absorb Brunei. The Rajah was expected to die soon, whereupon all outstanding matters could be settled.

60. Complete figures for Brunei's trade in the early years of the British Residency are not available; but most went through Labuan, for which the following statistics are available:

(1) Brunei: Trade with Labuan (1907-21).

Year	Exports to Labuan ($ Straits)	Imports from Labuan ($ Straits)
1907	50,926	65,349
1908-12	n.a.	
1913	442,930	133,243
1914	448,087	102,558
1915	538,276	134,932
1916	618,227	118,885
1917	648,738	142,351
1918	587,574	187,564
1919	765,569	316,178
1920	917,629	585,306
1921	759,567	406,308

(2) Brunei: Total Trade (1916-1921).

Year	Total Exports ($ Straits)	Total Imports ($ Straits)
1916	734,254	254,756
1917	952,260	189,451
1918	1,033,734	362,853
1919	1,134,864	614,061
1920	1,173,252	722,678
1921	791,028	410,854

Source: CO 824/1 Brunei Annual Report, 1906-21

61. The figure for imports into Brunei Town in 1884 is given elsewhere as $135,054.69 (CO 144/59: 13622). Total exports from Brunei State to Singapore carried in European ships amounted to $273,559.76 during the same year. Figures are available, also, for 1883, when imports into Brunei Town from Singapore totalled $111,854 (L20,506) compared with exports, likewise, of $106,544 comprised $68,411 (CO 144/58: 13016). Total trade, Consul Treacher estimated, was twice the value of that exported to Singapore. The figures, for example, did not include $19,092, representing the value of 3,182 tons of coal exported from Muara by Cowie.

62. After 1906, as mentioned above (note 59), monopolists were expropriated, and a new import tariff introduced. Duties did not cover many articles previously taxed, and, in many cases, imposed a duty of 5% instead of 10%. Retail prices began to fall (CO 144/80: 35280, M.S.H. McArthur to Secretary to High Commissioner, No. 150/06, 28 June 1906, paragraph 3).

63. Muara ('Brooketon') was, and remains, part of Brunei territory.

64. Exports of coal and cutch were as follows (values in Straits' dollars):

232

Year	Coal Exports Tons	Value	Cutch Exports Cwt.	Value
1906	14,533	n.a.	30,982	n.a.
1910	n.a.	n.a.	48,076	228,639
1915	22,633	148,730	50,128	237,400
1920	17,000	296,000	41,800	355,300
1925	10,337*	98,202*	52,000	234,000
1930	Nil	Nil	49,880	220,080
1935	25	200	51,500	177,910
1938	54	459	33,600	152,366

* 1924 figures

Year	Total Exports Value
1906	n.a.
1910	n.a.
1915	543,707
1920	1,173,252
1925	1,859,736
1930	807,449
1935	3,778,655
1938	6,580,482

There were no figures for the trade of the entire State of Brunei until 1915. Exports from Brunei Town totalled $78,909 in 1908 and $245,639 in 1910. Cutch exports amounted to $69,576 in 1908; coal exports were valued at $51,230 in 1907.

Source: compiled by author, mainly from Brunei Annual Reports.

65. The River Pandaruan is a short stream, 24 miles in length, which enters the sea about 13 miles from the Brunei capital. In 1884 Pengiran Muda Muhammad Tajudin (d. 1916) transferred the tulin rights to A.H. Everett (1849-1898), who, in turn, handed over the rights to Sir Charles Brooke (in about 1888). The Rajah "never looked on that as a very safe

233

transfer--I consider that it stands in the same light as Brooketon--all rights except the governing ones and the flag." Nevertheless he treated Pandaruan virtually as a part of Sarawak.

In 1906, shortly after assuming office as British Resident in the sultanate, McArthur expressed the opinion that Pandaruan possibly belonged to Brunei and "should not be given up to Sarawak." Nothing further happened, however, until tulin land claims had been settled (1910-11) and the Brunei Government became anxious to alienate land for rubber planting. It became essential, therefore, for the international frontier to be clearly defined. In 1912 a temporary boundary was established, which left the entire Pandaruan basin in Sarawak hands. A settlement was reached under which the Brunei Government would collect all the import, and half the export, duties of Pandaruan, Sarawak to retain only half of the export duties. Final settlement was achieved in February 1920, when the Pandaruan River itself became the international frontier between Brunei and Sarawak.

For further details, see A.V.M. Horton, "The Pandaruan Issue 1884-1920," in Sarawak Gazette (July 1984, pp. 26-30).

66. See notes 60 and 64 (above). Bark continued to be obtained mainly from outside Brunei.

67. The trade of Temburong increased from $5,142 in 1909 to $18,628 in 1910. The principal products were sago, raw and prepared ($4,059 in 1909, c. $13,335 in 1910) and jelutong ($823 and $3,759). In 1911 the North Borneo Trading Company employed some 150 men, and two shipments of timber were made. But in the following year the company decided to discontinue the venture, which had proved unprofitable, principally because of their own incompetence. This resulted in a serious loss of revenue for the administration. An attempt to obtain sugar from nipah palms began successfully (in 1911) but had to be abandoned before the end of the year because of "mischief done by monkeys." By 1914 the first consignment of para rubber had been exported, in 1915, 31,775 lbs. worth $36,932. See also, note 17 (above).

68. Examples of trouble-makers who could not be
     held included Sahat (above, pp. 117-9) and Si
     Radin (p. 128-9). It seems likely that only a
     few such people created a disproportionate
     amount of havoc, because Brunei Malays
     retained a reputation for being extremely law-
     abiding after 1906. There was little serious
     crime.

69. In the 1847 U.K.-Brunei Treaty there was an
     "Additional Article" which ran as follows:

          His Highness the Sultan of Borneo
          agrees that in all cases when a
          British subject shall be accused of
          any crime committed in any part of
          His Highness's dominions, the person
          so accused shall be exclusively
          tried and adjudged by the English
          Consul-General, or other officer
          duly appointed for that purpose by
          Her Britannic Majesty; and in all
          cases where disputes or differences
          shall arise between British sub-
          jects, or between British subjects
          and the subjects of His Highness, or
          between British subjects and the
          subjects of any other foreign Power
          within the dominions of the Sultan
          of Borneo, Her Britannic Majesty's
          Consul-General or other duly-
          appointed officer shall have power
          to hear and decide the same, without
          any interference, molestation, or
          hindrance on the part of any
          authority of Borneo, either before,
          during or after the litigation (L.R.
          Wright, The Origins of British
          Borneo (Hong Kong: Hong Kong
          University Press, 1970, p. 209).

     A similar article (VII) may be found in the
     Protectorate Treaty of 1888:

          It is agreed that full and exclusive
          jurisdiction, civil and criminal,
          over British subjects and their
          property in the State of Brunei, is
          reserved to Her Britannic Majesty,
          to be exercised by such consular or
          other officers such as Her Majesty

235

shall appoint for that purpose. The same jurisdiction is likewise reserved to Her Majesty in the State of Brunei over foreign subjects enjoying British protection; and the said jurisdiction may likewise be exercised in cases between British or British protected subjects and the subjects of a third power, with the consent of their respective Governments.

In mixed cases arising between British and British-protected subjects and subjects of the Sultan, the trial shall take place in the court of the defendant's nationality; but an officer appointed by the Government of the plaintiff's nationality shall be entitled to be present at, and to take part in, the proceedings, but shall have no voice in the decision (Wright, op. cit., p. 214).

70. Burong Pingai, named ostensibly after the pet bird of a Johore princess which the people of the ward cared for, was notable for its traders and religious figures at this time.

71. Arthur Louis Keyser (1856-1924). Educated at Clifton College and at Thun (Switzerland). 1884: Private Secretary to Governor of Fiji. 1888-97: Malayan Civil Service. 1898-1900: Consul at Brunei. 1900-1920: Consul successively at Berbera, Quaila, Cadiz, Seville, Quito. Author of People and Places: A Life in Five Continents (London: Murray, 1922) and Trifles and Travels (London: Murray, 1923). Died 7 March 1924.

72. I.e. the 25th Muslim Ruler of Brunei. The origins of the sultanate remain obscure, but latest research suggests that the best candidate for the date of its foundation is 1515. Archaeological evidence indicates that Kota Batu has been settled since the seventh century; but it was not necessarily the capital of Muslim Brunei's predecessor States, known to the Chinese as Vijayapura and P'o-ni. See the research of R. Nicholl.

73. I am inclined to believe His Highness rather than the Acting Consul. Pengiran Anak Hashim was blamed by Rajah James Brooke for the murder of the pro-Sarawak faction in Brunei in 1845-6, when he was "probably in his late teens" (D.E. Brown, Structure, p. 54). If so, this would give him a date of birth not later than 1826: hence he would indeed have been about 80 in McArthur's day. If the Sultan was only 70 in 1904, on the other hand, he would have been only eleven at the time of the 1845-6 massacre.

74. McArthur appears to be on dubious ground here as well. Belfield, who visited Brunei a few months afterwards, commented:

> 27. I found His Highness's intelligence to be more acute than I expected. He shows no sign of intellectual weakness, and is only stupid or deaf when it suits him to misunderstand a representation made to him . . . I fancy that there is greater power of comprehension behind a somewhat immobile countenance than McArthur gave him credit for (FO 12/128, pp. 448-9, H.C. Belfield to Anderson, 5 June 1905, paragraph 27; also in CO 273/310, item 33426).

75. Sultan Hashim's alleged infringements of Treaty obligations included the appeal to the Sultan of Turkey (see note 79, below); the issue of coal concessions in Brunei, although the monopoly was already held by the Rajah of Sarawak; and the alleged mistreatment of Chinese British subjects, especially by Pengiran Tajudin during the Tutong Revolt of 1901 (other instances included the case of Soh Eng Gin, discussed above, p. 120).

76. This is undoubtedly true. Consider the following quotation, which gives the substance of Sultan Hashim's attitude: "From the day I set my hand to the Treaty of Protection (17 September 1888), I have not once received assistance or protection from Your Majesty's Government and I beg, with all deference, for Your Majesty's help. Not a single consul has

done anything to help strengthen my country. They all seem to help Sarawak and to try to hand over my country to Sarawak" (CO 144/77, 12955: Sultan Hashim to H.M. King Edward VII, 19 Jemadilawal 1320AH/24 August 1902).

77. This has the ring of truth. On 10 April 1906, when Sultan Hashim was suffering his final illness, McArthur reported that His Highness was not expected to recover and that this was causing "some unrest and a certain amount of intrigue" in Brunei. "The Kedayan population in particular is disturbed, and the various headmen of that race have been to the Istana to ask whether there is to be a successor on the throne in the event of the decease of the Sultan, or whether it is true that the country has been ceded to England (sic, United Kingdom) and that there will in future be no Sultan" (CO 144/80, 16495, McArthur to Elgin, 10 April 1906, paragraph 2). Other quotations to similar effect could be produced.

78. See above, pp. x-xi.

79. This letter, dated 27 Safar 1321 (15 March 1903), may be found in FO 572/37, p. 32. After expressing the joy with which Brunei Muhammadans had heard of the appointment of a Turkish Consul-General in Singapore, Sultan Hashim offered to surrender his country to Turkey because the Muslim religion in Brunei was "being ruined by the unbelievers." The Sultan of Turkey was informed, in addition, that "one of your servant's districts, named Limbang, has even been seized by an unbeliever, one Charles Brooke of Sarawak."
    The letter was intercepted by Consul Hewett, who described the allegations as "false and baseless," pointing out that in 1902 he "assisted the Sultan (of Brunei) to obtain timber for the new mosque in Brunei, free of cost or duty, from Sarawak territory." Sir Frank Swettenham considered that it was "hardly worthwhile" to intervene in the matter.

80. See below, notes 124, 125, (pp. 252-3).

81. See above, pp. 14-5.

82. On 11 September 1904 McArthur reported that the loan of $10,000 was made on the 8th instant:

> 2. Since that date His Highness' lapau has been thronged daily with creditors and courtiers and he informed me that he had only a few hundred dollars left, as he had been busily engaged paying off his most pressing creditors. The loan has evidently relieved him of a great deal of anxiety for his finances were at such a low ebb that he was even becoming anxious about his daily food. His change of demeanour now is very marked.

His Highness also managed to redeem the Trusan cession money from the Juatan Abu Bakar. (FO 12/126, p. 189 McArthur to Anderson, No. 40, 11 September 1904, paragraphs 1-3).

83. See above, p. 184 (note 56). A.B. Ward remembered Hewett as "an extra-ordinary great smoker" and an "excellent shot" (Rajah's Servant, p. 85).
According to Butterworth, (using his pen-name, P. Blundell) the dignified, "stand-offish" Hewett "belonged to one of Britain's [sic] oldest families. He had the interests of Brunei at heart. He had no personal ambitions to serve. He knew that the honour and welfare of the people of Brunei and their ruler would be safe in the hands of the Brooke family" (P. Blundell, The City of Many Waters, London: Arrowsmith, 1923, p. 203). Hewett was a man "who had spent most of his life in Borneo and who thoroughly understood the Malays, [and] did all he could in an unobtrusive way to forward the interests of Brunei (ibid., p. 121).
Butterworth felt that Brunei should have been handed over the Sarawak: "Anyone who saw the boats flocking round the Zahora [during the Rajah's visit to Brunei in 1906] knew at once where the hearts of the people of Brunei lay. The Rajah had his reward. Others had their rewards too for the push and superlative diplomacy they had displayed on behalf of the Brunei people. But their rewards were of a

239

more substantial nature." Unlike the high-minded Sir Charles Brooke and Hewett, "the Eastern services nowadays contain several officials of obscure antecedents, no morals and great ambitions. And some of these men viewed with great disfavour the high position attained by the Brooke family" (ibid., pp. 203-204).

84. Keyser, Consul 1898-1900, on the other hand, claimed that Brunei chiefs were agreed that "it would be inconvenient for a representative of Her Majesty's Government to be a spectator of the terrible corruption, cruelty and misrule which were common both to the Sultan and his chiefs" (FO 12/111, p. 212ff., paragraph 17).

     Keyser was obliged to abandon his attempt to reside in the sultanate because he had been "poisoned" by Brunei pengirans: "Dire results followed and for long months I lay helpless and in pain." He added: "I realized to the full that I was a very inconvenient white man in their midst." Sultan Hashim "endeavoured to comfort me by explaining that many people were poisoned daily in Brunei and that some of them occasionally recovered" (Trifles and Travels, pp. 149-150; People and Places, pp. 220-1).

     In view of McArthur's statement, this passage from Keyser need not be taken too seriously. The sultan's words might be interpreted to mean accidental food poisoning rather than attempted murder.

85. A.B. Ward, who remembered that Consul Hewett's official duties in Labuan were "not very onerous" (Rajah's Servant, p. 85). Sir Frank Swettenham, British High Commissioner for Brunei, pointed out the deleterious consequences of such lack of occupation:

          8. I do not believe that the exist-
          ing [1903] conditions in Brunei are
          "intolerable" and in my opinion you
          would hear little about the place if
          it were not that Sarawak is on one
          side, the Borneo Company on the
          other, and the British consul,
          having little to do, is inclined to
          dabble in matters which really do

240

not concern him (FO 12/122, p. 56ff.: Swettenham to Lansdowne, No. 15, Secret, 6 August 1903, paragraph 8--my emphasis added).

86. Pengiran Muhammad Salleh (d. 1912), Pengiran Pemancha c. 1898-1912. A "pale dignified gentleman dressed in black" (Blundell, The City of Many Waters, p. 63). On 10 October 1899 Keyser reported that the pengiran was "in open revolt of the Sultan and cares nothing for his orders." (He then quotes, in illustration, the case of Goh Ah Lye.). The consul suggested that the Pengiran Pemancha, along with his fellow wazirs, should be deposed and replaced by younger and more loyal chiefs (CO 144/73, 34409).

Sir John Anderson, writing in 1906, had the impression that the pengiran, along with the Pengiran Bendahara, seemed "cunning . . . selfish and cruel" (CO 144/80, 5578).

Pengiran Muhammad Salleh died "at a somewhat advanced age" on 2 December 1912, having been Joint Regent since the death of Sultan Hashim on 10 May 1906. The Brunei Annual Report for 1912 records that the late wazir had been a "pengiran of the old class, and though he acquiesced in British protection, he never conformed more than outwardly to the new order of things."

87. Pengiran Anak Besar (c. 1829-1917), Pengiran Bendahara (1883-1917) and Joint Regent (1906-1917). His father (Pengiran Tajudin) and uncles (including Pengiran Muda Hassim and Pengiran Budrudin) were victims of the anti-British, anti-Brooke purge of 1845-6. An adopted son and heir of Sultan Abdul Mumin (r. 1852-85), he married a daughter of Pengiran Temenggong (later Sultan) Hashim in 1882.

Keyser, writing in 1899, described him first as "a fairly honest minister of limited intelligence who has never been out of Brunei"; but later as "an old man" whose intellect was not "much clearer than that of the Sultan." In October 1899, when arguing for the removal of the wazir from office, Keyser reported that the Pengiran Bendahara was

241

the instigator of all the cattle
raids at Limbang. He has persis-
tently worked against the advice and
wishes of Her Majesty's Government.
. . . Some few years back he sold a
slave for human sacrifice. I could
enumerate many more of his notorious
acts, but suffice it to say that all
the present troubles in Tutong and
Belait [see above, pp. 14-5] are
mainly due to his extortions and the
taking of women and children as
slaves, in honour of the marriage of
his daughter. No reforms can be
expected with this man in the
country" (FO 12/102, p. 127ff.,
Keyser to Sir C. Mitchell, No. 119,
10 October 1899, paragraph 8--
enclosed in Mitchell to Foreign
Office, no. 48 [Political], 27
October 1899; also in CO 144/73
(34409).

Butterworth remembered the Pengiran
Bendahara as a "jolly-looking elderly Malay
with a face something like George Robey's"
(Blundell, p. 63).
Finally, McArthur commented in August 1904
that the pengiran was "the largest owner of
property in Brunei and has a large following.
He is said to be able to swat the Sultan as he
pleases" (FO 12/126, p. 175ff: McArthur to
Anderson, No. 41, 28 August 1904, paragraph
4).

88. Pengiran Di-Gadong Muhammad Hassan (d. 1900),
was the brother of the Pengiran Bendahara, and
held his office from 1883 until his death. No
successor was appointed until the late 1960s.
In 1887 he was described as the leader of the
opposition to Sultan Hashim. Keyser, when
arguing for his removal in October 1899,
claimed that he was "a man of no intelligence
and stone deaf." At that time he was within a
few months of death.

89. A number of points arise out of this chapter,
most notably McArthur's failure to mention the
actual successor. Of the people he mentioned,
Pengiran Muda Omar Ali Saifudin died in August
1905, while Pengiran Muda Muhammad Tajudin

lived on until 1916 (see p. 221, above, note 18).

In April 1906 the dying Sultan Hashim nominated his eldest legitimate son, Pengiran Muda Muhammad Jemalul Alam, as his heir. The choice was ratified unanimously by the State Council (see above, pp. 41-2). The Honourable Sir Steven Runciman appears to be incorrect when he states that the nomination was made "on the advice of the British Resident" (S. Runciman, The White Rajahs (Cambridge: Cambridge University Press, 1960, p. 199). A Regency operated until 1918, when Sultan Muhammad Jemalul Alam was installed as Yang Dipertuan. Knighted in 1920, he survived only until 1924. His son Seri was the late Begawan Sultan of Brunei who died on 7 September 1986.

90. See also above, p. 213, notes 20 and 21; and D.E. Brown, op. cit., pp. 39-40.

91. As late as 1884 there had been only two sago manufacturers in Brunei (CO 1444/58, item 13016, W.H. Treacher to Lord Derby, No. 63 (Labuan) 10 June 1884).

92. Pengkalan Tarap: that is, Limbang Village (cf. p. 213, note 20, above).

93. CO 604/1 Sarawak Gazette 4 June 1904, p. 129. The report ran as follows:

> At the commencement of the month (April 1904) Haji Tarip and about 40 men . . . women and children moved in from Brunei and applied to live in Limbang. The men are blacksmiths of Brunei and the Pengiran Bendahara's hamba [;] they stated that there are some more of them to come yet. The reason for their coming is the common one of the pengiran's family attempting to take away the young girls from their relatives. They have settled down river below the station and have started building their smithies.

It will be noted that although the official history of the first two Rajahs Brooke mentions the flight to Limbang of these

243

people, their subsequent return to the Sultanate is omitted (Baring-Gould and Bampfylde, A History of Sarawak under its Two White Rajahs [London: Southeran, 1909], p. 361, fn. 1).

94. In fact Sultan Hashim addressed numerous letters on this subject to London. McArthur means, presumably, that no British official had attempted to present the Brunei case to the British Government.

95. Noel Penrose Trevenen (c. 1853-1901). "Distinguished himself" in the Straits Settlements Civil Service, 1874-1890. Governor Sir Cecil Smith, whose private secretary he was, "thought highly of him" (FO 12/93, minute by Sir G. Dallas, 3 January 1894). 1890-98: Consul in Borneo. 1898: November 30: "appointment terminated" (for failure to answer official correspondence and for suspected embezzlement; he was also a drunkard).

On his fact-finding mission to Limbang in 1891, Trevenen was accompanied, also, by two chiefs representing Brunei: the Pengiran Kerma Indra and the Orang Kaya Di-Gadong. He concluded that the headmen and Bisayas, having been "independent" of Brunei since 1884, would not have reverted willingly to the Sultan's rule (FO 12/87, p. 286ff. Trevenen to third Marquess of Salisbury, No. 4 (Political), 30 April 1891; also in CO 144/68, item 12133).

96. In 1941, the occasion of the Brooke Centenary, the third Rajah sought to make amends for the abrogation of the Limbang "feudal" rights. The sultan was offered a lump sum of $20,000 plus an annuity of $1,000, but this deal was blocked by the High Commissioner, Sir T.S.W. Thomas GCMG OBE (1879-1962). In addition, the surviving heirs of former tulin owners were offered shares of $60,000 down plus $6,000 annually; these payments were actually made.

After the Pacific War, the new British colonial Government in Sarawak undertook to uphold the Rajah's wishes and policies as far as possible. It was agreed that Sultan Ahmad Tajudin (r. 1924-50) would receive an ex-gratia payment of $6,000 for the years 1942-7 and annuity of $1,000 until his death, when no further payment would be made to his successor.

With regard to <u>tulin</u> rights, it became clear that the document which had been used as the basis for settlement in 1941 was a forgery and many claimants were left disgruntled. A new settlement was arranged, requiring an immediate payment of $28,048.92 and $4,674.82 annually thereafter. The Governor of Sarawak, Sir C. Arden-Clarke (1898-1962), proposed "to try at the first favourable opportunity to arrange for the commution of these annual payments, save that made to the Sultan for his lifetime" (CO 938/5, file 3: Governor's Deputy to CO, No. 58, 19 November 1948).

See also (below) note 99.

97. Alfred Hart Everett (1849-98): scientist, commercial speculator and colonial civil servant. 1885: Consul for Sarawak in Brunei and Resident of Trusan. 1869: first came to the East to examine the Sarawak cave deposits. 1872-6 and 1885-90: Sarawak Civil Service. 1878-83: British North Borneo Service, 1890: retired, 1 March. 1898: died, 18 June. Concerning the Pandaruan, see above, note 65 (p. 233).

Concerning mineral concessions, see above, note 7 (p. 209).

98. Tarling discounts McArthur's contention that the annexation of the Limbang arose out of a plot by the <u>Pengiran Di-Gadong</u> (<u>Britain, The Brookes and Brunei</u> [Kuala Lumpur: Oxford University Press, 1971], p. 409).

In March 1890 the <u>Orang Kaya Di-Gadong</u> (not to be confused with the <u>wazir</u>) was sent from Brunei to find out what the Rajah was doing in Limbang. He replied: "Here I am, ruler of Limbang. If the Sultan wishes to negotiate, let him negotiate. If he wishes to attack me, he may do so; he will find me armed and ready for him . . . ." (CO 273/166, item 9843: <u>Inche</u> Muhammad to Acting Governor, Straits Settlements, 31 March 1890).

99. The official report may be found in CO 604/1 <u>Sarawak Gazette</u> 2 August 1904. The text was written by D.J.S. Bailey and dated 27 June 1904 (pp. 152-6). The narrative refers to much burning of houses, stores of padi and

rice by Government forces, not to mention
looting, crop destruction, and scorched earth
tactics. The following quotation gives the
tone:

> In summing up [the results of one
> foray] Mr. Owen reckons 21 long-
> houses, not including farm huts
> (<u>damper</u>) and sheds (<u>langkau</u>), were
> completely destroyed, large stores
> of <u>padi</u> and rice burnt, live stock
> consumed, and in short the whole
> Engkari country devasted [<u>sic</u>]
> without the loss of a single man.
> The loot was chiefly in the shape of
> Klasa mats, a few common jars, a
> little brassware, and odds and ends
> such as are usually found in Dayak
> huts.

For more accessible accounts of the
background to the Batang Lupar expedition, see
Crisswell, <u>Rajah Charles Brooke</u>, pp. 127-31;
Bampfylde, <u>A History of Sarawak</u>, pp. 377-90;
and Baring-Dould and Runciman, <u>The White
Rajahs</u>, pp. 223-5.

100. The Governor of North Borneo, E. Birch,
agreed: Sultan Hashim's refusal to accept the
cession money was "a grand instance of royal
pride" (FO 12/120, p. 160ff.). A.B. Ward,
(<u>Rajah's Servant</u>, p. 68), on the other hand,
declared that the sultan personally stood to
receive little of the proferred $6,000
annually. A clue is provided by the 1941
settlement (cf. note 96, above): it will be
seen that Sultan Ahmad Tajudin received only
one-seventh of the annuity offered by Sarawak.
In these circumstances, Sultan Hashim's
"refusal" of the Limbang cession money was
less "striking," perhaps, than supposed by
McArthur.

101. Cf. above, pp. 47-8.

102. McArthur reported that Lisang and Batung,
<u>tulin</u> property of the <u>Pengiran Bendahara</u>, were
within the Limbang watershed. He informed the
sultan that while the Rajah of Sarawak had
control over the main river, he naturally
claimed its tributaries. The Acting Consul

feared that it was "impossible [for him] to take any action in the matter without re-opening the whole Limbang question" (FO 12/126, pp. 201-205). In fact, however, Brunei Town itself lies within the Limbang watershed, as Sarawak maps acknowledged by including it in Sarawak territory. Sir Charles, therefore, would appear to have been attempting to occupy as much of the Limbang watershed as he could achieve with impunity.

103.   H.C. Brooke-Johnson (1873-1950). 1894-1902: Sarawak Civil Service. 1897: Acting post-master-General. 1898: Assistant Treasurer. 1900: Treasurer. 1902: retired because of disagreement with Rajah. 1902-05: Lawas. Expelled from the Sarawak Club. An "adventurer" (according to Sir Charles Brooke). Service with the Royal Navy during First World War.

104.   I.e. the Governor, who was always referred to by the British Government as "Principal Representative of the BNBC in Borneo," pre-sumably to deny him the status of a regular governor under the Colonial Office. This practice continued until North Borneo became a British Colony in 1946.

105.   In the first paragraph of his Report (p. 99, above) McArthur mentions that Lawas could no longer be considered part of Brunei. It may appear somewhat surprising, therefore, that he should have devoted a section of his Report to a consideration of the Lawas issue. An extract from a letter written by McArthur to Sir Frank Swettenham on 13 December 1904 (CO 273/300 645 04/05) provides a clue. On learning that Lawas was about to be trans-ferred from North Borneo to Sarawak, McArthur commented:

> I am sure the Sultan will never forgive the British Government if they acquiesce in this transaction, for he hates the Rajah and will be most annoyed when he learns that he has acquired further rights and consolidated his claim on the remnant of Brunei. If the trans-action is submitted for Foreign

247

Office approval, I think that
approval ought not to be given
without very full consideration of
all the circumstances. The Lawas is
a very important river.

The BNBC exchanged the sovereign rights to
Rajah Charles in October 1904 in exchange for
L5,000 and the Rajah's coal rights in North
Borneo. The Foreign Office, Crisswell
comments, "still hopeful of seeing Brunei
absorbed [by Sarawak], gave its consent"
(Rajah Charles Brooke, p. 195). Subsequently,
Brooke-Johnson demanded compensation of
$15,000 down and further monthly installments
for the loss of rights in Lawas held by
himself and the heirs of Pengiran Abubakar.
Eventually the Rajah was compelled to pay
$6,000 annually in compensation (Crisswell, p.
198). He was also required to compensate
Brooke-Johnson "for loss of employment"
(Ibid., p. 199). See also Tarling, Britain,
the Brookes and Brunei, pp. 527-39.

106. See above, p. 215 (note 23).

107. In my opinion, McArthur's interpretation here
is incorrect. Cowie was granted three successive leases. The first, dated 13 March 1882,
gave him the right, for ten years, to mine
coal in Muara Damit and exclusive rights "to
export or sell to any ship the coal in the
territory of His Highness the Sultan of
Brunei, that is, from Tanjong Nosong (the
southern boundary of Kimanis Bay) on the north
up to and in the Tutong River." Clause Five
added that if a seam of coal were found in the
Sultan's dominions outside Muara, Cowie would
have the right of first refusal to work such a
deposit.
     A second agreement, amending the first,
was signed on 9 January 1884. Cowie was now
granted the monopoly of working coal in Muara
district (rather than mere permission as
theretofore) and throughout the territory
between Tanjong Nosong and Tutong (where
formerly he had only the right to "export or
sell (coal) to any ship," and first option to
work any seam). The lease was extended to
twenty years from 1882, with an option for a
further twenty.

Further modifications were made in a third lease, concluded on 4 May 1887. Change had become necessary because of the transfer, since 1884, of Trusan to Sarawak and of the coast between Cape Nosong and Sipitong to North Borneo. The boundaries of Cowie's concession were now defined as Muara Damit and all the pasisir-pasisiran within Brunei territory, i.e. from Sipitong to the River Bumbun and from Cape Puan to the River Tutong.

These rights were transferred to Sir Charles Brooke on 6 September 1888, for L25,000.

> In brief, he had exclusive rights to all coal except that west of the "River" Tutong. (It is not quite clear to the present writer whether the term "river" is used here to denote the stream itself or the district. In other words, the land between the true left bank of the Tutong and the boundary with Belait district may or may not be included within the area of the concession.)

The letter from Sir Charles Mitchell (referred to by McArthur) may be found in FO 12/102, p. 106ff. (No. 46 Political) and in CO 144/73, item 34409.

108. In fact Brooketon continued to sustain considerable losses (totalling between $52,000 and $95,000 annually from 1904 until 1913) and unsaleable coal was often left piling up (CO 604/1 Sarawak Gazette 2 July 1907, p. 159). Mining in Labuan ceased in 1911, Labuan Coalfields Ltd. (a reconstruction of the Central Borneo Company) going into liquidation in 1916. Production at Brooketon appears to have been significantly higher after 1911 (except 1912) than it had been before that date. The mine was closed finally in November 1924. The chief markets for Brooketon coal, according to the Sarawak Government Gazette dated 1 April 1925 (CO 604/10), were Singapore and Manila.

109. See CO 144/77 (16635) FO to CO, 6 May 1903, encl. Hewett to Lansdowne, 28 March 1903; and CO 144/77 (34409) FO to CO, 12 September 1903, encl. Hewett to High Commissioner, 25 June

1903. See also: CO 604/1 <u>Sarawak Gazette</u> 2
May 1903, p. 82 and ibid, <u>Sarawak Gazette</u> 5
June 1906, p. 141 (diary entry for 6 May
1906).

The coal at <u>Buang Tawar</u> was said to be "of
the best and hardest" quality "resembling more
to anthracite than to the bituminous coal of
. . . Brooketon." The seams were well drained
and easily accessible and mining continued
until October 1917. Production fluctuated
between one and two thousand tons annually;
and, like Brooketon, the mine ran consistently
at a loss.

In 1903 a spring of oil was struck at the
mine, but the oil, instead of increasing
profits, simply hampered the winning of coal.
The Sarawak Government continued to collect
the oil until at least 1928; the "usual flow"
was four barrels a <u>month</u>.

110. See above, note 109.

111. Brunei's pre-oil revenue (plus the proportion
of land revenue) was as follows: (figures are
in Straits' dollars).

Year	(1) Land Revenue	(2) Total Revenue	(1) as % of (2)
1907	3,200	51,777	16.16
1910	12,145	77,051	15.76
1915	14,343	129,529	11.07
1920	24,973	206,253	12.11
1925	42,986	345,573	12.44

Source: <u>Brunei Annual Reports</u> (CO 824/1).

112. Cf. p. 79 (paragraph 7) and p. 199 (footnote
10): above.

113. According to the 1911 Census (CO 531/3: 34002)
there were 4,931 Kedayans, and only 4,641 in
1921. In the same interval "Tutongs"
increased from 1,667 to 2,391. Census cate-
gories at this time were somewhat vague. It
is likely, therefore, that the Kedayans did
not decline in number but simply described
themselves (or were described) under a

different name.

114. See above, p. 229 (note 60) and below, p. 257 (note 141).

115. There are several corroborations of this opinion. Apart from Sir Hugh Clifford's 1902 article "A Dying Kingdom" (<u>Macmillan's Magazine</u>, LXXXVI, May-Oct. 1902, pp. 106-114), see Mitchell (FO 12/102, p. 181ff. and FO 12/101, p. 207); Trevenen (FO 12/97, po. 160ff.); Keyser (CO 144/73, 24234 and CO 144/74: 17694); and Hewett (CO 144/75: 14092). Even thoughtful Bruneians will admit that, but for the introduction of a Resident, Brunei would have been completely absorbed by Sarawak.

116. The "establishment" of British Protection in 1904 would have been impossible, since the sultanate had been a protectorate of the United Kingdom since September 1888. McArthur means the appointment of a Resident with powers over internal administration, British control formerly having been limited to foreign affairs and certain specific rights of interference in Brunei's domestic matters.
    McArthur repeats this mistake later: see, for example, paragraph 143 (p. 175).

117. By April 1882 the amount subscribed in shares to the Chartered Company was L362,010. Out of this amount had to be met the claims of the Provisional Association; for running expenses the company could count on no more than L150,000. Governor Treacher had spent already one-fifth of this, as well as all the locally-raised revenue. Retrenchment became the order of the day, but local deficits continued. After 1895 Cowie sponsored a number of high-cost projects, such as the telegraph and railway, following which the Chartered Company was plunged into debt. Yet dividends continued to be paid: two percent in 1899-1904; three percent in 1905; four percent in 1907 and five percent in 1909-14. In 1902 Cowie appealed to the Colonial Office for a loan, but was refused. A boom in rubber after 1905 helped the company; but in 1924 its debt stood at L1,649,800, the payment of dividends, financed by borrowing, having continued even

during the post-World War I slump.

118. This is confirmed by Belfield in his 1905
Report (CO 273/310: 33426). Cf. also Sir
Charles Brooke's letter to the Foreign Office,
dated 14 March 1899:

> I trust that something may shortly
> be done to depose and pension off
> the Sultan and five or six of the
> chiefs around him and to permit me
> to devote the rest of my years in
> putting the small portion of terri-
> tory which is under Brunei--although
> we hold considerable influence over
> it--in as good order as now exists
> along the line of coast under
> Sarawak rule (FO 12/105, p. 40).

119. See above, pp. 205-6 (note 1).

120. Given the acquiescence of the British Govern-
ment (which, by Treaty, was responsible for
Brunei's foreign policy), I imagine that Sir
Charles would have regarded his annexation of
Limbang as having been legalized already.

121. For the actual trade figures in the early
years of the Residential System, see above,
note 60.

122. The Rajah already had a real monopoly of coal
in Brunei (apart from Belait district)--see
above, p. 248 (note 107).

123. 1901.

124. In the letter under reference Lord Lansdowne
informed His Highness that the state of
affairs in Belait and Tutong had been "a
matter of grave concern to His Majesty's
Government and it appeared to them a matter of
plain duty that they should use their best
influence to restore order in the interests of
the suffering inhabitants of the disturbed
districts and to establish a better form of
Government." Hence Hewett had been authorized
to lay before His Highness the terms offered
by Sir Charles Brooke which "were likely to
conduce to the prosperity and just administration of the territories concerned." His

Majesty's Government learned "with sincere regret" that Sultan Hashim was unwilling to entertain the Rajah's offer (FO 12/124, p. 9, Lord Lansdowne to Sultan of Brunei, 26 February 1903, my emphasis added).

125. Cf. Hewett who reported that the Sultan was perfectly willing to accept the Rajah's terms and, moreover, begged him to persuade the mentris (junior ministers), who were adamant in their opposition, to agree also (CO 144/76: 40636, Hewett to Lansdowne, No. 15 confidential, 10 July 1902, paragraph 3, my emphasis added).

126. See above, pp. 40-7.

127. Cf. above, p. 45.

128. Article I of the 1888 Treaty, which was dated the 17th (rather than the 18th) of September, provided that British Protection "shall confer no right on Her Majesty's Government to interfere with the internal administration of (Brunei)" except in certain defined instances. Any dispute connected with the succession was to be referred to the United Kingdom for settlement (Article II). Brunei's foreign policy was to be conducted by His Majesty's Government (III). British subjects, commerce and shipping were to enjoy the same rights, privileges and advantages in the sultanate as their Brunei equivalents (V). No cession of territory was to be made without British consent (VI). Extra-territorial jurisdiction was to continue (VII).

Article III of the Treaty ran partly as follows: "if any difference should arise between the Sultan of Brunei and the Government of any other State, the Sultan of Brunei agrees to abide by the decision of Her Majesty's Government and to take all necessary measures to give effect thereto." If this clause is interpreted to mean that Sultan Hashim was obliged to acquiesce in the Brooke State's seizure of Limbang because the annexation had been approved by the United Kingdom, what was the point of his having signed the Treaty?

129. See above, p. 216, note 25. The 1887 lease, when held by Cowie, was not recognized by Her Majesty's Government; but after its transfer to the Rajah, nothing further was said.

130. For Kota Batu, see above, p. 219 (note 31).

131. This letter is in FO 12/118, p. 73ff. The sultan and wazirs were to be granted annuities of $12,000 and $6,000 respectively by the Rajah, these amounts to be reduced in half after the deaths of the existing office-holders. They were to be allowed to fly their flags and receive the ordinary salute as in Brunei and try cases among their personal following. Their titles were to remain as before, along with the Sarawak and North Borneo cession monies. Payment was to be made directly: no assignment would be recognized.

   Hewett declared that these terms repre-sented a "most generous offer" on the part of the Rajah and might be regarded as the outcome of the "intimate friendship" that had existed for many years between Sir James Brooke and the present Rajah (on the one hand) and members of the Brunei Royal Family (on the other). Hewett added that the advantages of the proposal, if carried out, were obvious. The Sultan and his family and the two wazirs would enjoy financial security; and under "the wise and humane" Government of the Rajah, "justice--a thing unknown in Brunei hitherto-- will be within the reach of everyone. Life and property will be secured to all and every form of oppression and extortion will at once disappear." Hewett could not doubt that the offer would prove acceptable to His Highness.

   Sir Frank Swettenham was skeptical: the terms offered would hardly relieve the Sultan from poverty and reference to their generosity "must be exaggerated language." If the British Government considered "that the Sultan of Brunei can properly sell the country of which he is the titular Ruler, and the only aim is to secure the highest price possible, the North Borneo Company or the British Government might be willing to offer better terms." Stubbs minuted that "cession to Sarawak would seem to be a better course than either of the alternatives suggested by Sir Frank Swettenham."

132. The Sultan's letter under reference ran as follows:

> I have been told that Mr. Hewett had informed His Excellency the High Commissioner that I am willing to hand over Brunei and its territories to the Rajah of Sarawak. This is absolutely untrue. The proposal originated with Mr. Hewett and it was he who advised and pressed me to hand over Brunei and its territories to the Rajah of Sarawak. I absolutely refuse to be governed by the advice of Mr. Hewett or to accept his suggestion. . . . (FO 12/126, pp. 158ff. Sultan Hashim to Acting Consul, 29 Rabialachir 1322 AH, encl. in McArthur to Secretary to High Commissioner, 15 July 1904).

133. The only census taken in Sarawak before the Second World War was in 1871, when the population numbered 128,679, of whom 52,519 were Malays. Bampfylde estimated the population in c. 1909 at about 416,000 of whom 100,000 were Malays and Melanaus, 250,000 were Ibans, Land Dayaks, Kayans and Kenyahs, and the balance were mainly of Chinese.

   Malays, however, played an important political role in the Brooke State (see Pringle, Rajahs and Rebels, p. 323) because the Rajah "was neither able nor willing to import a large number of European administrators, and since in general, no other element in the population was culturally equipped to exercise magisterial functions." But Sir Charles Brooke "became" an Iban: "I know the Dayak mind and feeling much better than I do my own . . . countrymen" (ibid., p. 178). He loved war and appeared happiest when leading Ibans on expeditions upriver. Indeed, it was as a war-leader to which he enjoyed his great reputation (R. Nicholl, in Brunei Museum Journal, 1983, pp. 236-7).

134. CO 604/1 Sarawak Gazette 2 August 1904, pp. 152-6. For a flavour of the proceedings, see above, note 99 (p. 245-6).

135. Cf. CO 144/73 (23569) Brooke to Keyser, 14 June 1899:

> The wishes of Her Majesty's Government shall be complied with by me so far as possible in relation to the coastline still under the Sultan's rule, but the state of anarchy, and, in fact, cruelty and injustice to the unfortunate inhabitants, should be stopped, and <u>this cannot be done without a certain amount of force being used in bringing His Highness the Sultan to terms</u> [emphasis added].

136. See p. 254, note 131 (above).

137. The Sultan of Brunei received a monthly allowance of $1,000 until 1934, when the amount was increased to $1,500, plus an extra allowance towards the cost of servants, etc. A further rise to $2,000 per month was implemented. In 1939 a sum was voted to enable His Highness to provide himself with a motor car. The Civil List amounted to $37,438 in 1940 and $38,128 was voted for 1941. These rises were made possible by the new oil wealth. There were, however, continual disputes between sultan and Resident on the subject, the former considering that he was receiving insufficient to support his dignity. Nowadays there is no limitation on the sums which the Brunei Sultan lavishes upon himself, witness the $350,000,000 palace just completed. However his His Majesty General Sir Hassanal Bolkiah II is said to be popular, (though he is not prepared to have this popularity tested in a democratic election), and the new palace is regarded, perhaps, as a symbol of Brunei's new status in the world.

138. For the <u>tulin</u> rights question, see above, pp. 54-5.

139. See FO 12/126, p. 173ff. The <u>Pengiran Bendahara</u>, however, was most unsatisfied with the Residential System (above, pp. 42-4).

140. See FO 12/127, p. 92ff. Villiers to Brooke, 1 January 1904 and Brooke to Villiers, 14

January 1904. Villiers suggested that the Rajah might improve his terms, for example, by offering to pay the Limbang cession money or by promising higher annuities as the revenue of Sarawak allowed. The Rajah replied that the Sarawak revenues would not stand any more strain on them "than in paying the sums I have laid down and seeing what the Brunei Government has been is and has been, I consider my offer liberal." This was, perhaps, a crucial miscalculation on the part of Sir Charles Brooke. He was never given a second chance.

141. In the years 1906-1911 Brunei arranged to receive loans totalling $500,000 from the Federated Malay States, of which $439,750 had been spent by 1914. The remaining $60,250 was not drawn. Ordinary revenue and expenditure were as follows (in $ Straits):

Year	Income	Expenditure
1907	51,777	93,334
1910	77,051	73,513
1915	129,529	114,518
1920	206,253	223,690
1925	345,573	245,286
1930	333,069	373,604
1935	813,532	786,201
1940	1,556,354	1,462,174

Source: Brunei Annual Reports (CO 824/1-2).

The Brunei National Debt was liquidated by the end of 1936. By 1959, at the end of the Residential Era, the annual revenue was $129,569,000; in 1979 revenue amounted to ($ Brunei) 2,753,000,000 (Borneo Bulletin, 5 January 1980). Much of the 1940 "expenditure," incidentally, represented funds invested on behalf of Brunei by the Crown Agents.

142. This is very true. Immediately after the Limbang annexation, for example, Sultan Hashim informed the Acting Governor of the Straits Settlements that "we . . . rest our hopes upon the protection of Her Majesty the Queen." In

1895 His Highness expressed astonishment that
Sarawak had been upheld in its possession of
Limbang and that the British Government "does
not agree with us, who are true and adhere to
the terms of the Treaty, as our conduct has
been straightforward and we have done no
wrong." In other words, Brunei had abided by
the terms of the 1888 Treaty and the United
Kingdom had a duty to do the same, by pro-
tecting Brunei from external aggression. In
1902 Sultan Hashim complained: "From the day I
set my hand to the Treaty of Protection, I
have not once received assistance or Protection from Your Majesty's Government . . . Not
a single consul has done anything to help
strengthen my country. They all seem to help
Sarawak and to try to hand over my country to
Sarawak" (Sources: respectively: CO 273/166:
9843; FO 12/92, p. 18ff.; and CO 144/77,
12955).

143. The Rajah Muda was (Sir) Charles Vyner Brooke
(1874-1963), GCMG 1928. Rajah of Sarawak,
1917-1946. As Rajah Muda in 1904 he must have
proved unsatisfactory, for the Second Rajah
did not retire finally until September 1916, a
few months before his death (17 May 1917).

144. In fact Sultan Hashim had agreed to accept a
Resident in 1887, when the suggestion had been
put before him by Sir Frederick Weld. The
British Government, on financial grounds,
refused to implement this proposal.

145. During McArthur's tenure as Resident, the
allowances paid to the sultan and wazirs did
indeed account for about half Brunei's total
income. In 1910 Lee-Warner proposed that when
the posts of Pengirans Bendahara and Pemancha
became vacant "there will be no need to
subsidize future [incumbents]--if such are
ever created--with more than $200 per·mensem
and a saving of nearly $8,000 per annum will
thus be effected" (Brunei Annual Report 1910,
p. 20). This proposal breached private
understandings which had been reached with the
wazirs in 1905 and was never implemented.

146. McArthur is somewhat unjust here. Labuan had
been acquired in 1847 as a "new Singapore."
British administration, however, had been

notoriously unsuccessful and extremely costly;
hence the Colonial Office had been only too
pleased, on 1 January 1890, to shift the
burden to the British North Borneo (Chartered)
Company, which governed the island until the
end of 1905.

When I quoted this passage from McArthur's
Report to A. Gilmour C.M.G. (Resident, Labuan
1928-9), he was distressed to find the
peaceful Kedayan farmers described as
"savages": in the 1920s there was practically
no crime "and I surely would have heard if
things had been greatly different a couple of
decades earlier" (letter to the author, 16
March 1984).

McArthur, when returning to Labuan in 1918
after an absence of ten years, noted that
little improvement had been made during the
interval (CO 531/12, 38835).

For an account of British incompetence in
Labuan in the nineteenth century, see James
Pope-Hennessy, Verandah: Some episodes in the
Crown Colonies 1867-1889 (London: Allen and
Unwin, 1964, pp. 57-109).

147. The BNBC was invited to return Labuan without
fuss or else to face an investigation into
alleged misgovernment (Cf. 1896, when C.P.
Lucas had minuted: "Labuan cannot be taken
back from the Company without practically
breaking up the Company . . ."--CO 144/70:
10680).

148. For the financial circumstances of the BNBC,
see above, p. 251 (note 117).

149. This was exactly the policy of C.P. Lucas in
the Colonial Office. McArthur's Report
strengthened his hand.

150. See above, p. 206 (note 2).

151. See above, pp. 54-8.

152. For the mode of taxation actually adopted, see
above, pp. 58-60.

ABBREVIATIONS

BMJ	Brunei Museum Journal
BMPC	British Malayan Petroleum Company
CH	Companion of Honour (UK decoration)
CBC	Central Borneo Company
CMG	Commander of the Order of St. Michael and St. George
CO	Colonial Office
CUP	Cambridge University Press
DCL	Doctor of Civil Law
DO	District Officer
FMS	Federated Malay States
FO	Foreign Office
GCMG	Knight Grand Cross of the Order of St. Michael and St. George
GCVO	Knight Grand Cross of the Royal Victorian Order
HH	His Highness
HM	His/Her Majesty
ITC (ITS)	Island Trading Syndicate (1900-11), renamed Island Trading Company (1911-57)
JMBRAS	Journal of the Malayan (later Malaysian) Branch of the Royal Asiatic Society
JSBRAS	Journal of the Straits Branch of the Royal Asiatic Society
KCB	Knight Commander of the Order of the Bath
KCMG	Knight Commander of the Order of St. Michael and St. George
MCS	Malayan Civil Service
MP	Member of Parliament
OAG	Office Administering the Government
OB	Order of the Bath (in ascending order: CB KCB GCB)
OBE	Order of the British Empire (in ascending order: MBE OBE CBE DBE/KBE GBE)
OMG	Order of St. Michael and St. George (in ascending order: CMG DCMG/KCMG GCMG)
OUP	Oxford University Press
PC	Privy Councillor
PRO	Public Record Office (Kew, United Kingdom)
PWD	Public Works Department
r	reigned

RVO	Royal Victorian Order (in ascending order: MVO LVO CVO DCVO/KCVO GCVO)
$	Straits' Dollar (value fixed at L0.12 from 1906)
SCS	Sarawak Civil Service
SG	Sarawak Gazette
SMJ	Sarawak Museum Journal
SPDK	Member, First Grade, Order of Kinabalu (Sabah)
SS	Straits Settlements
SSAC	Sarawak State Advisory Council
UMS	Unfederated Malay States (Brunei, Johore, Kedah, Kelantan, Perlis and Trangganu)

GLOSSARY

adat: customary law
amanat: will (i.e. final testament)
atap: roofing, especially of thatch
baba: Chinese born in Malaya
chandu: prepared opium
cheteria: "a major order of traditional (Brunei) noble officials ranking beneath the wazirs"*
daerah: district
dagang serah: forced trade tax (abolished 1906)
Dato Di-Gadong: Resident headman of Tutong district
hakim: judge
hamba: servant, follower, slave*
hukum kanun: Muslim administrative law*
hukum sharia: Muslim religious law
imam: leader of prayer in a mosque
inche (or awang): Mr.
istana: palace
Jawatan abu Bakar: one of the pehin
jelutong: a kind of wild rubber tree (its rubber is used in making chewing gum, its timber is valuable)
kajang: palm frond used in roofing, baskets and mats
kampong: village
Kampong Ayer: 'River Village' (Brunei Town)
kathi: Muslim religious judge
kati: catty (16 tahils or 1.33 lbs.)
kerajaan: appanages (land and serfs) of the crown (abolished 1906)
ketua: village elder
khatib: reader and preacher in a mosque
kuripan: appanges (land and serfs) of a wazir (abolished 1906)
lapau: Sultan's audience hall

---

* Definitions marked with an asterisk are derived from D.E. Brown, Brunei: The Structure and History of a Bornean Malay Sultanate (Special Monograph of the Brunei Museum Journal, Vol. 2, No. 2, 1970), pp. 26-11.

mui tsai: (Ch) "little sister," Chinese household 'slave'

nibong: tall tufted palm

ondong-ondong: traditional written law of Brunei

Orang Bukit: 'Hill People'

Orang Kaya: "literally 'rich man,' a common element in non-noble titles of office"*

padang: plain, playing field

padian: traditional fish market in Brunei Town

pehin: "a non-noble of sufficiently high rank to have been inaugurated with chiri, sacred formula"*

penghulu: headman

pengiran: a 'noble'

Pengiran Bendahara: highest-ranking wazir

Pengiran Di-Gadong: second-ranking wazir (post vacant 1900-68)

Pengiran Pemancha: third-ranking wazir

Pengiran Shahbandar: highest-ranking cheteria, but of similar status de facto as a wazir

Pengiran Temenggong: fourth-ranking wazir (post vacant 1885-1967)

pengkalan: landing place

pertolongan: tax imposed on the occasion of a birth, marriage or death in an overlord's family (abolished 1906)

pikul: 100 katis (133 lbs.)

prahu: boat

pulau/pulo: island

Rajah Muda: heir to the throne (Sarawak)

rakyat: general public

rotan: rattan (cane)

selesilah: genealogy

sireh: betel vine

tahil: 1 1/2 ounces

tanah: land, soil

terusan: channel

tongkang: sea-going barge

towkay: (Ch) businessman

tulin: private hereditary property, land and serfs (abolished 1906-11)

ulun: domestic servant/slave

wazir: "the four highest noble officials beneath the Sultan"*

SOURCES

PRIMARY SOURCES

Public Record Office, Kew

(a) Colonial Office Series:

CO 144	Labuan
CO 273	Straits Settlements
CO 531	Brunei (1907-26), British Borneo (1927-46) and British North Borneo (1946-51)
CO 537	Supplementary
CO 604	Sarawak Gazette (1903-51)
CO 717	Malay States
CO 824	Brunei Sessional Papers (1906-60)
CO 874	British North Borneo Company
CO 938	Sarawak (1946-51)
CO 943	Brunei (1946-51)
CO 1022	South East Asia

(b) Foreign Office Series:

FO 12	Borneo and Sulu
CO 572	Borneo and Sulu: Print of Correspondence

(c) Annuals:

Colonial Office List
Foreign Office List
Who's Who

(d) Decennials:

Dictionary of National Biography
Who Was Who

Rhodes House, Oxford

Brooke Family   Brooke Papers: Sarawak State Advisory Council Correspondence, 1912-17 (Mss Pac s83)

Sir C.V. Brooke   F. Kortright correspondence, 1916-31 (Mss Pac s74)

Fr. A.F. Owen   "D.A. Owen, 1880-1952: A Memoir,"
C.J.   (Mss Pac s103).

Datuk R.N.   "From the Depths of My Memory,"
Turner   unpublished autobiography, 3 vols., 1976 (Mss BE s454).

Published Government Reports

Wilford, G.E. The Geology and Mineral Resources of Brunei and Adjacent Parts of Sarawak, with Descriptions of the Seria and Miri Oilfields (Brunei: Brunei Press, 1961).

Wilson, R.A.M. The Geology and Mineral Resources of the Labuan and Padas Valley Areas (Kuching: Government Printing Office, 1964).

Unpublished Government Reports

Bevington, E.R. The Economy and Development of the State of Brunei, June 1956 (copy courtesy of its author).

Hickling, R.H. Memorandum upon Brunei Constitutional History and Practice, confidential 1955 (copy courtesy of Eussoff Agaki).

Newspapers

Borneo Bulletin (Kuala Belait)
The Daily Telegraph (London)
Straits Times (Singapore)
Sunday Telegraph Magazine (London)
The Times (London)

Magazines

1926-1973   British Malaya/Malaya/Malaysia: the journal of the Association of British Malaya.

BIBLIOGRAPHY

Books

Baring-Gould, S. and Bampfylde, C.A. A History of
    Sarawak Under its Two White Rajahs 1839-1908
    (London: Southeran, 1909).

Bassett, D.K. British Attitudes to Indigenous
    States in South East Asia in the Nineteenth
    Century (University of Hull: SE Asian Centre,
    Occasional Paper No. 1, 1980).

Belcher, E. (Admiral, Sir). Narrative of the
    Voyage of HMS Semarang 1843-6 2 vols. (London:
    Reeve, Bonham and Reeve, 1848).

Black, I.D. A Gambling Style of Government: The
    Establishment of Chartered Company Rule in
    Sabah, 1878-1915 (Kuala Lumpur: Oxford
    University Press, 1983).

Blundell, P. The City of Many Waters (London:
    Arrowsmith, 1923).

Brown, D.E. Brunei: The Structure and History of
    a Bornean Malay Sultanate (Special Monograph
    of the Brunei Museum Journal, Vol. 2, No. 2,
    1970).

Bruce, C. Twenty Years in Borneo (London:
    Cassell, 1925).

Crisswell, C.N. Rajah Charles Brooke: Monarch of
    All he Surveyed 1829-1927 (London: Oxford
    University Press, 1978).

Emerson, R. Malaysia: A Study in Direct and
    Indirect Rule (Kuala Lumpur: University of
    Malaya Press, 1964).

Financial Times. Rubber Producing Companies
    Capitalized in Sterling (London: Financial
    Times. Editions published in 1915, 1924,
    1936, 1944 and 1946).

Fitzgerald, C.P. A History of East Asia
    (Harmondsworth: Penguin, 1974).

Gullick, J.M. Indigenous Political Systems of Western Malaya (London: Athlone, Revised Edition, 1965).

Hall, D.G.E. A History of South-East Asia (London: Macmillan, Third Edition, 1968).

Harper, D.G.E. The Discovery and Development of the Seria Oilfield (Bandar Seri Begawan: Star Press, 1975).

Heussler, R. British Rule in Malaya: The Malayan Civil Service and its Predecessors, 1867-1942 (Oxford: Clio Press, 1981).

Irwin, G. Nineteenth Century Borneo: A Study in Diplomatic Rivalry (Singapore: Moore, 1965).

Keppel, H. (Sir). The Expedition to Borneo of HMS 'Dido' for the Suppression of Piracy (London: Chapman and Hall, 1847).

Keyser, A.L. People and Places: A Life in Five Continents (London: Murray, 1922).

_____. Trifles and Travels (London: Murray, 1923).

Maxwell, A.R. Urang Darat: An Ethnographic Study of the Kadayan of Labu Valley, Brunei (Ann Arbor: University Microfilms, 1981).

Maxwell-Hall, J. Labuan Story: Memoirs of a Small Island Near the Coast of Borneo (Jesselton: Chung Nam, 1958).

Mills, L.A. British Rule in East Asia (London: Oxford University Press, 1959).

Nicholl, R. European Sources for the History of the Sultanate of Brunei in the Sixteenth Century (Bandar Seri Begawan: Star Press, 1975).

Pope-Hennessy, P. Verandah: Some Episodes in the Crown Colonies (London: Allen and Unwin, 1964).

Porter, B. The Lion's Share: A Short History of British Imperialism (London: Longman, 1975).

268

Pringle, R. Rajahs and Rebels: The Ibans of Sarawak under Brooke Rule 1841-1946 (London: Macmillan, 1970).

Reece, R.H.W. The Name of Brooke: The End of White Rajah Rule in Sarawak (Kuala Lumpur: Oxford University Press, 1982).

Runciman, S. (Sir). The White Rajahs: A History of Sarawak 1841-1946 (Cambridge: Cambridge University Press, 1960).

Rutter, O. British North Borneo: An Account of its History, Resources and Native Tribes (London: Constable, 1922).

Stock Exchange. The Stock Exchange Official Intelligence (1920, and annually thereafter. Renamed The Stock Exchange Official Yearbook in c. 1933).

Tarling, N. Britain, The Brookes and Brunei (Kuala Lumpur: Oxford University Press, 1971).

Tregonning, K.G. A History of Modern Sabah (Singapore: University of Malaya Press, 1965).

Voon Phin Keong. Western Rubber Planting in South East Asia 1876-1921 (Kuala Lumpur: Penerbit University, Malaya; 1976).

Ward, A.B. Rajah's Servant (Ithaca, NY: Cornell University Press, 1966).

Winstedt, R.O. (Sir). The Malays: A Cultural History (London: Routledge and Kegan Paul, Revised Edition, 1950).

Wright, L.R. The Origins of British Borneo (Hong Kong: Hong Kong University Press, 1970).

Articles

Bigelow, P. "The Last of a Great Sultan," Harper's Monthly Magazine, Vol. CXIII (1960), pp. 716-22.

Black, I.D. "The Ending of Brunei Rule in Sabah," JMBRAS 1968 (Part II), pp. 176-92.

Brassey, T. (Sir). "North Borneo," The Nineteenth Century (Vol. XXII, July-December 1887), pp. 248-56.

Brown, Carrie C. "An Early Account of Brunei by Sung Lien," Brunei Museum Journal (1972), pp. 219-31.

Brown, D.E. "The Coronation of Sultan Jemalul Alam 1918," Brunei Museum Journal (1974), pp. 166-79.

_____. "Maps and the History of Brunei," Brunei Museum Journal (1973), pp. 88-90.

Butcher, J.G. "The Demise of the Revenue Farm System in the Federated Malay States," Modern Asian Studies (1983), pp. 387-412.

Carroll, J.S. "Berunai in the Boxer Codes," JMBRAS 1982, Part II, pp. 1-25.

Cator, G.E. "Brunei," Asian Review, Vol. 34 (1939), pp. 736-44.

_____. "I Remember: A Malayan Cadet in 1907," British Malaya (February 1941), p. 160.

Cave, B.J. "The Postage Stamps of Brunei 1895-1941: A Philatelic Outline," Brunei Museum Journal (1977), pp. 107-28.

Christie, E. "The First Tourist: Astana Guest, Kuching 1904" (Diary of Miss E. Christie) in Sarawak Museum Journal (1961), pp. 43-9.

Clifford, H. (Sir). "A Dying Kingdom," Macmillan's Magazine (May to October 1902), pp. 106-114.

Crisswell, C.N. "The Origins of the Limbang Claim," JSEAS Vol. 2, No. (1971), pp. 218-28.

_____. "The Establishment of a Residency in Brunei," Asian Studies (April 1972), pp. 95-107.

_____. "Pengiran Anak Hashim's Role in Brunei
Affairs Prior to his Accession to the Throne
in 1885," Sarawak Museum Journal (1977), pp.
41-54.

Davidson, J.A. "Postal Service in Brunei's Water
Town," Brunei Museum Journal (1976), pp. 87-
95.

_____. "Brunei Coinage," Brunei Museum Journal
(1977), pp. 43-81.

Harrisson, T. and Harrisson, B. "Kota Batu in
Brunei: An Introductory Report," Sarawak
Museum Journal Vol. VII, No. 8 (December
1956), pp. 283-318.

Hickling, R.H. "Brunei Silver," Corona, Vol. 7
(1955), pp. 294-8.

Hipkins, J.R. "The History of the Chinese in
Borneo," Sarawak Museum Journal (1971), pp.
109-53.

Horton, A.V.M. "The Pandaruan Issue (1884-1920),"
Sarawak Gazette (July 1984), pp. 26-30.

_____. "The Brunei Smallpox Epidemic of 1904,"
Sarawak Museum Journal (1984), pp. 89-99.

_____. "Brunei, Sarawak and the Kota Batu
Lands (1903-1907)," Brunei Museum Journal
(1985), pp. 62-74.

Hughes-Hallet, H. "A Sketch of the History of
Brunei," JMBRAS, Vol. XVIII, Part 2 (1940),
pp. 23-42.

Janardanan, E.C. "Brunei Malay Rubber
Beginnings," Sarawak Museum Journal (1962),
pp. 598-9.

Ibrahim, Abdul Latif bin Haji. "Padian - Its
Market and the Women Vendors," Brunei Museum
Journal (1970), pp. 39-51.

_____. "Variations and Changes in the Names
and Locations of the Wards of Brunei's Kampong
Ayer Over the Last Century," Brunei Museum
Journal (1971), pp. 56-73.

Leys, P. "Observations on the Brunei Political System, 1883-5," JMBRAS, Vol. 41, Part 2 (1968), pp. 117-130 (with notes by R.M. Pringle).

Lim, J.S. "A Short Account of Sago Production in Kuala Balai - Belait," Brunei Museum Journal (1974), pp. 143-55.

_____ and P.M. Shariffuddin. "Charcoal Production in Brunei," Brunei Museum Journal (1975), pp. 201-20.

_____. "Brunei Brass: The Traditional Method of Casting," British Museum Journal (1976), pp. 142-6.

Jibah, Matassim bin Haji. "Pengiran Indera Makhota Shahbandar Muhammad Selleh and James Brooke," Brunei Museum Journal (1978), pp. 38-51.

Nicholl, R. "Brunei and Camphor," Brunei Museum Journal (1979), pp. 52-68.

Ongkili, J.P. "Pre-Western Brunei, Sarawak and Sabah," Sarawak Museum Journal (1972), pp. 1-20.

Saunders, G.E. "James Brooke and Asian Governments," Brunei Museum Journal (1973), pp. 105-117.

Shariffuddin, P.M. "The Kedayans," Brunei Museum Journal (1969), pp. 15-23.

Stubbs, R.E. (Sir). "Two Colonial Office Memoranda on the History of Brunei" (edited and annotated by D.E. Brown) in JMBRAS, Vol. XLI, Part 2, (1968), pp. 83-116.

_____. "Sir James Brooke and Brunei," Sarawak Museum Journal (1963), pp. 1-12.

Tarling, N. "Britain and Sarawak in the Twentieth Century: Raja Charles, Raja Vyner and the Colonial Office," JMBRAS, Vol. 43, Part II (1970), pp. 25-52.

_____. "The Entrepot at Labuan and the Chinese," J. Ch'en and N. Tarling (eds.) Studies in the Social History of China and SE Asia (Cambridge: Cambridge University Press, 1970).

_____. "Sir Cecil Clementi and the Federation of British Borneo," JMBRAS, Vol. 44, Part 2 (1971), pp. 1-34.

Treacher, W.H. "British Borneo." "Part I," JSBRAS, Vol. 20, Part 1 (1889), pp. 13-74; "Part II," JSBRAS, Vol. 21, Part 2 (1890), pp. 19-121.

Tregonning, K.G. "The Partition of Brunei," Malaya (August 1958), pp. 27-31.

Watson, A.C. "Notes on the History of Bubongan Dua-Belas. The British High Commissioner's Residence in Brunei," Brunei Museum Journal (1982), pp. 37-104.

Wodak, E. "Old Brunei Coins," Sarawak Museum Journal, Vol. VIII, No. 11 (June 1958), pp. 278-92.

Wright, L.R. "Sarawak's Relations with Britain, 1858-1870," Sarawak Museum Journal (1964), pp. 628-48.

_____. "The Partition of Brunei," Asian Studies (1967), pp. 282-303.

Typescripts

Nicholl, R. Brunei Rediscovered, A Survey of Early Times (Paper Read at the Eighth Conference of the International Association of Historians of Asia at Kuala Lumpur, 25-29 August 1980, 15 pp. - copy courtesy of its author).

273

110-22, 132, 149-55,
  175-7, 222, 250;
  trade, 122-6, 200-1,
  231-4.
Brunei River, 106-7,
  112-3.
Brunei Town: land
  capital, 66-7, 69-70,
  220-1; and Limbang,
  138-9; school, 68;
  mentioned, xiii, 106,
  108-9, 114, 132, 149.
  See also Kampong Ayer.
Buang Tawar, 61, 108,
  215, 217-9, 250. See
  also Berembang and
  coal.
buffaloes, 50, 81. See
  also cattle raids.
Bugal, O.K. Pemancha, 84.
Bukit Chawit. See Bukit
  Sawat.
Bukit Sawat, 82, 84, 128,
  136, 152.
Burok. See Burut, Si.
Burong Pingai, 129, 226,
  236.
Burut, Si, 120, 228-9.
Butcher, J.G., 59.
Butterworth, F.N. (1875-
  1952): biography, 181-
  2; uses pen-name of P.
  Blundell, 182;
  mentioned, 8, 45, 62,
  212-3, 220, 239-40,
  242.

Campbell, D.G. (1867-
  1918) CMG: biography,
  35; and mission to
  Brunei (1905), 35-7.
Cator, Sir G.E. (1884-
  1973) KBE CMG, 65, 71-
  2, 195.
cattle raids, 117-20.
Central Borneo Company
  (1887-98): biography,
  204; mentioned, 209,
  249.
cession monies, 35, 58,
  166. 231.

chandu, 59.
Cheok Boon Seok, 59,
  192.
Cheok Yu, 56, 59, 112.
Chermin, Pulau, 107-8.
Chevalier, H. (c. 1860-
  1923), 34-5, 45, 47.
Chi Ki Yi, 82.
Chinese: attitude to
  Residency, 121-2,
  164; school, 68;
  traders, 134, 164,
  200-1, 230; mention-
  ed, 28, 53, 109-10,
  115, 120-2, 128, 164-
  5, 221, 230.
cholera, 220.
Chua Cheng Hee, 56, 59,
  110, 122-4.
Clarke, Province (North
  Borneo), 99, 144-7,
  158.
climate, 100-1.
coal, 49-52, 61, 64, 70,
  101, 106-7, 126, 147,
  159, 209, 216. See
  also Brooketon and
  Buang Tawar.
coinage, 25, 70, 128.
Commons, House of, 46.
communications, 101-2,
  131, 158, 172-3.
courts of law, 53, 66,
  69, 128-30, 235-6.
Cowie, W.C. (c. 1847-
  1910): biography,
  216; and British
  North Borneo Company,
  251; coal leases,
  215, 248-9, 253-4;
  mentioned, 107, 159,
  206-7, 209.
craft industries, 61-2,
  193.
Crane, H.A., 108, 217-8.
crime, lack of, 66, 226-
  7.
Crisswell, C.N., 6.
Crummey, H.G., 66.
Customs Enactment
  (1906), 58.

277

smallpox.
Hewett, G. (1859-1932):
    biography, 184, 202;
    character of, 239-40;
    plan for Brunei's
    future, 21-3, 160,
    165-8, 252-3; men-
    tioned, 15-7, 84, 100,
    128, 134, 144-5, 160,
    162, 167-8, 203-4,
    215, 253-4.
hides, 81, 123.
Hose, Dr. C. (1863-
    1929), 99.

Ibans, 32, 163-4, 197.
Imam, Tuan, 65.
iron, 101, 200, 209.
Islamic law, 37-8.
Island Trading Syndicate,
    60, 63-4, 149, 212-3,
    221-2, 224-6. See
    also cutch.

Jambol, Pengiran, 228.
Jawatan Abu Bakar, 65,
    239.
Jeludin, Pengiran, 217-8.
jelutong, 199-201, 213,
    234. See also jungle
    produce.
Jessel, Sir C., 46, 190,
    207.
jungle produce, 27, 82,
    149, 212.

Kalam, Dato, 15-6, 18-9,
    201-2.
Kampong Ayer, 7, 27, 30,
    149, 220-1, 226-7,
    233-4. See also
    Brunei Town.
kathis, 37-8.
Kayans, 27, 163.
Kedayans, 19-20, 27-8,
    60, 101-2, 112-4, 126,
    149-50, 153, 169, 238,
    250-1, 259.
Kelakas, 148.
Kenyahs, 163.
kerajaan, 25-6, 102-3,

105, 110, 113, 127,
    132.
Kerma Indra, Pengiran,
    65.
Keyser, A.L. (1856-
    1924): biography,
    236; mentioned, 129,
    223, 229-30, 240-2.
Kota Batu, 108, 179,
    219.
Kupang, 179.
kuripan, 25-6, 84, 102-
    3, 104-5, 110, 113,
    127, 166-7, 230.

Labi, 198.
labor, 63, 149.
Labu, 52, 63, 105-6,
    137, 212-3.
Labuan, 81, 92-3, 113,
    131, 147-8, 158, 165,
    172-4, 196 258-9.
Laksamana, OK (office),
    65.
Land Code (1907), 63.
land revenue, 60.
Landsdowne, fifth
    Marquess of (1845-
    1927): biography,
    196; mentioned, 91,
    95, 252-3.
Lasip, O.K., 84.
Lawas, 99, 144-7, 247-8.
Lee-Warner, W.H. (b.
    1880) OBE, 26, 55.
Leong Ah Ng, 67.
leprosy, 66.
Limau Manis, 16, 64,
    109-10, 222.
Limbang: importance to
    Brunei, 30-1, 138-44;
    mentioned, 7, 10, 18,
    27, 30, 69, 83, 100,
    106, 115, 117-20,
    122, 124, 129-30,
    158, 246-7.
Lisang, 143, 246-7.
literacy, 68.
loans, 37.
Lucas, Sir C.P. (1853-
    1931) KCB KCMG:

Weld, Sir F. (1823-91),
45.
Wilford, Dr. G.E., 200,
208.

Yahya, Awang, 68.

Zahora (gunboat, 1894-
1927), biography, 218;
mentioned, 44, 239.

Printed and bound by CPI Group (UK) Ltd, Croydon, CR0 4YY

09/06/2025

14685965-0005